NAVIES IN THE AMERICAN REVOLUTION:

A Bibliography

by

Myron J. Smith, Jr.

American Naval Bibliography, Vol. I

The Scarecrow Press, Inc.
Metuchen, N.J.   1973

Library of Congress Cataloging in Publication Data

Smith, Myron J
   Navies in the American Revolution.

   (American naval bibliography, v. 1)
   1. United States--History--Revolution--Naval operations--Bibliography. I. Title. II. Series.
Z1238.S54   016.9733'5   72-10995
ISBN 0-8108-0569-3

Copyright 1973 by Myron J. Smith, Jr.

In any operation, and under all circumstances, a decisive naval superiority is to be considered as a fundamental principle, and the basis upon which every hope of success must ultimately depend.

--George Washington
to Count Rochambeau,
15 July 1780

American Naval Bibliography Series

by MYRON J. SMITH, JR.

Vol. I.	Navies in the American Revolution.	1973
Vol. II.	The American Navy, 1789-1860.	1974
Vol. III.	American Civil War Navies.	1972
Vol. IV.	The American Navy, 1865-1918.	1974
Vol. V.	The American Navy, 1918-1941.	forthcoming

CONTENTS

Publisher's Note	iv
Foreword by Alexander Kent	vii
Preface	ix
Bibliography	1
Appendix A: The Otter and the Defence: A 1776 Naval Episode in Maryland Waters	177
Appendix B: Vessels in the Public Service of The United States, 1775-1785	194
Subject Index	207

FOREWORD

I was very glad to be asked to write this foreword, partly because of my own personal involvement with all matters concerning maritime history, and also because it is a work which has been long awaited. As a writer both of naval fact and fiction I am well aware that many attempts to collect material for such a work have often led to empty criticism and bias. Where war of any kind is concerned it must be admitted that we are rarely able to see "the other side's point of view."

I think it is true to say that the American War of Independence proved to be a turning-point in naval strategy, and down over the years we can see where those hard-won lessons have born success, or have brought disaster by being ignored.

Under the pseudonym of Douglas Reeman I concentrate all my writing on contemporary naval matters and so I am perhaps more privileged than some in being able to discover where earlier examples of tactics and deployment have made their marks in our own lifetimes. When Cornwallis surrendered his army to Washington at Yorktown it was not for want of pluck or energy to fight. Had the British navy been able to drive the French fleet from the Chesapeake and continue to supply or evacuate the embattled troops, history would doubtless have to be rewritten. It would not have won the war, but it might have delayed the settlement. But wars are not won on "if onlys" and "maybes" and the British Admiral Graves stuck rigidly to his orders and the inflexible wording of the Fighting Instructions. If a Nelson or a Keppel had been in the vanguard we might have yet another interesting example of individual strategy to examine, rather than one of frustration and uncertainty.

Later at the Saintes, Admiral Rodney bent those same rules very slightly, but if it was enough to demolish the French fleet it was insufficient to delay the course of events and peace was signed. As the British Prime Minister said to a gloomy House of Commons, "A defensive war can only end in defeat."

But was that grim lesson of the absolute need to keep open supply lines at all times really learned? The disastrous campaign in the Dardanelles in 1915, and the later ones in Greece and Singapore in World War II leave it very much open to doubt.

What is made very clear in this work is the background and the events which allowed the ships and men to work as they did. Living in an age of sophisticated weaponry as we do, when the potential of such power has largely outstripped the minds of those who control it, we can find admiration, even awe for those sailors in wood and canvas who had to depend entirely on their own crude determination of affairs which because of poor communications were made all the more difficult to act upon. Yet with such poor resources they would often risk everything to secure their own kind of freedom.

I think that John Paul Jones put it into writing better than most, and I am more than content to sum up my admiration for this work in his words. "It seems to be a law inflexible and inexorable that he who will not risk cannot win."

Alexander Kent
September 29, 1972

PREFACE

During the past two centuries, thousands of monographs and articles have spilled out describing the military (land) operations of the American Revolution. For most Americans, knowledge of the role taken by the navies of Britain and her rebellious colonies--and after 1778, France, Spain, and Holland--is clouded. At best, it is often limited to the exploits of John Paul Jones.

The lack of important interpretations of the nautical conflict, termed "neglected" by such scholars as Dr. Higgenbotham and Mr. Clark, is serious. Newer studies, particularly concerning the various state navies and revisions of the older concepts of the Continental service, are needed. When the war afloat took on an international flavor after the signing of the Franco-American treaty of alliance, an even greater expanse was opened. While a few studies exist detailing the service off India of the brilliant French admiral, Pierre de Suffren, the literature for naval activities in geographical areas outside the Caribbean is severely limited. It is a sorry situation when the bulk of the standard administrative and operational naval histories for this period were composed before or during the early 1900's. The present volume is offered as an aid to those interested in correcting these deficiencies and also to those simply in search of reading material on a little known area of the past.[1]

In selecting references for this bibliography, some criteria were necessary. Basically, this volume is devoted to operational, administrative, and biographical data concerning the sea forces. Works on genealogy and exploration, particularly the voyages of Captain James Cook, have been excluded. To our ends, the following types of materials are represented: books and monographs; scholarly papers; periodical, magazine, or journal articles; some documents; important general works; doctoral and masters degree papers; and contemporary poetry pertaining to the navies, naval battles, or heroes. As seamen of several European nations took part in our Revolutionary struggle, the language of these references is not limited to English. The following species of material are not included: fiction; children's works; newspaper articles (unless reprinted by a periodical); and book reviews. Annotations of a non-critical nature are often supplied.

The approximately 1,600 numbered entries of this volume span the period between about 1770 and early 1972. The whole is arranged alphabetically by authors and titles. Joint (jt.)-author, compiler, and editor cross references are provided within the body of the text, each receiving an entry number. Where earlier editions have been reprinted, the symbol "Rpr." and the year of reissue follows the pagination data. The appendices and a subject index complete the work.

No tool of this nature, with its inevitable omissions, can hope to include the efforts of writers whose pens even now are being warmed by the heat of the up-coming Bicentennial.[2] To keep abreast of the newest naval research, a periodic search of the newer issues and editions of the following is recommended:

Air University Index to Military Periodicals. Maxwell Air Force Base, Ala.: Air University Library, 1949--. v. 1--.

Albion, Robert D. Naval and Maritime History: An Annotated Bibliography. 3rd ed. Mystic, Conn.: Marine Historical Assoc., 1963. 230p.
Two supplements to this valuable tool have been published; a new and revised 4th ed. is expected shortly.

America: History and Life--A Guide to Periodical Literature. Santa Barbara, Calif.: Clio Press, 1964--. v. 1--. Quarterly.

British Museum. Department of Printed Books. General Catalog of Printed Books: Additions. London: Clowes, 1963--.
A subject index is published every four years.

Dissertation Abstracts International. Ann Arbor, Mich.: University Microfilms, 1969--.
Begun over 30 years ago as Dissertation Abstracts. Refer to the "A" Schedule, "The Humanities and Social Sciences."

Historical Abstracts: A Quarterly, Covering the World's Periodical Literature, 1775-1945. Santa Barbara, Calif.:

Clio Press, 1955--. v. 1--.
Contains coverage of the United States to 1964 when America: History and Life was begun. Still useful for naval developments of the period in Europe.

"The Military Library." Military Affairs. Washington: American Military Institute, 1937--. v. 1--. Quarterly. Contains book reviews and periodical citations.

"Notable Naval Books of the Year." United States Naval Institute Proceedings. Annapolis: United States Naval Institute, 1950--. v. 76--.

Paris. Bibliothèque Nationale. Catalogue Général des Livres Imprimés de la Bibliothèque Nationale: Auteurs. Paris: Imprimerie Nationale, 1900--.

Readers' Guide to Periodical Literature. New York: H. W. Wilson, 1916--.
Includes some important historical journals.

United States. Library of Congress. Library of Congress Catalog. Books: Subjects. A Cumulative List of Works Represented by Library of Congress Printed Cards. Washington: US Government Printing Office, 1950--. Quarterly with annual cumulation.

_____. Navy Department. Naval History Division. U.S. Naval History: A Bibliography. 5th ed. Washington: U.S. Government Printing Office, 1969. 33p.
A new edition is expected shortly.

Writings on American History: A Bibliography of Books and Articles on United States History Published During the Year--. Various publishers, 1902--.
Not issued in 1904-1905, 1941-1947; latest volume is year 1959.

For those interested in books which will be published, your attention is directed to:

Forthcoming Books. New York: R. R. Bowker, 1966--. v. 1--.

In an area where little, if any, bibliographic control has previously existed, it is hoped that this guide will prove a worthy starting point for further exploration. For their aid and advice in its completion, the following persons and libraries are gratefully and appreciatively acknowledged: Enoch Pratt Free Library (Baltimore); Gettysburg College Library; Mr. W. Bart Greenwood, Librarian, Navy Department Library; Mr. Robert H. Land, Chief, General Reference Section, Library of Congress; Library of the Maine Historical Society; Library of the Rhode Island Historical Society; Dr. William J. Morgan, Head, Research Section, Naval History Division, Navy Department; Dr. Charles Schultz, former Librarian, Mystic Seaport; University of Delaware Library; University of Maryland Library; U.S. Army Military History Research Collection; U.S. Naval Academy Library; Huntington Public Library, Huntington, Ind.

For her aid in the preparation of this book, thanks are given my wife Susan.

This work is dedicated to the memory of all the departed salts who manned the vessels of those nations sailing in the storm-tossed seas which were our American Revolution. May they enjoy an important remembrance in the years ahead.

Huntington, Indiana
September 1972

Myron J. Smith, Jr.

Notes

1. The late expert on Revolutionary naval history, William B. Clark, made this point to the October 4, 1945 meeting of the State Society of the Cincinnati of Pennsylvania in a paper entitled "A Neglected Phase of Revolutionary History." Dr. Don Higginbotham's excellent new survey, The War of American Independence: Military Attitudes, Policies, and Practice, 1763-1789 (New York: Macmillan, 1971), reinforces it.

2. For writing ideas, one might consult this bibliography to learn what has been published and then check Dean C. Allard and Betty Bern, U.S. Naval History Sources in the Washington Area and Suggested Research Topics (3rd ed., Washington: U.S. Government Printing Office, 1970), pp. 61-72 and R. Ernest and Trevor N. Dupuy, The Encyclopedia of Military History. . . (New York: Harper, 1970), pp. 701-702, 708-725 to find what might be worthy of further investigation.

NAVIES IN THE AMERICAN REVOLUTION: A BIBLIOGRAPHY

1. Abbey, Katherine, "Peter Chester's Defense of the Mississippi After the Willing Raid." Mississippi Valley Historical Review, XXII (June 1935), 17-32.

2. Abbot, Henry L. Beginning of Modern Submarine Warfare under Captain Lieutenant David Bushnell. New York: Archon, 1966. 69p.
    Originally published in pamphlet form in 1881.

3. Abbot, Willis J. Blue Jackets of '76: A History of the Naval Battles of the American Revolution; Together with a Narrative of the War with Tripoli. New York: Dodd, Mead, 1888. 301p.

4. Abbott, John S. C. John Paul Jones. New York: J. A. Hill, 1904. 359p.

5. Abbott, Wilbur C. New York in the American Revolution. New York: Scribner's, 1929. 302p.
    Refers to New York City.

6. Abelard. Elegiac Epistles on the Calamities of Love and War, Including a Description of the Engagement between H. M. Ships, the Serapis and Countess of Scarborough, and the Enemy's Squadron under the Command of Paul Jones, Sept. 23, 1779. London: The Author, 1780. 17p.
    Reprinted as Extra no. 60 of The Magazine of History (1922), p. 37-54.

7. "An Account of the Proceedings of the British Fleet, Consisting of 36 Sail of the Line in an Action with the French Fleet, Commanded by Comte de Grasse off Dominique and Guardaloupe [sic] on the following days, vis:--[April 9-13, 1782]." Journal of the Royal United Service Institute, LXII 187-190.

8. [Active, sloop.] The Case of the Sloop Active, etc.

[Philadelphia: Hall and Sellers, 1779.] 27p.

9. Adams, Charles F. "Contemporary Opinion on the Howes." Massachusetts Historical Society Proceedings, XLIV (1911), 94-120.
The admiral and his brother, the general.

10. -----., ed. See Adams, John, no. 12.

11. [Adams, John.] The Adams Papers: Diary and Autobiography of John Adams. Edited by L. H. Butterfield, et al. 4 vols.; Cambridge: Belknap Press of Harvard University Press, 1961.

12. -----. Familiar Letters of John Adams and His Wife, Abigail Adams, During the American Revolution, with a Memoir of Mrs. Adams. Edited by Charles F. Adams. New York: Hurt and Houghton, 1876. 424p.

13. Adams, John. "John Adams on Warfare." Magazine of History, XXI (August 1915), 131-132.

14. -----. "The True Origin and Foundation of the American Navy." In Charles F. Adams, ed., The Works of John Adams, Second President of the United States: With a Life of the Author. Notes and Illustrations. 10 vols.; Boston: Little, Brown, 1850-1856., III, 7-12.

15. Adams, Nathaniel, ed. Annals of Portsmouth: Comprising a Period of Two Hundred Years from the First Settlement of the Town. Portsmouth, N.H.: The Author, 1825. 400p.
Some coverage of Continental shipbuilding.

15a. Adams, Randolph C. "Arnold's Expedition to Richmond, 1781." William and Mary Quarterly, 2nd Series, XII (July 1932), 187-190.
Unsuccessfully opposed by the Virginia State Navy.

16. -----. "The Cartography of the British Attack on Fort Moultrie in 1776." In William W. Bishop and Andrew Keogh, eds. Essays Offered to Herbert Putnam by His Colleagues and Friends on his Thirtieth Anniversary as Librarian of Congress, 5 April 1929. New Haven: Yale University Press,

1929. p. 35-46.

17. Adams, Scarritt. "The Loss of the Royal George, 1782." History Today, IX (December 1959), 837-840.

18. Adams, W. H. Davenport. Neptune's Heroes; or, The Sea Kings of Britain from Sir John Hawkins to Sir John Franklin. London: Griffith and Farran, 1861. 440p.
Features lengthy biographies of Howe and Rodney.

19. Adams, William F., comp. Commodore Joshua Barney. Many Interesting Facts Connected with the Life of Commodore Joshua Barney, Hero of the U.S. Navy, 1776-1812. With Valuable Records for Those in Search of Barney Family Connections. Springfield, Mass.: Priv. print., 1912. 228p.

20. Affaires de l'Angleterre et de l'Amérique. 15 vols. in 17.; Paris: 1776-1779.
For France what the Remembrancer was to Great Britain.

21. Agnew, J. L., jt. author. See Lee, F. D., no. 893.

22. Ahlin, J. H. "New England Rubicon: A Study of Eastern Maine during the American Revolution." Unpublished PhD Dissertation, Boston University, 1961.
Includes incidents afloat.

23. Albion, Robert G. Forests and Sea-Power; the Timber Problem of the Royal Navy, 1652-1862. Cambridge, Mass.: Harvard University Press, 1926. 485p.

24. -----, and Jennie B. Pope. Sea Lanes in Wartime: The American Experience, 1775-1942. New York: W. W. Norton, 1942. 367p.
Chpt. 2, "Gunrunning in the Revolution."

25. Alden, Carroll S. and Ralph Earle. "John Paul Jones." In their Makers of Naval Tradition. New York: Ginn, 1925. p. 1-36.

26. Alden, John R. The American Revolution, 1775-1783. The New American Nation Series. New York:

Harper and Brothers, 1954. 294p.
A good survey of the period.

27. -----. General Gage in America: Being Principally a History of His Role in the American Revolution. Baton Rouge: Louisiana State University Press, 1948. 313p.
Develops the idea that Gage proposed a naval blockade of the colonies early on instead of massive military operations ashore.

28. -----. The South in the Revolution, 1763-1789. Vol. III of The History of the South. Baton Rouge: Louisiana State University Press, 1957. 442p.
A standard work on this theatre.

29. -----., ed. See Ward, Christopher, no. 1527.

30. Alexander, Arthur J. "A Footnote on Massachusetts Deserters who went to Sea During the American Revolution." American Neptune, X (January 1950), 43-51.

31. Alexander, John K. " 'American Privateersmen in the Mill Prison during 1777-1782:' an Evaluation." Essex Institute Historical Collections. CII (October 1966), 318-340.
A critical review of the Applegate article below.

32. -----. "Forton Prison During the American Revolution: A Case Study of British Prisoner-of-War Policy and the American Prisoners' Response to that Policy." Essex Institute Historical Collections, CIII (October 1967), 365-389.

33. -----. "Jonathan Haskin's Mill Prison Diary: Can It Be Accepted at Face Value?" New England Quarterly, XL (December 1967), 561-564.

34. Alexander, Mary H. T. "Paul Jones and Lord Selkirk." The Beaver, CCLXXIV (June 1943), 4-7.

35. Alger, Philip R. "The Naval Academy Miniature of John Paul Jones." United States Naval Institute Proceedings, XXXI (September 1905), 585-597.

36. -----., trans. See Daveluy, R., no. 422.

37. Allaben, W. G. "The Alliance of 1778." Journal of American History, XXII (July 1928), 197-205.

38. Allan, John. Military Operations in Eastern Maine and Nova Scotia during the Revolution; Chiefly Compiled from the Journals and Letters of Col. John Allan, with Notes and a Memoir of Col. John Allan, by Frederic Kidder. Albany: J. Munsell, 1867. 336p. Rpr. 1970.

39. Allardyce, Alexander. Memoir of the Honourable George Keith Elphinstone. London: Blackwood, 1882. 432p.

40. Allen, Gardner W. Captain Hector McNeill of the Continental Navy. Boston: Mass. Historical Society, 1922. 108p.
Includes his "autobiographical sketch" and an alphabetical list of officers and men of the ship Boston.

41. -----. "Esek Hopkins." New England Quarterly, IX (December 1936), 483-485.

42. -----. Massachusetts Privateers of the Revolution. Massachusetts Historical Society Collections, v. 77. Boston: The Society, 1926. 356p.

43. -----. "Naval Convoys." Massachusetts Historical Society Proceedings, LVII (1924), 392-414.

44. -----. The Naval History of the American Revolution. 2 vols.; Boston: Houghton, Mifflin, 1913. Rpr. 1970.

45. -----. "State Navies and Privateers in the Revolution." Massachusetts Historical Society Proceedings, XLVI (1913), 171-191.

46. Allen, Joseph, ed. Memoir of the Life and Services of Sir William Hargood. Compiled from Authentic Documents Under the Direction of Lady Hargood. Greenwich, Eng.: Henry S. Richardson, 1841. 296p.

47. Almon, J., ed. See Great Britain, Parliament, no. 654.

48. -----., ed. See The Remembrancer, no. 1264.

49. "American Prisoners in Mill Prison, Plymouth, England, in 1782." South Carolina Historical and Genealogical Magazine, X (April 1909), 116-124.

50. 'The American Privateer Rattlesnake of 1781." Nautical Research Journal, XII (1964), 126.
Two sets of plans are featured.

51. "American Revolutionary Naval Service." New Hampshire Genealogical Record, IV (January 1907), 25-37.
Of the Continental frigates Raleigh and Boston.

52. Amerman, Richard H. "Treatment of American Prisoners during the Revolution." New Jersey Historical Society Proceedings, LXXVIII (October 1960), 257-275.

53. Ames, Edgar W. "Benedict Arnold--Patriot." New York State Historical Association Proceedings, XII (1913), 139-157.
Includes his activities on Lake Champlain.

54. Amory, Thomas C. The Life of Admiral Sir Isaac Coffin, Baronet, His English and American Ancestors. Boston: Cupples, Upham, 1886. 141p.

55. Anderson, Olive. "The Establishment of British Naval Supremacy at Sea and the Exchange of Naval Prisoners-of-War, 1779-1788." English Historical Review, LXXV (January 1960), 77-89.

56. -----. "The Impact on the Fleet of the Disposal of Prisoners of War in Distant Waters, 1689-1783." Mariner's Mirror, XLV (July 1959), 243-249.
Argues that not until the time of Rodney did the Royal Navy employ efficient efforts to get these men to ship aboard the King's ships.

57. -----. "The Treatment of Prisoners-of-War in Britain During the American War of Independence." Institute of Historical Research Bulletin, XXVIII (May 1955), 63-83.
Colonial seamen were not exchanged by the British

Anderson, R. C.

until relatively late into the contest.

58. Anderson, R. C. "French Masts and Spars in 1780." Mariner's Mirror, XLV (July 1959), 224-226.

59. -----., jt. editor. See Trevenen, James, no. 1472.

60. Anderson, Troyer S. The Command of the Howe Brothers During the American Revolution. New York: Oxford University Press, 1936. 368p.

61. Andre, Benoit, trans. See Jones, John P., no. 805.

62. Andrews, Allen. Proud Fortress: The Fighting Story of Gibraltar. New York: Dutton, 1959. 220p. Chpt. 6, "The Great Siege."

63. Andrews, John. History of the War with America, France, Spain, and Holland, Commencing in 1775 and Ending in 1783. 4 vols.; London: J. Fielding, 1785-1786.

64. Andros, Thomas. The Old Jersey Captive; or, a Narrative of the Captivity of Thomas Andros. In a Series of Letters to a Friend.... Boston: W. Peirce, 1833. 80p.

65. [Angell, Israel.] Diary of Colonel Israel Angell, Commanding the Second Rhode Island Continental Regiment During the American Revolution, 1778-1781. Edited by Edward Field. Providence: Rhode Island Historical Society, 1899. 176p. Rpr. 1971.
Records the Franco-American attempts, especially during the 1779 visit of D'Estaing, to control the colony of Rhode Island.

66. The Annual Register: A Review of Public Events at Home and Abroad for the year--. London, 1758--. v.1--.

67. Anthiaume, A. "Le Comte de Grasse et La Prise de Yorktown." Mer et Colonies, XXVI (January 1924), 2.

68. Applegate, Howard L. "American Privateersmen in the Mill Prison During 1777-1782." Essex Institute Historical Collections, XCVII (October 1961), 303-320.

69. Archer, Jonathan. "Copy of a Letter Written from Mill Prison, England, September 25, 1778." Essex Institute Historical Collections, VI (1864), 113-114.
By a captive American seaman.

70. Armbruster, Eugene L. The Wallabout Prison-ships, 1776-1783. Brooklyn, New York: The author, 1920. 29p.

71. Ashe, S. A. "Some New Light on John Paul Jones." South Atlantic Quarterly, XVII (January 1918), 44-57.
Provides "new evidence" why he left Betsey in the West Indies in 1773, moved to Virginia, and changed his name.

72. Ashmore, Otis, ed. "Account of the [1779] Siege of Savannah, from a British Source." Collections of the Georgia Historical Society, V (1901), 129-139.

73. Aspin, Jehoshapat. Naval and Military Exploits Which Have Distinguished the Reign of George the Third, Accurately Described and Methodically Arranged. London: S. Leigh, 1812. 784p.
Includes some naval actions of the Revolution, particularly those in which the British came out on top.

74. Aspinall, Algernon. West Indian Tales of Old. London: Duckworth, 1912. 259p.
The siege of St. Kitts and the Battle of the Saintes featured.

75. [Arnold, Benedict.] "Benedict Arnold's Plan for Privateering, 1782." Edited by John M. Norris. William and Mary Quarterly, XIII (January 1956), 94-96.
Two unfruitful memos to the Earl of Shelburne.

76. Arnold, Isaac N. The Life of Benedict Arnold: His Patriotism and His Treason. Chicago: Jansen, McClurg, 1880. 444p.

77. Arnold, James N. "Journal of the Committee Who Built the Ships Providence and Warren for the United States in 1776." Magazine of History, III (November-December 1908), 249-254, 311-323; IV

Auger, Helen

(January-April 1909), 1-6, 63-79, 133-140, 195-202.

78. Auger, Helen. The Secret War of Independence. New York: Buell, Little, 1956. 381p.

79. Austin, Mary S. Philip Freneau, the Poet of the Revolution. Edited by Helen K. Vreeland. Detroit: Gale, 1968. 285p.

80. Azoy, A. C. M. "Palmetto Fort, Palmetto Flag." American Heritage, VI (October 1955), 60-64, 99.
The unsuccessful British attack on Fort Moultrie in 1776.

81. Baird, George W. The Father of the American Navy. N. p., n. d. 18p.

82. Balch, Thomas. The French in America During the War of Independence of the United States, 1777-1783. 2 vols.; Philadelphia: Porter & Coates, 1891-1895.

83. Balderston, Marion. "The Flag John Paul Jones Really Fought Under." Huntington Library Quarterly, XXXIII (January 1969), 77-83.
Discounts part of the traditional story.

84. Ballagh, James C., ed. See Lee, Richard Henry, no. 896.

85. Ballard, George A. "Hughes and Suffren." Mariner's Mirror, XIII (October 1927), 348-356.

86. -----. "The Last Battlefleet Struggle in the Bay of Bengal." Mariner's Mirror, XIII (April 1927), 124-144.
Suffren vs. Hughes covered on pages 130-144.

87. -----. Rulers of the Indian Ocean. Boston: Houghton, Mifflin, 1928. 319p.
Based, in part, on his Suffren articles in the Mariner's Mirror.

88. Ballesteros [Gaibrois], Manuel. "Participation de Espana en la Independencia de Estados Unidos." Revista Cubana, XXXI (1957), 29-48.

89. Bamford, Paul W. "France and the American Market in Naval Timber and Masts, 1776-1786." Journal of Economic History, XII (Winter 1952), 21-34.

90. Bancroft, George. History of the United States of America, From the Discovery of the Continent. Rev. ed. 6 vols.; Boston: Little, Brown, 1876. Rpr. 1970.

91. Banks, James Lenox. David Sproat and Naval Prisoners in the War of the Revolution, with Mention of William Lenox, of Charleston. New York: Knickerbocker Press, 1909. 127p.

92. [Barham, Charles M.] Letters and Papers of Charles, Lord Barham, Admiral of the Red Squadron, 1758-1813. Edited by John K. Laughton. Publications of the Navy Records Society, v. 32, 38, 39. 3 vols.; London: The Society, 1907-1911.
Known as Sir Charles Middleton, Controller of the Royal Navy, during the American Revolution.

93. Barnes, G. R., jt. editor. See Sandwich, John M., 4th Earl of, no. 1325.

94. Barnes, James. "The Personal Appearance of John Paul Jones." Appleton's Booklovers Magazine, VI (July 1905), 106-118.

95. -----. "The Tragedy of the Lost Commission." Outlook, LXXIII (January 3, 1903), 71-83.
On the tribulations of Gustavus Conyingham.

96. Barnes, John S., ed. The Logs of the Serapis-Alliance-Ariel, under the Command of John Paul Jones, 1779-1780, With Extracts from Public Documents, Unpublished Letters and Narratives, and Illustrated with Reproductions of Scarce Prints. Publications of the Naval History Society, v. 1. New York: Printed for the Society by De Vinne Press, 1911. 138p.

97. -----., ed. See Fanning, Nathaniel, no. 515.

98. Barnett, John. "Lord Rodney." In his Fighting Admirals. London: Smith, Elder, 1910. p. 214-250.

99. Barney, Mary, ed. Biographical Memoir of the Late Commodore Joshua Barney, from Autographical Notes and Journals in Possession of His Family and Other Authentic Sources. Boston: Gray & Bowen, 1832. 328p.

100. Barras, Jacques-Melchior Saint-Laurent, Comte de. Memoirs. 2 vols. [London: 1893.] His squadron joined De Grasse in the Chesapeake in September 1781 bringing heavy French cannon from Newport for the siege.

101. [Barrington, Samuel.] The Barrington Papers. Selected from the Letters and Papers of Admiral the Hon. Samuel Barrington and Edited by David Bonner-Smith. Publications of the Navy Records Society, v. 71, 81. 2 vols.; London: Printed for the Navy Records Society, 1937.

102. -----. "Some Letters of Admiral the Honorable Samuel Barrington, III." Mariner's Mirror, XX (January 1934), 67-84.

103. Barritt, M. K. "The Navy and the Clyde in the American War, 1777-1783." Mariner's Mirror, LVIII (February 1969), 33-42.

104. Barrow, John. An Autobiographical Memoir of Sir John Barrow, Bart.; Late of the Admiralty; Including Reflections, Observations, and Reminiscences at Home and Abroad from Early Life to Advanced Age. London: Murray, 1847. 515p.

105. -----. "Rodney's Battle of 12th April [1782]." The Quarterly Review, XXXIX (January 1830), 50-79.

106. -----. The Life of Richard Earl Howe ... Admiral of the Fleet and General of Marines. London: Murray, 1838. 432p.

107. Barrow, Thomas C. Trade and Empire; the British Customs Service in Colonial America, 1660-1775. Cambridge, Mass.: Harvard University Press, 1967. 336p.

108. Bartlett, John R. A History of the Destruction of His Majesty's Schooner Gaspee in Narragansett Bay on

the 10th of June 1772. Accompanied by the Correspondence Connected Therewith; the Action of the General Assembly of Rhode Island Thereon, and the Official Journal of the Proceedings of the Commission of Inquiry Appointed by King George III on the Same. Providence: A. C. Greene, 1861. 183p.

109. Barthold, Allen J. "'Gazette François,' Newport, Rhode Island, 1780-81." Bibliographic Society of America Papers, XXVIII, Part I (1934), 64-79.
Printed by the French fleet off Newport in those years.

110. Barton, John A. "The Battle of Valcour Island, 1776: Benedict Arnold's Defence." History Today, IX (December 1959), 791-99.

111. -----. "The Battle of Valcour Island. From the Life of Admiral Viscount Exmouth, by Edward Osler, Esq. London, 1835." Bulletin of the Fort Ticonderoga Museum, II (1930-1932), 163-168.

112. Bauer, K. Jack. Ships of the Navy, 1775-1969: Volume I, Combat Vessels. Troy, New York: Rensselaer Polytechnic Institute, 1970. 359p.
Tabulations of the basic statistics.

113. Baugh, Daniel A. British Naval Administration in the Age of Walpole. Princeton, N.J.: Princeton University Press, 1965. 557p.

114. -----. "Sir Samuel Hood: Superior Subordinate." In George A. Billias, ed. George Washington's Opponents: British Generals and Admirals in the American Revolution. New York: Morrow, 1959. p. 291-326.

114a. Baumann, E. D. "Het Bezoek van Paul Jones aan ons Land in 1779." Tijdschrift voor Geschiedenis, Land- en Volkenkunde, XIX (1904), 249-272.
A Dutch scholar's investigation of Jones in the Texel.

115. Baxter, W. T. The House of Hancock: Business in Boston, 1724-1775. Harvard Studies in Business History, v. 10. Cambridge, Mass.: Harvard University Press, 1945. 321p.

Beatson, Robert

Contains an excellent account of the seizure of the merchantman Liberty by HMS Romney in June 1768.

116. Beatson, Robert. Naval and Military Memoirs of Great Britain from 1727 to 1783. 6 vols.; London: Printed for Longman, Hurst, Rees, and Orme, 1804.
Military refers to "combined operations" by sea and land forces.

117. Beattie, Donald W. and J. Richard Collins. Washington's New England Fleet: Beverly's Role in its Origin, 1775-77. Salem, Mass.: Newcomb & Gauss, 1969. 67p.

118. Beaufort, W. H. de. Brieven van en aan Joan Derck van der Capellen van de Poll. Utrecht: Kemink and Zoon, 1879. 854p.

119. Beaurepaire, Chevalier Quesnay de. Memoirs. [Paris, 1788?]
Served aboard Le Sagittaire in the Chesapeake.

120. Becke, Louis and Walter Jeffery. Admiral [Arthur] Phillip, the Founding of New South Wales. New York: Longman, Green, 1899. 336p.
Some comment on his earlier life, including his 1783 failure to arrive in the West Indies in time for the Battle of the Saintes.

121. [Becker, Gottfried Wi.] John Paul Jones, der Kühne Seemann und Gründer der Amerikanischen Marine. Leipsig, 1826.

122. Begnaud, Allen E. "British Operations in the Caribbean and the American Revolution." Unpublished PhD Dissertation, Tulane University, 1967.

123. Bell, Charles H. "The Privateer General Sullivan." New England Historical and Genealogical Register, XXIII (1869), 47, 181, 289.

124. Bellas, Henry H. "The Defenses of the Delaware River in the Revolution." Wyoming Historical and Geological Society Proceedings and Collections, V (1900), 47-73.

125. Belmont, Perry. Naval Supremacy during the American Revolution. Brussels: Imprimerie P. and E. De Bie, 1931. 36p.
A pamphlet in English.

126. Bemis, Samuel F. The Diplomacy of the American Revolution. New York: D. Appleton, 1935. 293p.

127. "Benedict Arnold." In Gamaliel Bradford, ed. Damaged Souls. Boston: Houghton Mifflin, 1922. p. 19-50.

128. Benjamin, Samuel G. W. "Our Naval Heroes." Riverside Magazine for Young People, IV (July 1870), 296-300.
Includes John Paul Jones and the Bonhomme Richard.

129. Benz, Francis E. Commodore Barry, Navy Hero. New York: Dodd, Mead, 1950. 241p.

130. [Berthier, Alexandre.] "Alexandre Berthier's Journal of the American Campaign: The Rhode Island Sections." Trans. Marshall Morgan. Rhode Island History, XXIV (July 1965), 77-88.
In letters to a French friend, Berthier described conditions in the colony in 1780-81, with particular emphasis on naval and privateering activities.

131. Beson, Philip. "Narrative." Massachusetts Historical Society Proceedings, V (1862), 357-360.
Beson served aboard colonial privateers, 1777-1783, was captured, spent some time in Mill Prison, escaped, and returned to privateering.

132. Besson, Maurice. Le Comte d'Estaing, Colonel aux Indies, Gouverneur de Saint-Dominique, Vice-Amiral sons la Guerre d' Independance. Paris: Larose, 1931. 144p.

133. [Biddle, Charles.] Autobiography of Charles Biddle, Vice President of the Supreme Executive Council of Pennsylvania, 1745-1821. Edited by James S. Biddle. Philadelphia: E. Claxton, 1883. 423p.
Includes his dealings with the Pennsylvania State Navy.

Biddle, Edward

134. Biddle, Edward. "Captain Nicholas Biddle, 1750-1778." United States Naval Institute Proceedings, XLIII (September 1917), 1993-2003.

135. Biddle, James S., ed. See Biddle, Charles, no. 133.

136. [Biddle, Nicholas.] "Letters of Captain Nicholas Biddle." Edited by William B. Clark. Pennsylvania Magazine of History and Biography, LXXIV (July 1950), 348-405.
Captain of the ill-fated Continental frigate Randolph.

137. Bigelow, John, Ed. See Franklin, Benjamin, no. 565.

138. Bigot de Morogues, Sebastion F. Tactique Navale, ou, Traité des Evolutions et des Signaux, etc. Paris, 1763. 481p.

139. -----. Naval Tactics; or, a Treatise of Evolutions and Signals. Translated by a Sea Officer. London: W. Johnston, 1767. 152p.
A basic French tactical text well-read by both sides in the era of the American Revolution.

140. Billias, George A. "Beverly's Seacoast Defenses During the Revolutionary War." Essex Institute Historical Collections, XCIV (April 1958), 119-131.

141. -----. General John Glover and His Marblehead Mariners. New York: Holt, 1960. 243p.
Those who ferried Washington over the Delaware.

142. -----. "Marbleheaders Save the Day at Keps Bay." New England Social Studies Bulletin, XV (1957-1958), 21-23.
How General Glovers marine regiment saved Washington at New York.

143. -----. "Soldier in a Longboat." American Heritage, XI (February 1960), 56-59, 89-94.
How General John Glover's Marblehead fishermen, an "amphibious regiment," rowed Washington and company across the Delaware.

144. "Bills for Outfitting Washington's Four Schooners at Beverly." In U.S. Navy Department, Naval History

Division. Naval Documents of the American Revolution. Edited by William B. Clark, et al. Washington: U.S. Government Printing Office, 1964--. II, 1379-1385.
The Continental vessels Hancock, Franklin, Lee, and Warren.

145. "Biographical Memoirs of Arthur Philip, Esq." Naval Chronicle, XXVII (January to July 1812), 1-9.

146. "Biographical Memoirs of Benjamin Caldwell, Esq." Naval Chronicle, XI (January to July 1804), 1-9.
Commanded frigate Rose during Revolution.

147. "Biographical Memoirs of Captain Edward Riou." Naval Chronicle, V (January to July 1801), 482-93.

148. "Biographical Memoirs of Captain John Hunter." Naval Chronicle, VI (July to December 1801), 349-67.
Examined channels of Delaware River so British fleet could ascend. Commanded Berwick in the West Indies.

149. "Biographical Memoirs of Captain Joseph Ellison." Naval Chronicle, XIX (January-July 1818), 1-30.

150. "Biographical Memoirs of Captain Richard Dacres." Naval Chronicle, XXVI (July-December 1811), 353-84.

151. "Biographical Memoirs of Charles Edmund Nagent, Esq." Naval Chronicle, X (July to December 1803), 441-68.

152. "Biographical Memoirs of Commodore Sir Samuel Hood." Naval Chronicle, XVII (January to July 1807), 1-37.
A lt. aboard Barfleur at the Battle of the Chesapeake.

153. "Biographical Memoirs of Commodore William Locker." Naval Chronicle, V (January to July 1801), 97-121.
Commanded frigate Lowestoffe in W. Indies during Revolution.

Biographical

154. "Biographical Memoirs of Earl Howe." Naval Chronicle, I (January to July 1799), 1-24.

155. "Biographical Memoirs of George Young, Knt." Naval Chronicle, XXXI (January to July 1814), 177-183.

156. "Biographical Memoirs of John Knight, Esq." Naval Chronicle, XI (January to July 1804), 425-31.
Conned Howe's fleet through "the most intricate channels."

157. "Biographical Memoirs of Philip D'Auvergne, Duke of Bouillon." Naval Chronicle, XIII (January to July 1805), 169-91.

158. "Biographical Memoirs of Rear Admiral John Willett Payne." Naval Chronicle, III (January to July 1800), 1-38.
Served under Howe at New York.

159. "Biographical Memoirs of Rear Admiral Sir John Borlase Warren." Naval Chronicle, III (January to July 1800), 333-59; XXVI (July to December 1811), 89-132.
In command of frigate Ariadne, fought spirited engagement with Dunkirk privateer L'Aigle in 1781.

160. "Biographical Memoirs of Robert Roddam, Esq." Naval Chronicle, IX (January to July 1803), 253-268.
Commanded Cornwall, 74, in 1777.

161. "Biographical Memoirs of Sir Edward Pellow, Bart." Naval Chronicle, XVIII (July-December 1807), 441-466.

162. "Biographical Memoirs of Sir Erasmus Gower, Knt." Naval Chronicle, IV (July to December 1800), 257-89; XXV (January to July 1811), 452-53; XXX (July to December 1813), 265-301.
Served on Prince William, 64, under Rodney.

163. "Biographical Memoirs of Sir George Collier, Knt." Naval Chronicle, XXXII (July-December 1814), 265-96, 353-400.

164. "Biographical Memoirs of Sir Henry Trollope, Knt."

Naval Chronicle, XVIII (July to December 1807), 353-64.
In command of Rainbow frigate that captured French frigate La Hebe off the Isle of Bas, September 4, 1782.

165. "Biographical Memoirs of Sir Home Riggs Popham, Km. & Krs." Naval Chronicle, XVI (July-December 1806), 265-306, 352-379.

166. "Biographical Memoirs of Sir Hyde Parker, Bart." Naval Chronicle, V (January to July 1801), 281-307.

167. "Biographical Memoirs of Sir Isaac Coffin, Bart." Naval Chronicle, XII (July to December 1804), 1-12.
Second Lieutenant of Adamant during Revolution.

168. "Biographical Memoirs of Sir James Saumarez, Bart." Naval Chronicle, VI (July to December 1801), 85-116.

169. "Biographical Memoirs of Sir John Colpoys, Kb." Naval Chronicle, XI (January to July 1804), 265-72.

170. "Biographical Memoirs of Sir John Lockart Ross, Bart." Naval Chronicle, VI (January to December 1801), 1-33.
Commanded Shrewsbury at Ushant.

171. "Biographical Memoirs of Sir John Orde, Bart." Naval Chronicle, XI (January to July 1804), 177-207.
Led British fleet at Penobscot, 1779.

172. "Biographical Memoirs of Sir Nathan Dance, Knt." Naval Chronicle, XII (July to December 1804), 345-349.

173. "Biographical Memoirs of Sir Peter Parker, Bart." Naval Chronicle, XII (July to December 1804), 169-86.

174. "Biographical Memoirs of Sir Richard King, Bart." Naval Chronicle, XII (July to December 1804), 433-47.
Commanded Pallas in 1777.

Biographical 19

175. "Biographical Memoirs of Sir Richard Onslow, Bart." Naval Chronicle, XIII (January to July 1805), 249-59. Commanded St. Albans in West Indies.

176. "Biographical Memoirs of Sir Robert Calder, Bart." Naval Chronicle, XVII (January to July 1807), 89-115; XXVII (July to December 1812), 441-52.

177. "Biographical Memoirs of Sir Robert Kingsmill, Bart." Naval Chronicle, V (January to July 1801), 189-212. Commanded Vigilant, 64.

178. "Biographical Memoirs of Sir Roger Curtis, Bart." Naval Chronicle, VI (July to December 1801), 261-76.
Howe's fleet captain.

179. "Biographical Memoirs of Sir Thomas Louis, Bart." Naval Chronicle, XVI (July to December 1806), 177-93.

180. "Biographical Memoirs of Sir Thomas Pasley, Bart." Naval Chronicle, IV (July to December 1800), 349-65.

181. "Biographical Memoirs of Sir William Sidney Smith, Knt." Naval Chronicle, IV (July to December 1800), 445-477.

182. "Biographical Memoirs of the Honourable George Cranfield Berkeley." Naval Chronicle, XII (July to December 1804), 89-112.

183. "Biographical Memoirs of the Honourable Robert Digby." Naval Chronicle, XI (January to July 1804), 89-99.
Rear Ad. during the Rev.

184. "Biographical Memoirs of the Honourable Samuel Harrington." Naval Chronicle, IV (July to December 1800), 169-98.

185. "Biographical Memoirs of the Honourable William Cornwallis." Naval Chronicle, VII (January to July 1802), 1-25.

186. "Biographical Memoirs of the Late August Lord

Keppell." *Naval Chronicle*, VII (January to July 1802), 277-318, 389-437.

187. "Biographical Memoirs of the Late Captain Edward Thompson." *Naval Chronicle*, VI (July to December 1801), 437-61; VII (January to July 1802), 93-106.
Commanded *Hyaena* frigate in Revolution.

188. "Biographical Memoirs of the Late Captain James Newman Newman." *Naval Chronicle*, XXX (July to December 1813), 361-95.

189. "Biographical Memoirs of the Late Captain John Cooke." *Naval Chronicle*, XVII (January to July 1807), 353-66.
Aboard Howe's *Eagle* at age 13.

190. "Biographical Memoirs of the Late John MacBride, Esq." *Naval Chronicle*, XIX (January-July 1808), 265-72.

191. "Biographical Memoirs of the Late Lord (Constantine John Phipps) Mulgrave." *Naval Chronicle*, VIII (July to December 1802), 89-110.
One of commissioners in office of Lord High Admiral.

192. "Biographical Memoirs of the Late Right Honourable George Brydges, Lord Rodney." *Naval Chronicle*, I (January to July 1799), 349-96.

193. "Biographical Memoirs of the Late Sir Frederick Thesiger." *Naval Chronicle*, XIV (July to December 1805), 441-55.
Aide de Camp of Rodney at Saintes.

194. "Biographical Memoirs of the Late Sir Hugh Pallister, Bartonet." *Naval Chronicle*, XXXIX (January-July 1818), 89-112.

195. "Biographical Memoirs of the Right Honourable John Jervis, Earl of St. Vincent." *Naval Chronicle*, IV (July to December 1800), 1-42.

196. "Biographical Memoirs of the Right Honourable Lord (G. K. Elphinstone) Keith." *Naval Chronicle*, X (July to December 1803), 1-23.

Biographical 21

197. "Biographical Memoirs of the Right Honourable Lord Gardner Gardner." Naval Chronicle, VIII (July to December 1802), 177-98.
Commanded Duke under Rodney at the Saintes.

198. "Biographical Memoirs of the Right Honourable Lord Hugh Seymour." Naval Chronicle, II (July to December 1799), 357-73.
Cmdr. of Latona, 36.

199. "Biographical Memoirs of the Right Honourable Lord Nelson of the Nile, Kb." Naval Chronicle, III (January to July 1800), 157-89.
This part of a longer series highlights his service under Sir P. Parker in W. Indies in 1780's.

200. "Biographical Memoirs of the Right Honourable Samuel Lord Viscount Hood." Naval Chronicle, II (July to December 1799), 1-47.

201. "Biographical Memoirs of the Right Honourable Thomas Lord Graves." Naval Chronicle, V (January to July 1801), 377-408.

202. "Biographical Memoirs of the Right Honourable William Carnegie, Earl of Northesk, Esq." Naval Chronicle, XV (January to July 1806), 441-49.
Lieutenant aboard Rodney's ship at Saintes.

203. "Biographical Memoirs of the Right Honourable William Lord Hotham." Naval Chronicle, IX (January to July 1803), 341-57.

204. "Biographical Memoirs of the Right Honourable William Lord (Veldegrave) Radstock." Naval Chronicle, X (July to December 1803), 265-83.
Commanded frigate Pomona, 28.

205. "Biographical Memoirs of William Albany Otway, Esq." Naval Chronicle, XXXI (January-July 1814), 441-444.
Served aboard frigate Lark during Revolution.

206. "Biographical Memoirs of William Cornett, Esq." Naval Chronicle, XV (January to July 1806), 1-13.
First lieutenant of Robust at Battle of Chesapeake.

207. "Biographical Memoirs of William Truscott, Esq." Naval Chronicle, XXX (July to December 1813), 177-79.

208. "Biographical Sketch of Commodore John Barry." Portfolio, 3rd Series, II (July 1813), 1-10.

209. "Biographical Sketch of the Late Captain John Whitley." Naval Chronicle, IX (January to July 1803), 196-98.
Commanded cutter Rattlesnake.

210. Bird, Harrison. Navies in the Mountains. The Battles on the Waters of Lake Champlain and Lake George, 1609-1814. New York: Oxford University Press, 1962. 361p.

211. Blanchard, Amos. American Military and Naval Biography: Containing the Lives and Characters of the Officers of the Revolution; Together with Some of the Most Eminent Statesmen of that Interesting Period. To which are Added, the Life and Character of Benedict Arnold and the Circumstances of the Capture, Trial, and Execution of Major Andre. Cincinnati: Robinson & Fairbank, 1832. 604p.
Part II: Naval Officers in the American Service.

212. Blanchard, W., ed. See Keppell, August K., no. 821.

213. Bland, Schuyler O., author. See United States, Yorktown Sesquicentennial Commission, no. 1499.

214. [Bland, Theodore.] "Letter of Colonel Theodore Bland to Thomas Jefferson." Magazine of History, VII (March 1908), 175-176.
Describing military and naval events around Yorktown in 1781.

215. Blane, Gilbert. Account of the Battle between the British and French Fleets in the West Indies on April 12, 1782, in a Letter to Lord Dalrymple, British Minister at the Court of Warsaw. (London: 1782.)
An eyewitness account of Rodney's private physician.

216. -----. A Narrative of Facts Connected with the Manoeuvre [sic] of Breaking the Enemy's Line on the 12th of April. London: Samuel Bentley, 1830. 16p.

[Blatchford, John]

217. [Blatchford, John.] The Narrative of John Blatchford, Detailing his Sufferings in the Revolutionary War, while a Prisoner with the British. With an Introduction and Notes by Charles I. Bushnell. New York: Priv. print, 1865. 138p. Rpr. 1971.

218. -----. Narrative of Remarkable Occurances, in the Life of John Blatchford, of Cape Anne, Mass., Containing his Treatment in Nova Scotia, the West Indies, Great Britain, France, and the East Indies, as a Prisoner in the Late War. New London: T. Green, 1788. 22p.
    The first edition of this prisoner's story.

219. Bloomster, Edgar L. Sailing and Small Craft Down the Ages. 2nd ed. Annapolis: U.S. Naval Institute 1940. 280p.
    Useful drawings and data on the vessels and rigs available in the era of the Revolution.

220. [Boardman, Francis.] "Journal of Francis Boardman, Sloop Adventure." In U.S. Navy Department, Naval History Division. Naval Documents of the American Revolution. Edited by William B. Clark, et al. Washington: U.S. Government Printing Office, 1964--. IV, 1485-1488.
    The vessel was captured by H.M.S. Falcon on March 8, 1776.

221. Boardman, Rev. Samuel W. Log Book of Timothy Boardman; kept on Board the Privateer Oliver Cromwell, During a Cruise from New London, Ct., to Charleston, S.C., and Return, in 1778; also, a Biographical Sketch of the Author. Albany: J. Munsell, 1885. 85p.

222. Boatner, M.M. Encyclopedia of the American Revolution. New York: McKay, 1966. 1287p.

223. Bolander, Louis H. "Arnold's Retreat from Valcour Island." United States Naval Institute Proceedings, LV (December 1929), 1060-1062.

224. -----. "A Forgotten Hero of the Revolution." United States Naval Institute Proceedings, XXII (April 1928), 119-128.
    Lambert Wickes.

225. -----. "The Frigate Alliance, the Favorite Ship of the American Revolution." United States Naval Institute Proceedings, XLIII (September 1937), 1249-1258.

226. -----. "Two Notes on John Paul Jones." United States Naval Institute Proceedings, LIV (July 1928), 546-549.
    I "His Qualifications as an Officer"; II "His Birthplace."

227. Bolton, Reginald P. The Bombardment of New York and the Fight for Independence on the Waters of New York City Against the Seapower of Great Britain in the Year 1776. (New York: 1915.) 75p.

228. -----. "The British Navy in the [American] Revolution." Magazine of History, II (1905), 223-227, 311-314.
    A useful survey.

229. Bon Homme Richard (ship). The Log of the Bon Homme Richard. Mystic, Conn.: Marine Historical Association, Inc., 1936. 61p.

230. Bonner-Smith, David. "Byron in the Leeward Islands, 1779." Mariner's Mirror, XXX (January 1944), 38-48, 81-92.

231. -----. "The Case of the Sartine." Mariner's Mirror, XXI (July 1935), 305-322.
    Concerns Roddam Home's action off Cape St. Vincent in 1780.

232. -----, ed. See Barrington, Samuel, no. 101.

233. Bonsal, Stephen. When the French Were Here: A Narrative of the Sojourn of the French Forces in America, and Their Contribution to the Yorktown Campaign, Drawn from Unpublished Reports and Letters of Participants in the National Archives of France and the Ms. Division of the Library of Congress. New York: Doubleday, 1945. 263p. Rpr. 1968.

234. Boromé, Joseph A. "Dominica During the French Occupation, 1778-1784." English Historical Review,

LXXXIV (January 1969), 36-58.
Brief account of the island's capture precedes an elaboration of the rule.

235. Boucher, Odet J. Histoire de la Derniere Guerre, Entre la Grande Bretagne, et les Etats-Unis de l'Amerique, la France, l'Espagne, et Hollande. Paris: Brocas, 1787. 358p.
Pro-allied verdict.

236. Boudinot, Elias. "Report on American Prisoners of War in New York." William and Mary Quarterly, 3rd Series XIII (July 1956), 379-393.

237. Bourdé de Villehuet, Jacques. Le Manoeuvrier, ou, Essai sur la Théorie et la Pratique de Mouvements du Navire et des Evolutions Navales. Paris, 1765. 407p.
A basic French tactical text well-read by both sides in the era of the American Revolution.

238. Boutet de Monvel, Roger. La Vie Martiale du Bailli de Suffren. Paris, 1929. 244p.

238a. Bowie, Julia V. W. "The Burning of the Peggy Stewart." American Monthly Magazine, XXXV (December 1909), 1181-1183.

239. Bowles, Francis T. "America's Debt to De Grasse." Massachusetts Historical Society Proceedings, LX (1927), 235-250.

240. Bradford, Gershom. "Nelson in Boston Bay." American Neptune, XI (October 1951), 239-244.
During the Revolution.

241. Brady, Cyrus T. Commodore Paul Jones. Great Commanders, ed. by James Grant Wilson. New York: D. Appleton, 1900. 459p.

242. -----. "John Paul Jones: The Formost Sea Fighter of the Revolution." Munsey's Magazine, XVI (July 1905), 453-461.

243. Branch, Joseph G., jt. editor. See Jones, William R., no. 810.

244. Breaking the Line. Statement of Facts in the Nature of Memoir, Leading to and Connected with the Great Battle of the 12th of April 1782, Between the Fleet of Great Britain, Commanded by the Late Lord Rodney, and That of France, under the Compte [sic] de Grasse. By an Old Naval Officer, who Served under Lord Rodney, and was Lieutenant of a Seventy-four gun Ship on that Occasion. Cheltenham: J. J. Hadley, 1830. 52p.
Author, who signs his appended letters "G. C.," claims to have been aboard H. M. S. Hercules.

245. Brebner, John B. The Neutral Yankees of Nova Scotia: A Marginal Colony during the Revolutionary Years. New York: Columbia University Press, 1937. 388p.

246. Breen, K. C. "The [British] Navy and the Yorktown Campaign, 1781." Unpublished M. Phil. Thesis, University of London, 1966.

246a. Brenton, Edward P. The Naval History of Great Britain from the Year 1781 to 1836. 2 vols.; London: H. Colburn, 1837.
The Battle of the Saintes included.

247. Brewington, Marion V. "American Naval Guns, 1775-1785." American Neptune, III (January-April 1943), 11-18, 148-158.

248. -----. "The Battle of Delaware Bay, 1782." United States Naval Institute Proceedings, LXV (February 1939), 231-240.

249. -----. "The Designs of Our First Frigates." American Neptune, VIII (January 1948), 11-25.
Those ordered by the Continental Congress on December 13, 1775, an example of which is the Maryland ship Virginia.

250. -----. "The Sailmaker's Gear." American Neptune, IX (October 1949), 278-296.

251. -----. "The State Ship General Greene." Pennsylvania Magazine of History and Biography, XL (April 1936), 229-241.

252. -----. "Washington's Boats at the Delaware Crossing." American Neptune, II (April 1942), 167-170.

253. Bridport, Alexander N. and Alexander N. Hood. "Hood." In G. E. Marindin, ed. Our Naval Heroes. London: Murray, 1901. p. 247-273.

254. "Brief Account of the Desolation made in Several of the West India Island by the Late Hurricane." Gentlemens Magazine, L (1780), 620-623.
By the large storm of late 1780.

255. British Naval Biography, Comprising the Lives of the Most Distinguished Admirals, from Howard to Codrington, with an Outline of the Naval History of England from the Earliest Period to the Present Time. London: Scott, Webster & Geary, 1839. 665p.

255a. Brooke, George M. "The Virginia Navy in the American Revolution." DAR Magazine, XLIV (March 1960), 187-191.

256. Brooke, Richard. Liverpool as it was During the Last Quarter of the Eighteenth Century, 1775-1800. London: J. R. Smith, 1853. 558p.
Home port for English privateers during the American Revolution.

257. Brooks, Walter F. History of the Fanning Family. 2 vols.; Worcester, Mass.: Priv. print, 1905.
Features a complete biography of Nathaniel, who served under John Paul Jones.

258. Broomfield, J. H. "Lord Sandwich at the Admiralty Board: Politics and the British Navy, 1771-1778." Mariner's Mirror, LI (February 1965), 7-17.

259. -----. "The Keppel - Palliser Affair, 1778-1779." Mariner's Mirror, 47 (August 1961), 195-207.

260. Brown, Anne S. K. "Rhode Island Uniforms of the Revolution." Military Collector and Historian, X (Spring 1958), 1-10.
Dress of a Rhode Island Naval Officer, p. 5.

261. Brown, Charles W. John Paul Jones of Naval Fame:

A Character of the Revolution. Chicago: M. A. Donohue, 1902. 271p.

262. Brown, Gerald S. The American Secretary: The Colonial Policy of Lord George Germain, 1775-1778. Ann Arbor: University of Michigan Press, 1963. 246p.
    Highlights his difficulties with Admiral Howe.

263. -----. "The Anglo-French Naval Crisis, 1778: A Study of Conflict in the North Cabinet." William and Mary Quarterly, 3rd Series XIII (January 1956), 3-25.

264. -----, ed. See Howe, Richard, no. 752.

265. Browne, William H., et al. eds. Maryland Archives. 70 vols. +; Baltimore: Maryland Historical Society, 1883--.

266. Brumbaugh, Catherin E. B. "Report on the British Prison Ship Jersey, February 2, 1781." D. A. R. Magazine, XLIV (April 1914), 237-239.

267. Bryan, Dan. "Commodore John Barry." Irish Sword, II (Summer 1956), 249-256.

267a. Bryant, Samuel W., ed. "H. M. S. Gaspee: The [1772] Court-Martial." Rhode Island History, XXV (January 1966), 65-72.
    Excerpts from the proceedings.

268. Buell, Augustus C. Paul Jones, Founder of the American Navy: A History. 2 vols.; New York: Scribner, 1900.
    Much of this work a product of the author's imagination.

269. -----., ed. See Kilby, John, no. 829.

270. Bulger, William T. "The British Expedition to Charleston, 1779-1780." Unpublished PhD Dissertation, University of Michigan, 1957.

271. Bullocke, John G., ed. See Tomlinson, Robert and Nicholas, no. 1466.

272. Burney, William. The Naval Heroes of Great Britain; or, Accounts of the Lives and Actions of the Distinguished Admirals and Commanders who have Contributed to Confer on Great Britain the Empire of the Ocean. London: R. Phillips, 1806. 435p.

273. "The Burning of Falmouth, now Portland, Maine, October 18, 1775." Historical Magazine, XV (March 1869), 202-203.

274. "The Burning of the Peggy Stewart." American Monthly Magazine, XVI (February 1900), 128-131.

275. Bushnell, Charles I., ed. See Blatchford, John, no. 217.

276. -----., ed. See Hawkins, Christopher, no. 724.

277. Butler, Charles. "On the Legality of Impressing Seamen." The Pamphleteer, XXIII (1824), 225-287.
Revision of a 1777 essay.

278. Cahill, Thomas P. The Famous Tracys of Newburyport, Massachusetts. Somerville, Mass.: Captain Jeremiah O'Brien's Memorial Associates, 1942. 12p.
Revolutionary privateers.

279. Caldwell, Margaret N. "Samuel Tucker--Revolutionary Patriot." Nautical Research Journal, III (August 1951), 97-102.
A Continental naval officer.

280. Calef, John. The Siege of Penobscot by the Rebels; Containing a Journal of the Proceedings of His Majesty's Forces ... under ... General Francis McLean, and of Three ... Sloops-of-War ... when Besieged by ... Rebel Land Forces under ... General Solomon Lovell. London: G. Kearsley, 1781. 44p. Rpr. 1970.

281. Caley, Percy B. "Dunmore: Colonial Governor of New York and Virginia, 1770-1782." University of Pittsburgh Bulletin, XXXVII (January 15, 1941), 54-61.

282. Calkin, Homer L. "James Leander Cathcart and the

United States Navy." Irish Sword, III (Summer 1958), 145-152.
Cathcart served in the Revolution, 1779-1782.

283. Calkins, Carbs G. "American Admirals in the British Navy." United States Naval Institute Proceedings, XXXV (1909), 685-713.
Highlights Sir Benjamin H. Carew, 1760-1834.

284. Callahan, North. Royal Raiders: The Tories of the American Revolution. Indianapolis: Bobbs-Merrill, 1963. 288p.
Including some who operated afloat.

285. Callender, Geoffrey A. R. "Admirals Keppel, Rodney, and Howe." In his Sea Kings of Britain. 3 vols.; London: Longmans, 1907-1911. III, 1-33, 34-118, 119-176.

286. -----. The Naval Side of British History. London: Christophen, 1924. 305p. Rpr. 1952.

287. -----. "With the Grand Fleet in 1780." Mariner's Mirror, IX (1923), 258-270, 290-304.

288. Callo, Joseph, Jr. "Sea Power: A Lost Legacy." Navy, VII (April 1964), 20-24.

289. Calmon-Maison, Jean J. R. L'Amiral d'Estaing. Paris: Calmann-Levy, 1910. 513p.
The French admiral who aided the colonies, if somewhat poorly, only to end a victim of the French Revolution in 1794.

290. Cameron, A Guyot. "Admiral de Grasse and American Gratitude." Minute Man, XXIV (January 1930), 330-334.
Believes the Frenchman forgotten.

291. [Campbell, Archibald.] "Letters and Memoranda of Sir Archibald Campbell, Prisoner-of-War, Captured in Boston Bay, June 17, 1776." Edited by Archibald M. Howe. Bostonian Society Publications, XII (1915), 65-95.

292. Campbell, John. Lives of the British Admirals, Containing a New and Accurate Naval History, from the

Campbell, Randolph B.

Earliest Periods ... With a Continuation Down to the Year 1779, Including the Naval Transactions of the Late and Present War. 4 vols.; London: Alexander Donaldson, 1779.

293. Campbell, Randolph B. "The Case of the Three Friends an Incident in Maritime Regulation during the American Revolution." Virginia Magazine of History and Biography, LXXIV (April 1966), 190-209.
Problems in controlling Colonial privateers, highlighted by the capture of a British schooner in North Carolina waters.

294. Candler, Allen D., ed. The Revolutionary Records of the State of Georgia. 3 vols.; Atlanta: Franklin-Turner, 1908.

295. "Captain R. N." "The Coming Struggle for Sea Power. The United States Navy." United Service Magazine, CLV-CLVI (February, April, May 1907), 588-599, 1-13, 117-130.
This part of a longer series by an anonymous author devoted to the Revolution. As much of article based on Buell's Jones, the value is questionable.

296. "Capture of the Packet Schooner Dispatch by the Privateer Tyrannicide." Essex Institute Historical Collections, XLII (January 1906), 40.

297. Carleton, William R. "New England Masts and the King's Navy." New England Quarterly, XII (March 1939), 4-18.

298. Caron, Max. L'Amiral de Grasse. Introduction par Mgr. Gibier. Les Gravuves ont ete Executees sur Bois par Mm. Bauchart, freres. Paris: Tequi, 1919. 275p.

299. -----. Admiral De Grasse, One of the Great Forgotten Men. Boston: Four Sea, 1924. 253p.

299a. Cartel pour l'Exchange General de Tous les Prisoniers Pris en Mer, Entre la France & la Grande-Bretagne & Amenes en Europe. A Paris: de l'Imprimerie Royale, 1780. 23p.

300. Cassell, Frank A. Merchant Congressman in the Young Republic: Samuel Smith of Maryland, 1752-1839. Madison: University of Wisconsin Press, 1971. 312p.
 A little data on his Revolutionary career.

301. Castex, Raoul V. P. L'Envers de la Guerre de Course: la Vérité sur l'Enlèvement du Convoi de St.-Eustache par Lamotte-Piquet (Avril-Mai 1781). Paris: L. Fouraier, 1912. 55p.
 The fate of the booty taken by Rodney at St. Eustatius in February, 1781.

302. -----. Les Idées Militaire de la Marine du XVIIIme Siecle: Du Ruyter à Suffren. Paris: L. Fouraier, 1911. 371p.
 French naval strategy up to and including the time of the American Revolution.

303. -----. La Manoeuvre de la Praya (16 Avril 1781). Studie Politique, Stratégique, et Tactique (d'Apres de Nombreux Documents Inédits). Paris: L. Fouraier, 1913. 416p.

304. Caughey, John W. "Bernardo de Galvez and the English Smugglers on the Mississippi, 1777." Hispanic American Historical Review, XII (February 1932), 46-58.

305. -----. Bernardo de Galvez in Louisiana, 1776-1783. Publications of the University of California at Los Angeles in Social Science, no. 4. Berkeley: University of California Press, 1934. 290p.
 Includes his support of American quasi-naval adventures on the Mississippi River.

306. -----. "Louisiana Under Spain, 1762-1783." Unpublished PhD Dissertation, University of California at Berkeley, 1929.
 Exploits of Bernardo de Galvez in the Revolution.

307. -----. "The Panis Mission to Pensacola, 1778." Hispanic American Historical Review, X (1930), 480-489.

307a. -----. "Willing's Expedition Down the Mississippi,

Caulkins, C. G.

1778." *Louisiana Historical Quarterly*, XV (January 1932), 5-36.

308. Caulkins, C. G. "The American Navy and the Opinions of One of its Founders, John Adams, 1735-1826." *United States Naval Institute Proceedings*, XXXVII (June 1911), 453-483.

309. Caulkins, Frances M. *The History of New London, Connecticut. From the First Survey of the Coast in 1612, to 1852.* New London: The Author, 1852. 679p.
Much on privateering and naval activities of the Revolution. A 2nd edition, revised to 1860, adds nothing.

310. -----. *The History of Norwich, Connecticut, from its Settlement in 1660 to January 1845.* Norwich: T. Robinson, 1845. 359p.
The ill-fated Continental frigate Confederacy was constructed there.

311. Cavaliero, Roderick. "Admiral Suffren in the Indies." *History Today*, XX (July 1970), 472-481.

312. Chadwick, French E. "The American Navy, 1775-1815." *Massachusetts Historical Society Proceedings*, XLVI (1913), 191-208.

313. -----. "Sea Power: The Decisive Factor in Our Struggle for Independence." In *The Annual Report of the American Historical Association, 1915.* Washington, D.C.: Government Printing Office, 1916. p. 171-189.

314. -----., ed. See Graves, Thomas, no. 646.

315. Chadwick, John W. "The Battle of Long Island." *Harper's New Monthly Magazine*, LIII (August 1876), 333-346.
Includes a discussion of Mugford's adventures and the Wallabout prison ships.

316. Chapelle, Howard I. "The Design of the American Frigates of the Revolution and Joshua Humphreys." *American Neptune*, IX (July 1949), 161-168.

317. -----. History of the American Sailing Navy. New York: Norton, 1949. 558p.
Includes useful plans, dimensions, and "biographical data" for Continental warships.

318. -----., jt author. See Stegmann, George H., no. 1406.

319. Chapin, Howard M. "Some Recently Found Flag Items." Colonial Society of Massachusetts Publications, XXXII (1937), 521.525.
Notes from the 1775 day book of ship chandler James Wharton of Philadelphia with references to early American naval flags.

320. "Chaplains of the French Navy [in American waters]." American Catholic Researches, VII (July 1911), 250-257.
List.

320a. Chapman, Fredrik Henrik af. Architectura Navalis Mercatoria: A Fascimile of the Famous Eighteenth-Century Treatise on Shipbuilding. New York: Praeger, 1971.
Bicentennial edition of a volume first published in 1768. Reproduces drawings and theories of a significant naval architect, bringing together for the first time Architectura Navalis Mercatoria and the author's explanatory text, Treatise on Shipbuilding, published a few years later. Systematically classifies ships into types and presents Chapman's own as well as his contemporaries' scientific findings. Some of the drawings are reproduced as foldout diagrams to permit an uninterrupted view of the designs. Chapman (1721-1808) was Chief Shipbuilder to the Swedish Navy and Admiral of the Kariskrona Naval Dockyard.

320b. Charnock, John. Biographia Navalis; or, Impartial Memoirs of the Lives and Characters of Officers of the Navy of Great Britain from the Year 1660 to the Present Time. 6 vols.; London: Faulder, 1794-1798.
A chronological history of the Royal Navy woven around the lives of its distinguished officers.

321. -----. History of Marine Architecture. 3 vols.;

Clerkenwell, England: Bye & Law, 1803.
Vol. III, Ships of the British Navy, 1700-1800, lists major vessels and their fates to that date.

321a. Charron, William. A Description of the Freedom Box, Voted by the City of London, to the Hon. Augustus Keppel. To which is Prefixed a Succinct Account of His Public Services. London: The Author, 1779. 22p.

322. "A Chart of the Coast of New England from Beverly to Scituate Harbour, Including the Ports of Boston and Salem." London Magazine, XLIII (1774), 168.

323. Chase, Thomas. Sketches of the Life, Character, and Times of Paul Jones. Richmond: C. H. Wynne, 1859. 58p.

324. Chatterton, Edward. King's Cutters and Smugglers, 1700-1855. Philadelphia: Lippincott, 1912. 425p.

325. Chenevix Trench, R. B. "An Eighteenth Century Invasion Alarm." History Today, VI (July 1956), 457-465.
 The Franco-Spanish plot of 1779.

326. -----. "National Service Two Centuries Ago: The Press Gang." History Today, VI (January 1956), 37-44.
 An explanation of its mechanics.

327. Chester, Colby M. "A Naval Affair of the Revolution." In Sons of the American Revolution, District of Columbia Society. Addresses Delivered and Papers Read Before the Monthly Meeting. Washington: The Society, 1912. p. 74-84.
 Also published in the American Monthly Magazine, XLI (July 1912), 1-4, 19. An account of the romance between the Groton, Conn., lass, Rebecca Chester, and Lt. John Reid, R. N.

328. -----. "The Volunteer Navy." Magazine of History, XIX (August-September 1914), 53-69.
 In the Revolution.

329. Chevalier, Louis E. Histoire de la Marine Française Pendant la Guerre de l'Independance Américaine,

Précédee d'une Etude sur la Marine Militaire de la France et sur ses Institutions Depuis le Commencement du XVIIe Siècle Jusqu 'a l'Année 1877. Paris: Hachette, 1877. 517p.

329a. Chidsey, Donald B. The American Privateers. New York: Dodd, Mead, 1962.

330. Churchill, Charles R. "Don Bernardo de Galvez; Governor of the Province of Louisiana." DAR Magazine, LVIII (October 1924), 597-604.

331. Clark, George L. Silias Deane: A Connecticut Leader in the American Revolution. New York: G. P. Putnam, 1913. 287p.

332. Clark, Thomas. Naval History of the United States: From the Commencement of the Revolutionary War to the Present Time. Philadelphia: M. Carey, 1815. 177p.
Title later changed to simply The Naval History of the United States; much of the data gleaned from participants.

333. Clark, William B. "American Naval Policy, 1775-1776." American Neptune, I (January 1941), 1-16.

334. -----. "The Battle of Words: A Naval Episode of the Revolutionary War." Minute Man, XL (October-December 1950), 5-12; XLI (February 1951), 5-8.
Press reports of the courts-martial of Captains Thomas Thompson of the Raleigh and Elisha Hinman of the Alfred.

335. -----. Ben Franklin's Privateers: A Naval Epic of the American Revolution. Baton Rouge: Louisiana State University Press, 1956. 198p.
Operations of three cruisers sent out by Franklin while representing the colonies in France.

336. -----. Captain Dauntless, the Story of Nicholas Biddle of the Continental Navy. Baton Rouge: Louisiana State University Press, 1949. 317p.

337. -----. "The Continental Brig Resistance." American Neptune, XIV (January 1954), 47-60.

Clark, William B.

338. -----. The First Saratoga, Being the Saga of John Young and His Sloop-of-War. Baton Rouge: Louisiana State University Press, 1953. 199p.

339. -----. Gallant John Barry, 1745-1803; The Story of a Naval Hero of Two Wars. New York: Macmillan, 1938. 530p.

340. -----. George Washington's Navy: Being an Account of His Excellency's Fleet in New England Waters. Baton Rouge: Louisiana State University Press, 1960. 275p.
Exploits of a small schooner force, 1775-1777.

341. -----. "John the Painter." Pennsylvania Magazine of History and Biography, LXIII (Autumn 1939), 1-23.

342. -----. Lambert Wickes, Sea Raider and Diplomat. The Story of a Naval Captain of the Revolution. New Haven: Yale University Press, 1932. 466p.

343. -----. "That Mischievous Holker: the Story of a Privateer." Pennsylvania Magazine of History and Biography, LXXIX (January 1955), 27-62.
A Philadelphia vessel, owned by Blair McClenachan, 1779-1783.

344. -----. A Neglected Phase of Revolutionary History. An Address Delivered at the 162nd Annual Meeting of the State Society of the Cincinnati of Pennsylvania on October 4th 1945. [Philadelphia: The Society, 1945.] 8p.
Contends the navy has been forgotten.

345. -----., ed. See Biddle, Nicholas, no. 136.

346. -----., ed. See Hutchinson, James, no. 762.

347. -----., ed. See United States, Navy Department, Naval History Division, no. 1497.

348. Claudel, Paul. "Yorktown et De Grasse." Legion d'Honneur, II (October 1931), 79-81.

349. Clerk, John. An Essay on Naval Tactics, Systematical

and Historical, with Explanatory Plates. 3rd ed., with Notes by Lord Rodney. Edinburgh: A. Black, 1827. 331p.
Precipitated a long debate over Rodney's "maneuver" of breaking the French line during the 1782 Battle of the Saintes.

350. -----. "A Statement of Facts." Mariner's Mirror, XX (October 1934), 475-495.
Reprint of the 1806 tract on the Battle of the Saintes.

351. Clinton, Henry. Memorandums, etc., etc., Respecting the Unprecedented Treatment which the Army have met with Respecting Plunder Taken After a Siege and of which Plunder the Navy Serving with the Army Divided Their More than Ample Share, Now Fourteen Years Since. London: 1794. 106p.
The Clinton-Arbuthnot feud after the fall of Charleston in 1780.

352. -----. Narrative of Co-Operations: A Narrative of Sir Henry Clinton's Co-Operation with Sir Peter Parker on the Attack of Sullivan's Island, in South Carolina, in the Year 1776, and with Vice-Admiral Arbuthnot, in an Intended Attempt Against the French Armament at Rhode Island, in 1780. London: 1781.
The general did not get along with the Royal Navy.

353. -----. The Narrative of Lieutenant-General Sir Henry Clinton, K.B., Relative to His Conduct During Part of his Command of the King's Troops in North America: Particularly to that which Respects the Unfortunate Issue of the Campaign of 1781. With an Appendix Containing Copies and Extracts of Those Parts of His Correspondence with Lord George Germain, Earl Cornwallis, Rear Admiral Graves, etc., which are Referred to Therein. London: Printed for J. Debrett, 1783. 115p.
A new version, edited by William B. Willcox, appeared in 1954, presenting more inclusive materials.

354. Clos, Jean Henri. The Glory of Yorktown. Yorktown, Va.: Yorktown Historical Society, 1924. 51p.
A brief narrative.

355. Clowes, Sir William L. ed. The Royal Navy: A History from the Earliest Times to the Present. 7 vols.; Boston: Little, Brown, 1897-1903.

356. Coakley, R. W. "Virginia Commerce During the American Revolution." Unpublished PhD Dissertation, University of Virginia, 1949.
Much on the British blockade.

357. Coffin, Joshua. A Sketch of the History of Newbury, Newburyport, and West Newbury, from 1635 to 1845. Boston: S. G. Drake, 1845. 416p.
Home of many Revolutionary privateers.

358. Coggins, Jack. Ships and Seamen of the American Revolution; Vessels, Crews, Weapons, Gear, Naval Tactics, and Actions of the War for Independence. Harrisburg, Pa.: The Stackpole Company, 1969. 224p.
Many illustrations.

359. Cole, W. A. "Trends in Eighteenth Century Smuggling." Economic History Review, 2nd Series X (1957-1958), 395-410.
Mostly in tea.

360. Coleman, Kenneth. The American Revolution in Georgia. Athens: University of Georgia Press, 1958. 352p.
The Siege of Savannah highlighted.

361. Coles, Robert R. "Historical Hempstead Harbor." Long Island Forum, XXXIII (1970), 160-164.
A Loyalist shelter during the Revolution.

361a. Colgate, H. A. "Trincomalee and the East Indian Squadron, 1746 to 1844." Unpublished M. A. thesis, University of London, 1959.
A vital cog in the Suffren campaigns.

362. [Collier, George.] A Detail of Some Particular Services Performed in America during the Years 1776, 1777, 1778, and 1779. Compiled from Journals and Original Papers Supposed to be Chiefly taken from the Journal kept on board the Ship Rainbow, Commanded by Sir George Collier while on the American Station during the Period; Giving a Minute Account

of Many Important Attacks on Towns and Places, Expeditions sent up Rivers, Skirmishes, Negotiations, etc. Printed for Ithiel Town, from a Manuscript Obtained by him while in London in the Summer of 1830. New York, 1835. 117p.

362a. -----. "Expedition to Portsmouth, Virginia, 1779." William and Mary Quarterly, 2nd Series XII (April 1932), 181-186.
Copies of British correspondence on their successful raid.

363. -----. "The Naval Descent Upon Virginia in 1779." Researcher, I (January 1927), 82-84.
Copy of a May 16, 1779, letter from Sir George Collier to General Sir Henry Clinton.

364. -----. "'To My Inexpressible Astonishment': Sir George Collier's Observations on the Battle of Long Island." New York Historical Society Quarterly, XLVIII (October 1964), 293-305.
On the British fleet's failure to cut-off the Colonials.

365. Collier, Thomas S. "The Revolutionary Privateers of Connecticut, with an Account of the State Cruisers, and a Short History of the Continental Navy Cruisers, built in the State, with Lists of Officers and Crews." New London County Historical Society Records and Proceedings, I (1893), 3-77.

366. Collins, Clarkson A., III, jt. author. See Roelker, William, no. 1298.

367. Collins, J. F. "Whaleboat Warfare on Long Island Sound." New York History, XXV (April 1944), 195-201.

368. Collins, J. Richard. "The Hannah-Nautilus Affair." Essex Institute Historical Collections, CIV (January 1968), 34-41.
"First documented naval engagement of the Revolution," October 10, 1775.

369. -----., jt. editor. See Beattie, Donald W., no. 117.

370. Colomb, Philip H. Naval Warfare, its Ruling

Colvile, R. F.

Principles and Practice, Historically Treated. London: W. H. Allen, 1891. 448p.
Some data on the period of the American Revolution.

371. Colvile, R. F. "Naval Personnel of the XVIIIth Century." Royal United Service Institute Journal, LXXVII (May 1942), 160-176.
Refers to British naval personnel, including those active at the time of the American Revolution.

372. Cometti, Elizabeth. "Depredations in Virginia During the Revolution." In Darrett B. Ratman, ed. The Old Dominion: Essays for Thomas Perkins Abernethy. Charlottesville: University of Virginia Press, 1964. p. 135-151.
Along the shores and inland by the forces of Governor Dunmore and General Benedict Arnold.

373. -----. "Impressment During the American Revolution." In Vera Largent, ed. Walter Clinton Jackson Essays in the Social Sciences by Members of the Faculty of the Women's College of the University of North Carolina. Chapel Hill: University of North Carolina Press, 1942. p. 97-109.

374. Commager, Henry S. and Richard B. Morris, eds. The Spirit of 'Seventy-Six: The Story of the American Revolution as Told by Participants. New York: Harper, 1958. 1,348p.
Chpt. 23 "Sea Battles and Naval Raids"; Chpt. 24 "Privateering."

375. "Commodore [Alexander] Gillon and the Frigate South Carolina." South Carolina Historical and Genealogical Magazine, IX (October 1908), 189-219.

376. Conn, Stetson. Gibraltar in British Diplomacy in the Eighteenth Century. Yale Historical Publications, no. 41. New Haven: Yale University Press, 1942. 317p.

377. Connecticut. The Public Records of the Colony of Connecticut, 1636-1776. Edited by J. H. Trumbell, et al. 15 vols.; Hartford: Case, Lockwood & Brainard, 1850-1890.

378. Contenson, Ludovic de. "La Capitulation de Yorktown et le Comte de Grasse." Revue d'Histoire Diplomatique, XLII (October-December 1928), 378-399.
Title misleading. Actually an edition of that part of the journal of the Marquis de Saint-Simon covering West Indies events of 1781 and the French admiral's northward voyage to Chesapeake Bay.

379. -----. "La Cooperation Franco-Americane Pendant la Guerre de l'Independance." Legion d'Honneur, II (October 1931), 103-106.
Includes the co-operation of the French fleet.

380. -----. "La Prise de Saint Christophe." Revue Histoire de Antilles, I (May 1929), 17-41.
Capture of St. Kitts by DeGrasse in 1782.

381. [Conyngham, Gustavus.] Letters and Papers relating to the Cruises of Gustavus Conyngham, a Captain of the Continental Navy, 1777-1779. Edited by Robert W. Neeser. Publications of the Naval History Society, Vol. 6. New York: The Society, 1915. 241p. Rpr. 1970.

382. Cooper, James F. The History of the Navy of the United States of America. 2 vols.; Philadelphia: Lea and Blanchard, 1839. Rpr. 1970.

383. -----. Lives of Distinguished American Naval Officers. 2 vols.; Philadelphia: Carey and Hart, 1846.
Includes lengthy biographies of Jones and Dale.

384. Copeland, Peter F. "The 'Hero' Galley, Virginia State Navy, 1776-1778." Military Collector and Historian, XVI (December 1964), 114-116.

385. -----., jt. author. See Zlatick, Marko, no. 1594.

386. Copplestone, Bennet. "The Burning of the Gaspee." Blackwood's Magazine, CCXIX (February 1926), 256-264.
In the Providence River, June 10, 1772.

387. "Copy from the Account Book of the Privateer Brig Sturdy Beggar." Essex Institute Historical Collections, XXVIII (1891), p. 183.

388. "Copy of a Letter from Philadelphia, July 6." Delaware History, VII (September 1957), 376-379.
On the capture of the brig Nancy in July 1776.

389. Corbett, Julian S., ed. Fighting Instructions, 1530-1816. Publications of the Navy Records Society, V. 29. London: The Society, 1905. 366p.
Part VII includes "The Permanent Instructions, 1703-1783."

390. -----., ed. Signals and Instructions, 1776-1794, with Addenda to Volume XXIX. Publications of the Navy Records Society, v. 35. London: The Society, 1908. 403p.
Directly concerned with the British warships and commanders on the North American station.

391. Cornish Chough, pseud. "Captain John Mead of the Fowey." Devon and Cornwall News and Quarterly, XXII (July 1943), 177-178.
H.M. frigate was very active on the American coast during the Revolution.

392. Cornwallis-West, George F. M. The Life and Letters of Admiral Cornwallis. London: R. Holden, 1927. 537p.

393. "Cost of Outfitting Washington's Schooner Lynch." In U.S. Navy Department, Naval History Division. Naval Documents of the American Revolution. Edited by William B. Clark, et al. Washington: U.S. Government Printing Office, 1964--. III, 1353-1365.

394. Cotten, Elizabeth. The John Paul Jones--Willie Jones Tradition: A Defense of the North Carolina Position. Chapel Hill: Heritage Printers, 1966. 118p.

395. Coulter, Jack L. S., author. See Keevil, John J., no. 814.

396. Cowell, Benjamin. Spirit of '76 in Rhode Island; or, Sketches of the Efforts of the Government and People in the War of the Revolution. Boston: A. J. Wright, Printer, 1850. 352p.

397. Cowper, John. "The Ship Marquis Lafayette." Researcher, II (July 1928), 117-123.

A Virginia privateer.

398. Coyle, John G. "The Suspension of Esek Hopkins, Commander of the Revolutionary Navy." American Irish Historical Society Journal, XXI (1922), 193-235.

399. Crawford, Mrs. Mary (MacDermot). The Sailor Whom England Feared: Being the Story of Paul Jones, Scotch Naval Adventurer and Admiral in the American and Russian Fleets. London: E. Nash, 1913. 424p.
    Jones was never an Admiral in the U.S. service.

400. Crerai, J. W. "The Story of the Black Prince." Vineland Historical Magazine, XXIV (1939), 186-193.
    Ship which became the Alfred.

400a. Creswell, John. British Admirals of the 18th Century: Tactics in Battle. London: Alley & Unwin, 1972.
    Includes the Battles of the Chesapeake, and of the Saintes.

401. Crimmins, John D. "Patriots Bearing Irish Names Who Were Confined Aboard the Jersey Prison Ship." Journal of the American-Irish Historical Society, VI (1906), 21-30.
    A list of names.

402. Crittenden, Charles C. "The Sea Coast in North Carolina History, 1763-1789." North Carolina Historical Review, VII (1930), 433-442.

403. -----. "Ships and Shipping in North Carolina, 1763-1789." North Carolina Historical Review, VIII (January 1931), 1-13.

404. Cross, F. E. "The Father of the American Navy." United States Naval Institute Proceedings, LIII (December 1927), 1296-1297.
    Contends the title belongs to no one person.

405. Crowell, E. P. The Commission of the Captain [Samuel Crowell] of a Salem Privateer in the Revolutionary War. Salem, Mass.: Essex Institute, 1884. 4p.

406. Crowninshield, B. B. An Account of the Private Armed Ship America of Salem. Salem, Mass.: Essex Institute, 1901. 76p.

407. "The Cruise of the Fair American." In Burton E. Stevenson, ed. Poems of American History. Boston: Houghton, Mifflin, 1936. p. 219-220.

408. Cubberly, Fred. "Fort George (St. Michael) Pensacola." Florida Historical Quarterly, VI (April 1928), 220-234.

409. Cugnac, Casper, Comte de. Yorktown (1781), Trois Mois d'Operations Combinees sur Terre et sur Mer dans une Guerre de Coalition. Nancy: Imprimerie Berger-Levrault, 1932. 45p.

409a. Cullen, Joseph P. "The Concise Illustrated History of the American Revolution." American History Illustrated, VI (April 1972), 1-65.

410. -----. "How Jones's Body was Discovered." American History Illustrated, I (April 1966), 20-22.

411. -----. "John Paul Jones--A Personality Profile." American History Illustrated, I (April 1966), 12-19.

412. Cummings, E. C. "Captain Daniel Tucker in the Revolution. An Autobiographical Sketch, with Prefatory Remarks...." Collections and Proceedings of the Maine Historical Society, 2d Series VIII (1897), 225-254.

413. Cunat, Charles. Histoire du Baille de Suffren. Rennes: Marteville et Lefas, 1852. 415p.

414. Cundall, Frank. "The Battle of the Saints." West India Committee Circular, XX (November 16, 1916), 452-453.

415. -----. "The Fate of a Convoy in 1782." West India Committee Circular, XVIII (August 25, 1914), 389.
    A number of Rodney's April 12 captures floundered in a hurricane on the return passage to England.

416. Cundall, H. M. "Admiral Lord Rodney in Jamaica."

Mariner's Mirror, XXIV (July 1938), 289-292.

417. Curzon, Richard Viscount. "Howe." In G. E. Marindin, ed. Our Naval Heroes. London: Murray, 1901. p. 194-218.

418. Cuvillier, Louis A. Admiral Frances Joseph Paul de Grasse, Hero of Yorktown. N. p., 1931. 20p.

419. Dale, Ida D. "St. Eustatius and the First Salute to the American Flag." Huguenot, II (November 1932), 9-11.

420. Dart, Henry P. "West Florida--the Capture of Baton Rouge by Galvez, September 21, 1779." Louisiana Historical Quarterly, XII (April 1929), 255-265.

421. Daughters of the American Revolution. Maine. Hanna Weston Chapter. Naval Battle of Machias, June 12, 1775. Machias: Parlin Printing Company, n. d. 14p.
    The Margaretta and the "Lexington of the Sea."

422. Daveluy, R. "A Study of Naval Strategy: Part Five, The War of American Independence." Trans. from the French by Philip R. Alger. United States Naval Institute Proceedings, XXXVI (June 1910), 391-428.

423. Davies, J. A. "An Inquiry into Faction Among British Naval Officers During the War of the American Revolution." Unpublished MA thesis, University of Liverpool, 1964.

424. Davies, Wallace E. "Privateering Around Long Island During the Revolution." New York History, XX (July 1939), 283-294.

425. Davin, Emmanuel. Suffren, Ce Qui N'a Pas Ou Peu Ete Dit Sur Aui. Precede d'Une Biographie de ce Prestigieux Marin Provencal. Paris: Societe d'Editions Geographiques, Maritimes et Coloniales, 1947. 140p.

426. Davis, Joshua. A Narrative of Joshua Davis, an American Citizen Who was Pressed and Served on Board Six Ships of the British Navy. Boston: 1811.
    Davis was captured when his ship, the privateer

Davis, Junius

Jason, was taken by the British in 1779.

427. Davis, Junius. Some Facts about John Paul Jones. Raleigh: Presses of Edwards and Broughton, 1906. 36p.

428. Davis, Nicholas D. The Battle off Dominica in 1782. [Dimerara, np., 1882.]
Battle of the Saints.

429. -----. The Capitulation to the French in 1782. [Georgetown, 1892.]
Capture of the colonies of Demerara, Essequibo, and Berbice by De Grasse, February 3, 1782.

430. -----. "The Fight between the Randolph and the Yarmouth." United Empire, New Series II (December 1911), 870-872.
Fought on March 7, 1778.

431. Davis, Ralph. The Rise of the English Shipping Industry in the Seventeenth and Eighteenth Centuries. London: Macmillan, 1962. 427p.
Plagued by Yankee privateers during the Revolution.

432. Dawson, Henry B., ed. Battles of the United States by Sea and Land. 2 vols.; New York: Johnson, Fry, 1858.

433. -----., ed. See Dring, Thomas, no. 469.

434. Dawson, Warrington. "Les 2112 Francais Morts aux Etats-Unis de 1777 a 1783 en Combattant pour l'Independance Americane." Societe des Americanistes Journal, New Series XXVIII, Fasc. 1 (1933), 1-154.
A list of French military and naval dead compiled from official sources.

435. Deane, Silas. An Address to the United States of North America. To Which is Added a letter to the Hon. Robert Morris, esq., with Notes and Observations. London: Printed for J. Debrett, 1784. 95p.
A defense of his conduct during his Paris mission.

436. -----. "Correspondence of Silas Deane, Delegate to

the First and Second Congress at Philadelphia, 1774-1776." Collections of the Connecticut Historical Society, II (1870), 127-363.

437. Deane, Silas. The Deane Papers: Correspondence Between Silas Deane, His Brothers, and Their Business and Political Associates, 1771-1795. Collections of the Connecticut Historical Society, v. 23. Hartford: The Society, 1930. 277p.

438. "Dedication Ceremonies for a Bronze Statue of Commodore John Barry, USN, at Wexford, Ireland, September 16, 1956." United States Naval Institute Proceedings, LXXXII (November 1956), 1024.

439. Defence (ship). "Ships Company Defence." Maryland Archives, XVIII (1900), 654-661.

440. Degouy, L'Amiral [?]. "Le Lieutenant General des Armees Navales, Comte de Grasse, et les Americaines (Operations Strategiques de 1781)." Vie Maritime, XXII (October 1928), 1-3.

441. -----. "Une Rehabilitation Militaire; L'Amiral de Grasse." Revue Politique et Parlementaire, CXL (July 1929), 123-136.

442. Deherain, Henri. Une Escale du Baille de Suffren dans les Dardanelles, 16-19 Janvier, 1773. Paris, 1925. 6p.
An early adventure of the great admiral, included within our time span.

443. De Kay, C. "The Burning of the Peggy Stewart." Outlook, LXXIX (January 7, 1905), 72-76.
A pre-Revolutionary incident in Maryland.

444. De Koven, Anna (Farwell). The Life and Letters of John Paul Jones, by Mrs. Reginald De Koven. 2 vols.; New York: Scribner, 1913.

445. Delaney, Norman C. "The Outer Banks of North Carolina During the Revolutionary War." North Carolina Historical Review, XXXVI (January 1959), 1-16.

446. Delaware Archives, Military and Naval Records. 5

vols.; Wilmington: Mercantile Printing Co., 1911-1916.

447. Derrick, Charles. Memoirs of the Rise and Progress of the Royal Navy. London: Sold by Blacks and Parry, 1806. 309p.

448. De Saudeuil, J. N. Jouin, trans. See Grenier, Jacques R. de, no. 668.

449. DesBarres, Joseph F. W. The Atlantic Neptune: Published for the Use of the Royal Navy of Great Britain. London, 1774-1784.
Number of volumes varies with dates.

450. Des Coutrils, C. C. "Une Croisiere en 1775." La Revue Maritime, #198 (Avril 1963), 456-58.

451. A Description of the Royal George; with the Particulars Relative to her Sinking. Portsmouth, Eng., 1782. 42p.

452. Deshon, John. "Letter." Publications of the Rhode Island Historical Society, New Series VIII. Providence: The Society, 1900. 214-216.
Tells how the Colonial warship Warren slipped through the blockade in 1778.

453. "D'Estaing and the Southern Campaign of 1779: the British Point of View set forth in the Annual Register for that Year." Journal of American History, XXIII (1929), 207-216.
The siege of Savannah.

454. Detail and Conduct of the American War, under Generals Gage, Howe, Burgoyne, and Vice Admiral Howe: With a very Full and Correct Statement of the Whole of the Evidence, as Given Before a Committee of the House of Commons: and the Celebrated Fugitive Pieces, which are Said to have Given Rise to that Important Enquiry. 3rd ed. London: Richardson and Urquhart, 1780. 190p.

455. Deux Ponts, Guillaume, Comte de. My Campaigns in America: A Journal, 1780-81. Tr. from the French ms, with notes, by Samuel A. Green. Boston: Wiggin, 1868. 176p.

The French text precedes the English; deals mainly with the French efforts at Newport and Yorktown.

456. Dickerson, Oliver M. "John Hancock: Notorious Smuggler or Near Victim of British Revenue Racketeers?" Mississippi Valley Historical Review, XXXII (March 1946), 517-540.

457. -----. The Navigation Acts and the American Revolution. Philadelphia: University of Pennsylvania Press, 1951. 344p. Rpr. 1971.

457a. Digby, William. The British Invasion from the North: Digby's Journal of the Campaigns of Generals Carleton and Burgoyne from Canada, 1776-1777. Introduction and Notes by James P. Baxter. New York: DeCapo, 1970. 412p.
Reprint of the 1887 edition; includes English preparations for the Valcour Island fight.

458. Dillon, Philip R. "The Strange Case of Admiral De Grasse, Forgotten by France and America." Pennsylvania Magazine of History and Biography, LI (July 1927), 193-206.

459. -----. "L'Independance Americaine et L'Amiral de Grasse." Mercure de France, CCXIII (August 1, 1929), 513-528.

460. Dodwell, Henry H. "The Carnatic, 1761-1784." In his The Cambridge History of India. 6 vols.; Cambridge: Cambridge University Press, 1922-1932. V, 273-293. Rpr. 1963.
"Hughes's actions against Suffren."

461. Dole, Ester M. Maryland During the Revolution. Baltimore: Waverly Press, 1941. 294p.
Some naval activities included.

462. Doniol, Henri. Histoire de la Participation de la France à l'Etablissement des Etats-Unis d'Amerique. Correspondence Diplomatique et Documents. 5 vols.; Paris: Imprimerie Nationale, 1886-1892. Rpr. 1967.

463. Dorlodot, Albert de. L'Aide Belge aux Insurgents Americains, 1774-1782. Verviers: Imp. P and A

Kaiser, 1951. 16p.

464. Douglas, Howard. Naval Evolutions. London: T. and W. Boone, 1832. 101p.
Claims his father, rather than John Clerk, originated Rodney's famous 1782 "maneuver."

465. Doune, Solomen. "Life on a Privateer, 1780." In The Building of the Republic, 1689-1783. Vol. II of Albert B. Hart, ed. American History as Told by Contemporaries. 5 vols.; New York: Macmillan, 1897-1929. p. 497-498.
By a doctor aboard the privateer Hope.

466. Dow, H. E. "Captain John Manley of the Continental Navy." United States Naval Institute Proceedings, LII (August 1926), 1554-1561.

467. Dowdell, Vincent J. "Captain Mugford and the Powder Ship." United States Naval Institute Proceedings, LXXXII (December 1956), 1358-1359.
On the capture of the British transport Hope by Mugford's schooner Franklin and the American's battle-to-the-death on April 6, 1776.

468. Drayton, John. Memoirs of the American Revolution, from its Commencement to the Year 1776, Inclusive; as Relating to the State of South Carolina, and Occasionally Referring to the States of North Carolina and Georgia. 2 vols.; Charleston: A. E. Miller, 1821.

469. Dring, Thomas. Recollections of the Jersey Prison-Ship; from the Original Manuscript of Thomas Dring, One of the Prisoners. [Rewritten] by Albert Greene, edited by Henry Dawson. Morrisana, N. Y. [Alvord printer] 1865. 201p.

470. [Duncan, Henry.] "Journals of Henry Duncan, Captain, R. N., 1776-1782." In John K. Laughton, ed. The Naval Miscellany. Navy Records Society Publications, v. 20. London: The Society, 1902. p. 105-219.

471. Du Perron, Joachim, Comte de Reval. Journal Particulier d'une Campagne aux Indes Occidentales (1781-82). Paris: H. Charles-Lavauzelle [1898]

287p.
By an officer of the French fleet present at the Battles of the Chesapeake and Saints.

472. Durieux, Joseph. "Conquete de l'Ile Sainte-Christophe en 1782." Carnet de La Sabretache, 3rd Series VII (November 1924), 507-519.

473. Duro, Cesárco F. Armada Española. 9 vols.; Madrid, 1895-1903.
Vols. 6-7 applicable; the standard Spanish naval history.

474. Duyckink, Evert A., ed. See Freneau, Philip, no. 584.

475. Dwight, T. W. "The American Flag and John Paul Jones." Magazine of American History, XXIV (October 1890), 269-272.

476. Earle, Ralph, jt. editor. See Alden, Carroll S., no. 25.

477. East, Robert A. Business Enterprise in the American Revolutionary Era. Studies in History, Economics, and Public Law, no. 439. New York: Columbia University Press, 1938. 387p.
Includes privateering.

478. Eastman, Ralph M. Some Famous Privateers of New England. Boston: State Street Trust Company, 1928. 87p.

479. Echt Verslag der Voornamste Levensbyzonderheden van John Paul Jones, zee Kapitein in Dienst der Vereenigde Staaten van Noord-America, Behelzende Deszelfs Menigvuldige Kygsbedryven, en verbaazende Lotgevallen in Engeland, Schotland, Ierland, Frankryk het Westindische Eilanden enj... Vit het Engelson Vertaald. Te Amsterdam, By Dirk Schnurman, Boekverkooper, of het Rokkin... 1780. 51p.

480. Eckenrode, Hamilton J. The Revolution in Virginia. Boston: Houghton, Mifflin, 1916. 311p. Rpr. 1964.

481. -----., author. See United States, Congress, Senate,

no. 1487.

482. Editors of Navy Times. "John Paul Jones." In their Great American Naval Heroes. New York: Dodd, Mead, 1965. p. 1-12.

483. Edson, M. A., Jr. "Eighteenth Century Gun Carriages and Fittings." Nautical Research Journal, XII (1964), 113-116.

484. [Eduardo, Miguel Antonio.] "Diary of Miguel Antonio Eduardo." In U. S. Navy Department, Naval History Division. Naval Documents of the American Revolution. Edited by William B. Clark, et al. Washington: U. S. Government Printing Office, 1964--. V, 1339-1351.
Adventures on the Chesapeake in 1776 during the last days of Dunmore's Virginia control.

485. -----. Een Niew Lied op de Groote Held Paul Jones: "Hier Komt Paul Jones aan Het is Soon Aardig Ventze." [Np:1779.] 4p.
A song composed in honor of Jones' arrival in the Texel with the pair of British warships taken off Flamborough Head.

486. Edwards, Henry S., trans. See Lomenie, Louis L. de, no. 930.

487. Edye, Lourenco. The Historical Records of the Royal Marines. London: Harrison, 1893. 607p.

488. Eight Views, Representing the Manoeuvers of the English and French Fleets on the Memorable 27th of July 1778. Accompanied by a Full Account of the Proceedings of the Two Fleets from the 23rd of the Same Month to the 28th. London: J. Bew, 1779. 16p.
The Battle of Ushant.

489. Ekins, Charles. Naval Battles, From 1744 to the Peace of 1814, Critically Reviewed and Illustrated. London: Baldwin, Cradock, and Jay, 1824. 425p.
Much praise of Admiral Rodney.

490. Eller, Ernest M. "From Across the Sea." United States Naval Institute Proceedings, LIX (October

1933), 1457-1462.
French naval aid during the Revolution.

490a. -----. "George Washington - Father of the American Navy." DAR Magazine, XCV (February 1961), 71-74.

491. -----. "Launching U.S. Power from the Sea: The Saga of U.S. Combined Operations Since 1775." Army Information Digest, XVI (July 1961), 44-55.

492. -----. "Sea Power in the American Revolution." United States Naval Institute Proceedings, LXII (June 1936), 777-789.

493. Ellery, William. "Letter." Publications of the Rhode Island Historical Society, New Series VIII. Providence: The Society, 1900. 222-224.
Ellery argued in 1778 against the colonies building large warships on the grounds that they would be quickly captured by the larger Royal Navy.

494. Ellis, Arthur B. American Patriotism on the Sea. Cambridge, Mass.: J. Wilson & Son, 1884. 15p.
Mostly concerned with the Revolution.

495. Ellsberg, Edward. "John Paul Jones: ... Just What This Country Needed." In John A. Garraty, ed. Unforgettable Americans. Developed as a Project of the Society of American Historians, by Allan Nevins. Great Neck, N.Y.: Channel, 1960. p. 81-85.

496. Elting, John R. "The Thompson Westcott Descriptions of Military Dress During the American Revolution." Military Collector and Historian, XII (Spring 1960), 1-5.
Dress of a Continental naval seaman, circa 1777, p. 5.

497. Emery, William M. "Captain Nathaniel Pope and the First Sea Fight of the Revolution." Old Dartmouth Historical Sketches, No. 51 (April 19, 1921), 8-15.

498. Emmons, George F. The Navy of the United States, from the Commencement, 1775 to 1853: A Statistical History of the United States Navy. With a Brief History of Each Vessel's Service and Fate....

To Which is Added a List of Private Armed Vessels, Fitted Out Under the American Flag.... Washington: Gideon, 1853. 208p.

Written under the authority of the Navy Department by a naval lieutenant.

498a. An Enquiry into the Nature and Legality of Press Warrants. London: J. Almon, 1770. 58p.

498b. An Enquiry into the Practice and Legality of Pressing by the King's Commission: Founded on a Consideration of the Methods in Use to Supply the Fleets and Armies of England. London: J. Almon, 1772. 60p.

500. Essex County, Massachusetts. "The Seacoast Defenses of Essex County in 1776." Essex Institute Historical Collections, XLIII (April 1907), 187-189.

501. Estaing, Charles Hector, Comte de. "A Declaration Addressed in the Name of the King of France to all the Ancient French in North America." Magazine of American History, XXII (November 1889), 427-429.

Translation of a document printed in French aboard the Lanquedoc of the admiral's fleet on October 28, 1778.

502. -----. "Siege of Savannah, 1779. General Orders of the Count d'Estaing for the attack by the Allied Forces, 8th and 9th October. Trans. from the Original ms in the possession of Frank Moore." Magazine of American History, II (September 1878), 548-551.

503. Evans, Edward J. "Time on Target--177 Years." Marine Corps Gazette, XXXVIII (February 1954), 36-39.

Marine artillery, 1775-1945.

504. "Events on Hudson's River in 1777, as Recorded by British [Naval] Officers in Contemporary Reports." Duchess County Historical Society Yearbook, XX (1935), 88-105.

505. Everett, Sidney. "The Chevalier de Ternay." New England Historical and Genealogical Register,

XXVII (October 1873), 404-418.

506. Extrait du Journal d'un Officer de la Marine d'Escadre de M. le Comte d'Estaing. N. p., 1782. 126p.

507. Ewan, N. R. Chevaux-de-Frize: Military Obstructions in the Delaware River During the Revolutionary War, Dredged up July 1941. Also an Account of the Chevaux-de-Frize in the Hudson River During the Revolution. Newport News, Va.: The Mariners Museum, 1944. 7p.

508. Fabre, Marc-Andre. "Le Lieutenant-General Comte d'Estaing." Revue Historique de l'Armee, XIII (1957), 37-43.
A recent French appraisal of his conduct during the American Revolution.

509. Fackenthal, B. F. 'The Great Chain at West Point and Other Obstructions Placed in the Hudson River during the War of the Revolution." Bucks County Historical Society Papers, VII (1937), 596-611.

510. Fagan, Louis S. "Samuel Nicholas, First Officer of American Marines." Marine Corps Gazette, XVIII (November 1933), 5-15.

511. [Fairbanks, John.] "John Fairbanks--His Journal. Contributed by Herbert Harris. The Privateer Wasp Journal, 1782." Collections and Proceedings of the Maine Historical Society, 2d series VI (1895), 139-144.

512. Fairburn, J. Fairburns Improved Edition of the Life of Paul Jones, English Corsair; Giving a Faithful Account of the Extraordinary Perils, Voyages, Adventures and Escapes of that Bold Pirate and Smuggler During the American War; from his Youth to his Death. London: the Author, n. d. 24p.

513. Fairlamb, George R., Jr. "The Revolutionary Navy." Minute Man, XXIII (January 1929), 418-422.

514. Falconer, William. A Universal Dictionary of the Marine. London: T. Cadell, 1784. 420p.
Reprinted in 1930 under the title Old Wooden Walls.

515. [Fanning, Nathaniel.] Fanning's Narrative; Memoirs of Nathaniel Fanning. Edited by John S. Barnes. Publications of the Naval Historical Society, v. 2. New York: Naval History Society, 1912. 258p. Rpr. 1968.
John Paul Jones as seen by one of his officers.

516. Farmer, Edward G. "A Series of Firsts--The Champlain Story." Nautical Research Journal, XIII (Summer 1965), 26-27.
Argues that the first naval battles of the Revolution were fought on this lake and not at Machais, Maine.

517. -----. "Skenesborough [New York]: Continental Navy Shipyard." United States Naval Institute Proceedings, XC (October 1964), 160-162.
Built most of Arnold's vessels used at Valcour Island.

518. [Farmer, Robert.] "Bernardo de Galvez's Siege of Pensacola in 1781 (as related in Robert Farmar's Journal)." Edited by James A. Padgett. Louisiana Historical Quarterly, XXVI (April 1943), 311-329.

519. Farnham, Charles W. "Crew List of the Privateer Independence, 1776." Rhode Island History, XXVI (October 1967), 125-128.

520. Farrère, Claude. Histoire de la Marine Française. Paris: Flammarion, 1956. 439p.

521. Farris, Sarah G. "Wilmington's Maritime Commerce, 1775-1807." Delaware History, XXIV (April 1970), 22-51.

522. Faucher de Saint-Maurice, Narcisse Henri Edouard. Notes Pour Servir a l'Histoire des Officiers de la Marine et de l'Armee Francais qui ont fait la Guerre de l'Independance Americaine. Quebec: Dimers, 1896. 287p.

523. Felt, Joseph B. Annals of Salem. 2nd ed. 2 vols.; Boston: J. Munroe, 1845-1849.
Revolutionary privateering highlighted.

524. Ferguson, Eugene S. Truxton of the Constellation:

The Life of Commodore Thomas Truxton, U.S. Navy, 1755-1822. Baltimore: Johns Hopkins University Press, 1956. 322p.
Includes his Revolutionary service.

525. Ferguson, Homer L. Salvaging Revolutionary Relics from the York River. Newport News, Va.: The Mariners Museum, 1939. 10p.

526. Field, Cyril. Britain's Sea Soldiers: A History of the Royal Marines. 2 vols.; Liverpool, Eng.: Lyceum Press, 1924.

527. Field, Edward. Esek Hopkins, Commander-in-Chief of the Continental Navy During the American Revolution, 1775-1778. Providence: Preston and Rounds, 1898. 280p. Rpr. 1970.

528. -----. Revolutionary Defences in Rhode Island: an Historical Account of the Fortifications and Beacons Erected During the American Revolution with Muster Rolls of the Companies Stationed Along the Shores of Narragansett Bay. Providence: R. I. Preston and Rounds, 1896. 161p.

529. -----., ed. See Angell, Israel, no. 65.

530. Field, Thomas W. The Battle of Long Island, with Connected Preceding Events, and the Subsequent American Retreat. With Authentic Documents. Memoirs of the Long Island Historical Society, v. 2. Brooklyn: The Society, 1869. 540p.

531. Fink, Leo G. Barry or Jones, "Father of the United States Navy": Historical Reconnaissance. Philadelphia: Jefferies and Manz, 1962. 138p.
Leans toward Barry.

532. "The First of the Submarines: Bushnell's 'American Turtle,' 1776," Magazine of History, IX (May-June, 1914), 242-246.

533. Firth, Charles H. Naval Songs and Ballads. Publications of the Navy Records Society, v. 33. London: Printed for the Navy Records Society, 1894. 387p.
Many were popular at the time of the Revolution.

534. Fiske, John. The American Revolution. 2 vols.; Boston: Houghton, Mifflin, 1891.

535. -----. "Paul Jones and the Armed Neutrality." Atlantic Magazine, XXX (December 1887), 786-805.

536. Fiske, Nathan. "French Naval Forces in the American Revolution." American Catholic Historical Research, III (January 1907), 25-34.

537. Fitch, Jabes. Diary of Captain Jabes Fitch. [New York? Prison-ship Martyrs' Monument Association, 1897?] 3p.
By a survivor of the Wallabout floating jails.

538. Fitchett, W. H. Nelson and His Captains: Sketches of Famous Seamen. London: Smith, Elder, 1902. 322p.
Portraits of Pellow, Saumarez, Edward Riou, and William Parker.

539. -----. "Rodney and De Grasse at the Battle of the Saints." Cornhill Magazine, LXXVII (April 1898), 433-445.

540. Fitzhugh, Percy K. The Story of John Paul Jones. New York: McLoughlin Brothers, 1906. 63p.

541. Fitzpatrick, John C. "A Sea Captain of the Revolution." DAR Magazine LIV (August 1920), 444-448.
Andrew Paton, skipper of the ship Lady Margareta, who took a miscel. cargo from Cadiz, Spain, to Edenton, North Carolina, in the winter of 1777-1778.

542. -----., ed. See Washington, George, nos. 1537 and 1539.

543. Fleming, Thomas. Beat the Last Drum: The Siege of Yorktown. New York: St. Martin's Press, 1963. 375p.

544. Fleuriot de Langle, Y. "Contribution de la Marine Française a la Victoire de Yorktown." Revue Maritime, CCLXXIII (1970), 177-183.
The Battle of the Chesapeake.

545. Flexner, James T. George Washington in the American Revolution (1775-1783). Vol. II of his George Washington. Boston: Little Brown, 1968. 599p.
Some mention of naval activities including an account of how the general "inaugurated the American navy" in 1775 by commissioning the Hannah, Captain Nicholas Broughton.

545a. Fogdall, Soren J. M. P. Danish-American Diplomacy, 1776-1920. University of Iowa Studies in the Social Sciences, v. 8. Iowa City: University of Iowa, 1922. 171p.

546. Folsom, William R. "The Battle of Valcour Island." In William R. Folsom, Vermonters in Battle, and Other Papers. Montpelier: Vermont Historical Society, 1933. p. 56-73.

547. [Foot, Caleb.] Reiminscences of the Revolution. Prison Letters and Sea Journal of Caleb Foot, Born 1750, Died 1787. Compiled by his Grandson and namesake, Caleb Foot. Salem, Mass.: Essex Institute, 1889. 33p.

548. Footner, Herbert. Sailor of Fortune: The Life and Adventures of Commodore Barney, U.S.N. New York: Harper, 1940. 323p.

549. Force, Peter, ed. American Archives. 9 vols.; Washington: The Author, 1837-1853.
The 4th Series, March 1774-July 1776, and the 5th Series, which ends in late 1776, are the most complete compilations of source material on American Revolutionary naval activities published prior to Clark's Naval Documents of the American Revolution.

550. Ford, Paul L. "Lord Howe's Commission to Pacify the Colonies." Atlantic Monthly, LXXVII (June 1896), 758-766.

551. Ford, Worthington C., ed. Defences of Philadelphia in 1777. Brooklyn: Historical Printing Club, 1897. 300p. Rpr. 1971.
American correspondence on the defense of the Delaware River against the British fleet.

552. -----. "Parliament and the Howes." Massachusetts

Historical Society Proceedings, XLIV (1911), 120-143.

553. -----., ed. See Lee, William, no. 899.

554. -----., ed. See United States, Continental Congress, no. 1489.

555. Forester, C. S. "The Battle of the Saintes." American Heritage, IX (June 1958), 4-9, 108.
By the author of the Hornblower saga.

556. Forsyth, Mary I. "The Burning of Kingston by the British on October 16th, 1777." New York State Historical Association Proceedings, XI (1912), 62-70.
Reprinted in the Journal of American History, VII (1913), 1137-1148.

557. Fort Moultrie Centennial; Being an Illustrated Account of the Doings at Fort Moultrie, Sullivan's Island, Charleston (S. C.) Harbor. 2 vols.; Charleston: Walker, Evans and Cogswell, 1876.
Celebration of the repulse of the British fleet in 1776.

558. Fortescue, John W. A History of the British Army. 13 v. in 14. New York: Macmillan, 1899-1930. Rpr. 1969.

559. -----. "St. Lucia, 1778." Macmillan's Magazine, LXXXV (1902), 419-427.

560. -----., ed. See George III, King of Great Britain, no. 616.

561. Foster, Joseph. "The Continental Frigate Raleigh." Granite Monthly, LX (November 1928), 558-566.
Built in New Hampshire.

562. France. Dictionnaire de Biographie Française. Paris: Letouzey, 1933--.
Eleven volumes completed to date.

563. -----. Reglement Concernant les Prises que des Corsaires Francais Conduiront dans les Ports des Etats-Unis de l'Amerique; et Celles que les

Corsaires Americains Ameneront dans les Ports de France. Du 27 Septembre, 1778. Paris: De l'Imprimerie Royale, 1778. 8p.

564. -----. Ministere Des Affaires Estrangeres. Combattants François de la Guerre Americaine, 1778-1783. Washington: Imprimerie Nationale, 1905. 453p. Rpr. 1969.

564a. -----. Statutes. Code des Prises; ou Recueil des Edits, Declarations, Lettres, Patents, Arrets, Ordonnances Dupuis 1400 Jusqu a Presents. 2 vols.; Paris: de l'Imprimerie Royale, 1784.
Codification of all the French prize rules to that date.

565. [Franklin, Benjamin.] The Complete Works of Benjamin Franklin. Compiled and Edited by John Bigelow. 12 vols.; New York: G P Putnam's Sons, 1904.

566. Fraser, Edward. Famous Fighters of the Fleet: Glimpses Through the Cannon Smoke in the Days of the Old Navy. New York: Macmillan, 1904. 322p.
Battle of the Saintes included.

567. -----. The "Londons" of the British Fleet. London: John Lane, 1908. 453p.
Individual ship histories; Graves flagship at the Battle of the Chesapeake went by that name.

568. Fraser, Henry S., ed. See Green, William, no. 661.

569. Free and Accepted Masons. Grand Lodge of the District of Columbia. John Paul Jones's Commemoration at Annapolis, April 24, 1906. Washington: Priv. print, 1907. 117p.
Jones was a member of this society.

570. Freeman, Douglas S. Leader of the Revolution. Vol. IV of his George Washington: A Biography. 7 vols.; New York: C. Scribners Sons, 1948-1957.

571. -----. Victory With the Help of France. Vol. V of his George Washington: A Biography. 7 vols.; New York: C. Scribners Sons, 1948-1957.

Freeman, Fred

572. Freeman, Fred, jt. author. See Roscoe, Theodore, no. 1302.

573. Fremantle, E. "Seapower and the American War of Independence." Royal United Service Institute Journal, LXII (August 1917), 471-505.

574. French, Allen. The First Year of the American Revolution. New York: Houghton Mifflin, 1934. 795p. Rpr. 1967.

575. -----. "The Hallowell-Graves Fisticuffs, 1775." Massachusetts Historical Society Proceedings, LXIII (1931), 23-48.

576. "The French in Newport, 1781." Newport Historical Magazine, II (January 1882), 176-178.

577. Freneau, Philip. "Barney's Invitation." In Harry H. Clark, ed. Poems of Freneau. New York: Harcourt, Brace, 1929. p. 80-81.
On his privateer Hyder Ali.

578. -----. The British Prisonship. A Poem in Four Cantos. Canto I: The Capture. II: the Prisonship. III: the Prisonship Continued. IV: the Hospital Prisonship. To Which is Added: A Poem on the Death of Captain N. Biddle who was Blown up in an Engagement with Yarmouth near Barbadoes. Philadelphia: F. Bailey, pr., 1781. 23p.

579. -----. "On Captain Barney's Victory Over the Ship General Monk, April 26, 1782." In Harry H. Clark, ed. Poems of Freneau. New York: Harcourt, Brace, 1929. p. 82-84.
A song.

580. -----. "On the Death of Captain Nicholas Biddle." In Harry H. Clark, ed. Poems of Freneau. New York: Harcourt, Brace, 1929. p. 35-36.
A 1781 poem on the loss of the Raleigh.

581. -----. "On the Memorable Victory Obtained by the Gallant Captain Paul Jones, of the 'Good Man Richard,' Over the 'Seraphis,' etc., Under the Command of Captain Pearson." In Philip M. Marsh, ed. The Freneau Sampler. New York: Scarecrow,

1963. p. 97-100.

582. -----. "On the New American Frigate Alliance." In Harry H. Clark, ed. Poems of Freneau. New York: Harcourt, Brace, 1929. p. 33-34.
A 1786 poem on Captain John Barry's final Continental command.

583. -----. The Poems of Philip Freneau, Poet of the American Revolution. Edited for the Princeton Historical Association by Fred L. Pattee. 3 vols.; New York: Russell and Russell, 1963.

584. -----. Poems Relating to the American Revolution. With an Introductory Memoir and Notes by Evert A. Duyckinck. New York: W. J. Widdleton, 1865. 288p.

585. -----. Poems Written and Published during the American Revolutionary War, and now Republished from the Original mms., Interspersed with Translations from the Ancients and other Pieces not Heretofore in Print. 3d ed. 2 vols.; Philadelphia: L. R. Bailey, pr., 1809.

586. -----. Some Account of the Capture of the Ship Aurora. New York: M. F. Mansfield & A. Wessels, 1899. 49p. Rpr. 1970.
The poet was serving aboard this privateer when she was taken by the British frigate Iris in 1780.

587. Frere, B. H. T., ed. See Spilsbury, John, no. 1395.

588. Frisbie, Nora G. "The Ships of the Continental Navy." DAR Magazine, CIV (February 1970), 124-130.

589. Frost, Holloway H. "Our Heritage from John Paul Jones." United States Naval Institute Proceedings, XLIV (October 1918), 2275-2332.

590. Frost, John. American Naval Biography: Lives of the Commodores and other Commanders Distinguished in the History of the American Navy. Philadelphia: the author, 1844. 450p.
Three additional editions, 1845, 1850, and 1854,

Frothingham, Thomas G.

under various titles. Revolutionary officers include Jones, Dale, Murray, Barry, Barney, and Nicholas Biddle.

591. Frothingham, Thomas G. "The Sequence that Led to Yorktown." United States Naval Institute Proceedings, LVII (October 1931), 1326-1330.

592. -----. "The Service of Marblehead to the United States Navy." United States Naval Institute Proceedings, LII (December 1926), 2413-2418.
On the Continental schooner Hannah, manned by Marblehead men.

593. G. A. M. "Sabotage in Portsmouth." Blackwood's Magazine, no. 1546 (August 1944), 103-109.
Jack the Painter.

594. Gaines, William H. "The Battle of the Barges." Virginia Cavalcade, IV (Autumn 1954), 33-37.
The 1782 contest in Chesapeake Bay.

595. Gale, Benjamin. "The American Turtle Built at Saybrook by David Busnell." Connecticut Historical Society Collections, II (1870), 315-318, 322-323, 333-335.

596. Galloway, Joseph. A Letter to the Right Honourable Lord Viscount H--e, on his Naval Conduct in the American War. London, 1779. 50p.
A criticism of Richard Howe's activities by the noted Pennsylvania Loyalist.

597. Galvez, Bernardo de. "Diario de las Operaciones de la Expedicion Contra la Plaza de Panzacola Concluida por las Armas de S. M. Catholica." Sociedad Economica de la Habana. Memorias. 2d ser, II (1846), 192-196, 249-268; III (1847), 66-72, 393-407.

598. -----. "Diary of the Operation of the Expedition Against the Place of Pensacola, Concluded by the Arms of His Catholic Majesty Under the Orders of Field Marshall Bernardo de Galvez." Louisiana Historical Quarterly, I (January 1917), 44-84.
The Spaniard used a few vessels in his attack.

599. -----. "Letters of General Don Bernardo de Galvez." Sons of the American Revolution. Louisiana Society. Yearbook, XLIV (1921), 106.

600. Gammage, Russell. "British Naval Uniforms, 1775-1783." Military Collector and Historian, XVI (Summer 1964), 49.

601. Gardiner, Asa B. The Order of the Cincinnati in France ("L'Ordre de Cincinnatus"). Its Origin and History: With the Military or Naval Records of the French Members who became such by Reason of Qualifying Service in the Army or Navy of France or of the United States in the War of the Revolution for American Independence. Providence: The Rhode Island Society of the Cincinnati, 1905. 243p.

602. Gardiner, Leslie. The British Admiralty. Annapolis: U.S. Naval Institute, 1968. 418p.
An administrative history of the Royal Navy including the period overseen by the Earl of Sandwich.

603. Gardner, Frank A. "Lincoln galley." Massachusetts Magazine IV (October 1911), 245-246.

604. -----. "State brigantine Active." Massachusetts Magazine II (October 1909), 234-236.

605. -----. "State brigantine Independence." Massachusetts Magazine II (January 1909), 44-47.

606. -----. "State brigantine Rising Empire." Massachusetts Magazine IV (July 1911), 179-182.

607. -----. "State ship Diligent." Massachusetts Magazine III (January 1910), 40-46.

608. -----. "State ship Mars." Massachusetts Magazine III (October 1910), 260-267.

609. -----. "State ship Protector." Massachusetts Magazine III (July 1910), 181-183.

610. -----. "State ship Tartar." Massachusetts Magazine IV (January 1911), 43-48.

611. -----. "State sloop Machias Liberty."

Massachusetts Magazine III (April 1910), 133-140.

612. -----. "State sloop Republic." Massachusetts Magazine II (July 1909), 168-171.

613. -----. "State sloop Winthrop." Massachusetts Magazine IV (April 1911), 110-118.

614. [Gardner, James A.] Recollections of James Anthony Gardner, Commander, R.N. (1775-1814). Edited by R. Vesey Hamilton and John K. Laughton. Publications of the Navy Records Society, v. 31. London: The Society, 1906. 287p.
Rpr. 1955 under the title Above and Under Hatches.

615. Garstin, Crosbie, ed. See Kelley, Samuel, no. 816.

616. George III. King of Great Britain. The Correspondence of King George III from 1760 to December 1783. Edited by John W. Fortescue. 6 vols.; London: Macmillan, 1927-1928.

617. George, John A. "Virginia Loyalists, 1775-1783." Richmond College Historical Papers, I (1916), 173-221.
Including those operating on Chesapeake Bay.

618. Germain, George. Correspondance du Lord G. Germain, Avec les Generaux Clinton, Cornwallis, et les Amiraux dans la Station de l'Amerique, Avec Plusieurs Letters Interceptees du General Washington, du Marquis de la Fayette & M. de Barras, Chef d'Escadre. Traduit de l'Anglais sur les Originaux Publies par Ordre de la Chambre des Paris. Berne: Chez la Nouvelle Societe Typo-Graphique, 1782. 304p.

619. Germiny, Marc, Comte de. "Les Brigandages Maritimes de l'Angleterre sous le Régne de Louis XVI. D'après des documents Nouveaux." Revue Quest. Historie, XC (1911), 54-85, 396-433.

620. Giambattista, M. D. "Captain Jeremiah O'Brien and the Machais Liberty." United States Naval Institute Proceedings, XCVI (February 1970), 85-87.

621. Gibbs, George F. "The Daring of John Paul Jones."

Cosmopolitan Magazine, XV (October 1901), 641-643.

622. Gilligan, Arthur E. "The Battle of Valcour Island." United States Naval Institute Proceedings, XCIII (October 1967), 157-160.

623. [Gillon, Alexander.] "Letters from Commodore Gillon in 1778 and 1779." South Carolina Historical Magazine, X (January-July 1909), 3-9, 75-82, 131-135.
Relating to his mission to France.

624. Gilpin, William. Memoirs of Josias Rogers, Esq., Commander of His Majesty's Ship Quebec. London: Cadell and Davis, 1808. 184p.
The same officer who lost the General Monk to Barney's Hyder Ali.

625. Gipson, Laurence H. The Coming of the Revolution, 1763-1775. The New American Nation Series. New York: Harper and Brothers, 1954. 287p.
Chronologically, the volume ahead of Alden's study.

626. "The Glorious 12th of April." West India Committee Circular, XIII (April 23, 1907), 199-200.
Battle of the Saintes.

627. Goepp, Edouard and Ectot, eds. La France Biographique Illustrée: Les Marins. 2 vols.; Paris: Farne, Jouvett, 1877.
Short pieces included on D'Estaing, De Grasse, and the Baille de Suffren.

628. Golder, Frank A. John Paul Jones in Russia. New York: Doubleday, 1927. 230p.

629. Gooding, Alfred. Portsmouth in the Eighteenth Century. Portsmouth, N.H., n.d.

630. Goodrich, Casper F. "Historical Instances of Scouting." United States Naval Institute Proceedings, XXIX (1903), 917-925.

631. -----. "Howe and D'Estaing: A Study in Coast Defense." United States Naval Institute Proceedings, XXII (1896), 577-586.

Goodwin, A.

632. -----. "The Naval Side of the American Revolution." In Naval Actions and Operations Against Cuba and Porto Rico, 1593-1815. Vol. XI of The Papers of the Military History Society of Massachusetts. Boston: The Stillings Press, 1901. pp. 29-63.

633. -----. "The Sailor in the Revolution." United States Naval Institute Proceedings, XXIII (1897), 459-486.

634. Goodwin, A., ed. The American and French Revolutions, 1763-1793. Vol. VIII of The New Cambridge Modern History. Cambridge: Cambridge University Press, 1957--. 748p.
Twelve of fourteen volumes thus far completed.

635. Goodwin, H. B. "The Navy of the Georges." Colburn's United Service Magazine, IV (1890), 178-190.

636. Goold, William. The Burning of Falmouth (now Portland), by Captain Mowatt, in 1775. Prepared at the Request of the [Maine Historical] Society, and Read Before It, February 19, 1873. Boston: 1873. 16p.
Reprinted from the New England Historical and Genealogical Register, 1873.

637. Gordon, Thomas. Principles of Naval Architecture, with Proposals for Improving the Form of Ships. London: T. Evans, 1784. 207p.

638. Gottschalk, Louis. Lady in Waiting: the Romance of Lafayette and Aglae de Hunolstein. Baltimore: Johns Hopkins University Press, 1939. 137p.
Also contains the John Paul Jones correspondence with Mlle. de Hunolstein.

639. Gould, Edward K. British and Tory Marauders on the Penobscot. Rockland, Me.: The Author, 1932. 46p.

640. [Goussencourt, Chevalier de.] "A Journal of the Cruise of the Fleet of His Most Christian Majesty, Under the Command of the Count de Grasse-Tilly, in 1781 and 1782." In John D. G. Shea, ed. The Operations of the French Fleet under the Count de Grasse in 1781-2, as Described in Two Contemporaneous Journals. Bradford Club Series, no. 3.

New York: The Club, 1864. p. 25-133. Rpr. 1971.

641. Grafton, Joseph. "Auction Sales in Salem of Shipping and Merchandise During the Revolution." Essex Institute Historical Collections, XLIX (April 1913), 97-124.

642. Graham, Gerald S. Empire of the North Atlantic: The Maritime Struggle for North America. Toronto: University of Toronto Press, 1950. 338p.

643. Grasse, Alexandre, Comte de. Memoire ... sur le Combat Naval du 12 Avril, 1782, Avec les Plans [8] des Positions Principales des Armees Respectives. [Paris: 1782.] 26p.
Reproduced in 1926 by the Massachusetts Historical Society as no. 211 of it's Americana Series.

644. -----. Notice Biographique sur L'Amiral Cte. de Grasse d'apres les Documents Inedits. [Paris, 1840.]

645. Graves, Clarence E., 4th Lord, and Frank Graves. "Graves." In G. E. Marindin, ed. Our Naval Heroes. London: Murray, 1901. p. 219-231.

646. [Graves, Thomas.] Graves Papers, and other Documents Relating to the Naval Operations of the Yorktown Campaign. Edited by French E. Chadwick. Publications of the Naval History Society, v. 7. New York: Naval History Society, 1916. 268p. Rpr. 1967.
Graves commanded the British fleet.

646a. Graves, William. Two Letters Respecting the Conduct of Rear Admiral [Thomas] Graves on the Coast of the United States, July to November, 1781. Morrisania, N.Y., n.d.

647. Gray, Ernest. "Naval Hygiene in the Eighteenth Century." Durham University Journal, New Series IV (June 1943), 98-101.

648. Great Britain. Admiralty. An Address to the Lords of the Admiralty, on their Conduct towards Admiral

Greathouse, Ronald H.

Keppel. London: J. Almon, 1778. 46p.

649. ----- -----. Instructions for the Conduct of the Ships of War, Explanatory of ... the Signals Contained in the Signal-Book, etc. London, 1776. 46p.

650. ----- -----. Instructions Given with Commissions for Seizing ships, etc., Belonging to Inhabitants of Rebellious Colonies, etc. St. James, March 27, 1777. [London: 1777] 4p.

651. ----- -----. A List of the Flag-Officers of His Majesty's Fleet. London, 1772. 26p.

652. ----- -----. Sailing and Fighting Instructions for His Majesty's Fleet. 2 parts. London, 1779.

653. ----- -----. Historical Manuscript Commission. Report on the Manuscripts of Mrs. Stopford-Sackville. 2 vols.; London: H. M. Stationery Office, 1904-1910.

Contains excerpts of correspondence from such British naval officers as Admiral Arbuthnot.

654. ----- -----. Parliament. The Parliamentary Register ... Proceedings and Debates of the House of Commons. Edited by J. Almon. 83 vols.; London: 1775-1804.

655. ----- -----. Royal Navy. Exercise of the Small Arms and Great Guns, for the Seamen on Board His Majesty's Ships. [London? 1765?] 44p.

656. ----- -----. Regulations and Instructions Relating to His Majesty's Service at Sea. Established by His Majesty in Council. 10th ed. London, 1766. 232p.

657. Greathouse, Ronald H. "The Battle of Valcour Bay: A Victorious Defeat." Marine Corps Gazette, XLII (November 1958), 16-18.

658. [Green, Ezra.] Diary of Ezra Green, M. D., Surgeon on board the Continental Ship-of-War Ranger Under John Paul Jones, from November 1, 1777 to Sept. 27, 1778.... Edited by George H. Preble. Boston: D. Clapp, 1875. 28p. Rpr. 1970.

659. [Green, John.] "American Prisoners in Mill Prison at Plymouth in 1782: Captain John Green's Letter." South Carolina Historical & Genealogical Magazine, X (April 1909), 116-124.

660. Green, Samuel A., trans. See Deux Ponts, Guillaume, Comte de, no. 455.

661. [Green, William.] "The Memoranda of William Green, Secretary to Vice Admiral Marriott Arbuthnot in the American Revolution." Edited by Henry S. Fraser. Rhode Island Historical Society Collections, XVII (1924), 54-64, 126-140; XVIII (1925), 112-128, 154-160.

662. Greene, Albert, author. See Dring, Thomas, no. 469.

663. Greene, Wallace M. "Piscataqua's Pirates." United States Naval Institute Proceedings, LVIII (February 1932), 241-244.

664. Greenwood, Isaac J. Bermuda During the American Revolution. Boston: Clapp, 1896. 6p.

665. -----. Captain John Manley, Second-in-Rank in the United States Navy, 1776-1783. Boston: Goodspeed, 1915. 174p. Rpr. 1970.

666. -----., ed. The Revolutionary Services of John Greenwood of Boston and New York, 1775-1783. New York: 1922. 155p.

667. Greer, James A. The Navy in the War of the American Revolution. District of Columbia Society, Sons of the American Revolution, Historical Papers, no. 1. Washington: The Society, 1898. 15p.

668. Grenier, Jacques R. de. The Art of War at Sea; or, Naval Tactics Reduced to New Principles. Translated by J. N. Jouin de Saudeuil. London, 1788.
Critical of the single line of battle; illustrated with examples from the "late war."

669. Grey, William. "Rodney." In G. E. Marindin, ed. Our Naval Heroes. London: Murray, 1901. p. 153-178.

670. Grieve, R. "Esek Hopkins, First Admiral of the American Navy." New England Magazine NsXXVII (November 1897), 346-362.
　　　The title is misleading.

671. Griffin, Martin I. J. "Commodore John Barry." In Annual Report of the American Historical Association for the Year 1895. Washington: Government Printing Office, 1896. p. 339-368.

672. -----. Commodore John Barry, "Father of the American Navy"; A Record of His Services for Our Country. Philadelphia: The Author, 1902. 424p.

673. -----. "John Barry, Commodore and Father of the American Navy." American Catholic Researches, New Series IV (April 1908), 97-192.

674. -----. The History of Commodore John Barry. Philadelphia, 1897. 251p.

675. Griffiths, D. M. "American Contribution to the Armed Neutrality of 1780." Russian Review, XXX (April 1971), 164-172.
　　　Naval.

676. Griswold, Charles. "Letter." American Journal of Science and Arts, II (November 1820), 94-101.
　　　The author knew Ezra Lee, pilot of the submarine Turtle, and tells of the Busnell craft's efforts in New York Harbor.

677. Grover, G. W. M. A Short History of the Royal Marines. Aldershot, Eng.: Gale & Polden, 1948. 68p.

678. Gruber, Ira D. "Admiral Lord Howe and the War for American Independence." Unpublished Ph.D. Dissertation, Duke University, 1966.

678a. -----. The Howe Brothers and the American Revolution. New York: Atheneum, 1972. 396p.

679. -----. "Lord Howe and Lord George Germain: British Politics and the Winning of American Independence." William and Mary Quarterly, 3rd Series, XXII (April 1965), 225-243.

The peace efforts of the admiral.

680. -----. "Richard Lord Howe: Admiral as Peacemaker." In George A. Billias, ed. George Washington's Opponents: British Generals and Admirals in the American Revolution. New York: Morrow, 1969. p. 233-242.

681. Gurn, Joseph. Commodore John Barry, Father of the American Navy. New York: P. J. Kenedy, 1933. 318p.

682. Guthorn, Peter J. American Maps and Map Makers of the Revolution. Monmouth Beach, N.J.: Philip Freneau Press, 1966. 48p.

683. Gwathmey, John H. Historical Register of Virginians in the Revolution: Soldiers, Sailors, Marines, 1775-1783. With an introduction by Dr. H. J. Eckenrode. Richmond: The Diets Press, 1938. 372p.

684. Haarran, Albert W. "The Spanish Conquest of British West Florida, 1779-1781." Florida Historical Quarterly, XXXIX (October 1969), 107-134.

685. [Hadden, James M.] Hadden's Journal and Orderly Books. A Journal Kept in Canada and Upon Burgoyne's Campaign in 1776 and 1777.... With an Explanatory chapter and notes by Horatio Rogers. Albany: J. Munsell, 1884. 581p.
The author was a lieutenant in the Royal Artillery and participated in the Battle of Valcour Bay.

686. Haggerty, J. J. "The Influence of British Naval Power upon the American Colonies." Army Quarterly, LXXXVIII (April 1964), 43-52.

687. Hagglund, L. F. "The Continental Gondola Philadelphia." United States Naval Institute Proceedings, LXII (May 1936), 665-669.

688. Haldane-Robertson, Langdon. "Some Philadelphia Ships Condemned at Jamaica During the Revolution." American Neptune, II (July 1942), 203-208.

689. Hale, Arthur. "The Yankee Privateer." In Burton E. Stevenson, ed. Poems of American History.

Hale, Edward E.

Boston: Houghton, Mifflin, 1936. p. 221-222.
A contemporary poem on the Providence.

690. Hale, Edward E. Franklin in France. From Original Documents, Most of Which are now Published for the First Time. 2 vols.; Boston: Roberts Brothers, 1887-1888.

691. -----. "Naval History of the Revolution." American Antiquarian Association Proceedings, New Series V (1889), 379-397.
Includes Arthur Hale's "The Yankee Privateer," p. 395-397.

692. Hale, Richard, Jr. "New Light on the Naval Side of Yorktown." Massachusetts Historical Society Proceedings, LXXI (1959), 124-132.

693. Hall, Clayton C. Baltimore: Its History and Its People. 3 vols.; New York: Lewis Historical Publishing Company, 1912.
Some Revolutionary privateering data.

693a. Hallock, David H. "Captain William Hallock, Continental Navy." DAR Magazine, LXVI (1932), 508-510.
A brief biography of the first commander of the Wasp.

694. Hamersly, Lewis R. List of Officers of the Navy of the United States and of the Marine Corps from 1775 to 1900. Edited by Edward W. Callahan. New York: L. R. Hamersly & Co., 1901. 749p. Rpr. 1969.

695. Hamersly, Thomas H. S., ed. Complete General Navy Register of the United States, from 1776-1887.... Containing the Names of all the Officers of the Navy, Volunteer and Regular ... 1776-1887. New York: The Editor, 1888. 934p.

696. Hamilton, Edward. Life of Paul Jones. Aberdeen: G. Clark & Son, 1848. 304p.

697. Hamilton, Edward P. Lake Champlain and the Upper Hudson Valley. Ticonderoga, N.Y.: Fort Ticonderoga Association, 1959. 47p.

698. Hamilton, Milton W. "Augustus C. Buell, Fraudulent Historian." Pennsylvania Magazine of History and Biography, LXXX (October 1956), 478-492.
A biographer of John Paul Jones noted chiefly for his fictions.

699. Hamilton, R. Vesey. "Hood." In John K. Laughton, ed. From Howard to Nelson: Twelve Sailors. London: Lawrence and Bullen, 1899. p. 361-396.

700. -----. "Rodney." In John K. Laughton, ed. From Howard to Nelson: Twelve Sailors. London: Lawrence and Bullen, 1899. p. 277-317.

701. -----., ed. See Gardner, James A., no. 614.

702. -----., ed. See Martin, Thomas Byam, no. 1002.

703. Hammersly, Sydney E. The Lake Champlain Naval Battles of 1776-1814. Hudson-Champlain, 1959, 350th Anniversary Edition. Waterford, N.Y.: 1959. 28p.
Valcour Island included.

704. Hammond, Otis G. "Ebenezer Hogg vs John Paul Jones." Magazine of History, I (July, 1905). p. 48-54.

705. Hamond, Andrew S., jt. author. See Montagu, John, no. 1053.

706. Hanks, Carlos C. "A Cruise for Gunpowder." United States Naval Institute Proceedings, LXV (March 1939), 324-327.
Hopkin's squadron in the West Indies.

707. Hanney, David. Rodney. New York: Macmillan, 1891. 222p.

707a. -----., ed. See Hood, Samuel, no. 742a.

708. -----. A Short History of the Royal Navy, 1217-1815. 2 vols.; London: Methuen, 1898-1909.
Vol. II, "1689-1815" applicable.

709. Hapgood, Hutchins. Paul Jones. The Riverside Biographical Series, no. 32. New York: Houghton,

[Hardy, Henry.]

Mifflin, 1901. 126p.

710. [Hardy, Henry.] Narrative of Events in Several Cruises of Captain Lambert Wickes, of the U. S. Brigantine Reprisal of 16 guns. [Washington, D. C.: H. Hardy, 1877.] 2p.

711. Hargreaves, Reginald. The Narrow Seas: A History of the English Channel, Its Approaches and Its Immediate Shores. London: Sidgwick and Jackson, 1959. 517p.

712. -----. "The Pea-Jackets." Navy, VII (January 1964), 20-24.

713. -----. "Submarine Offensive-A. D. 1776." Navy, VI (March 1963), 38-42.

714. Harlow, Vincent T. The Founding of the Second British Empire, 1763-1793. 2 vols.; New York: Longmans, Green, 1952.
Suffren's activities in volume one.

715. Harrington, V. D. "The New York Merchant on the Eve of the Revolution." Unpublished Ph. D. Dissertation, Columbia University, 1935.

716. Harris, Joseph. The Naval Atlantis; Pt. I, or, a Display of the Characters of Such Flag Officers as Were Distinguished during the Last War, by Nauticus, Jr. Pt. II, or, a Display of the Characters of Post-Captains who Served During the Late War. 2 vol. in 1.; London: Ridgway, 1788-1789.

717. [Harrison, Joseph.] "Joseph Harrison and the Liberty Incident." Edited by D. H. Watson. William and Mary Quarterly, 3rd Series XX (October 1963), 585-595.
By the collector of Boston Port on the seizure of Hancock's sloop in 1768.

718. Hart, Charles H. Robert Morris, the Financer of the American Revolution. A Sketch. Philadelphia: Historical Society of Pennsylvania, 1877. 15p.
Also prominent in Continental naval affairs.

719. -----. "The Sword Presented by Louis XVI to John

Paul Jones." United States Naval Institute Proceedings, XXXIII (June 1907), 712-715.

720. Hart, Francis R. Admirals of the Caribbean. New York: Houghton Mifflin, 1922. 203p.
Lord Rodney among others.

720a. Harvey, Margaret B. "Expedition of Captain James Willing." American Monthly Magazine, XX (February 1902), 105-110.
Down the Mississippi in 1778.

721. Hastings, George E. The Life and Works of Francis Hopkinson. Chicago: University of Chicago Press, 1926. 516p.
Poet and member of the Continental Navy Board.

722. Hatch, Marie M., ed. See Jervis, John, no. 785.

723. Haugen, R. N. B. "The Setting of Internal Administrative Communication in the United States Naval Establishment, 1775-1920." Unpublished Ph.D. Dissertation, Harvard University, 1953.
Concerned with the letting of contracts, not the passing of messages.

724. Hawkins, Christopher. The Adventures of Christopher Hawkins, Containing Details of his Captivity, a First and Second Time on the High Seas, in the Revolutionary War, by the British and his Consequent Sufferings and Escape from the Jersey Prison Ship. With an introduction and notes by Charles I. Bushnell. New York: Priv. print, 1864. 316p. Rpr. 1969.

725. Hayavadana Rao, Conjeeveram. History of Mysore, 1399-1799. 3 vols.; Bangalore: Superintendent of the Government Press, 1943-1946.
Suffren's activities covered in the third volume.

726. Hayes, Frederic H. "John Adams and American Sea Power." American Neptune, XV (January 1965), 34-45.
A discussion of his Revolutionary service on the Congressional Marine Committee featured.

727. Hayes, John D. "Washington and the Sea." Military

Haywood, Charles F.

Review, LI (July 1971), 60-66.

728. Haywood, Charles F. Minutemen and Mariners; True Tales of New England. New York: Dodd, Mead, 1963. 269p.

729. Haywood, Marshall De Lancey. "The State Navy of North Carolina in the War of the Revolution." North Carolina Booklet, XVII (July 1917), 48-56.

730. Haywood, Walter S. "The Penobscot Expedition." In Essays in Modern English History in Honor of Wilbur Cortez Abbott. Cambridge, Mass.: Harvard University Press, 1941. p. 221-253.

731. Hazard, Samuel, et al. Pennsylvania Archives. 138 vols.; Philadelphia: various publishers, 1852-1949.

732. Heath, William. Memoirs of Major-General Heath. Containing Anecdotes, Details of Skirmishes, Battles, and Other Military Events, During the American War. Written by Himself. Boston: Printed by I. Thomas and E. T. Andrews, 1798. 388p. Rpr. 1968.
    Considerable mention of French admirals D'Estaing, DeGrasse, and De Ternay.

733. Hedges, James B. The Browns of Providence Plantations: The Colonial Years. Studies in Economic History. Cambridge, Mass.: Harvard University Press, 1952. 336p.
    Includes the burning of the British revenue sloop Liberty in 1769 and the Gaspee Incident of 1772.

734. Heinl, Robert D. Soldiers of the Sea: The United States Marine Corps, 1775-1962. Annapolis: U.S. Naval Institute, 1962. 692p.
    Good coverage of Marine activities in the Revolution.

735. Herbert, Arthur, jt. author. See Hudson, Edward A., no. 757.

736. Herbert, Charles. A Relic of the Revolution, Containing a Full and Particular Account of the Sufferings and Privations of all the American Prisoners Captured on the High Seas, and Carried into Plymouth,

England, During the Revolution of 1776; with the Names of the Vessels Taken--the Names and Residence of the Several Crews, and Time of Their Commitment--the Names of Such as Died in Prison, and Such as Made their Escape, or Entered on board English men-of-war; Until the Exchange of Prisoners, March 15, 1779. Also an Account of the Several Cruises of the Squadron under the Command of Commodore John Paul Jones, Prizes Taken, etc. etc. Boston: C. H. Peirce, 1847. 258p. Rpr. 1968.
By a crewman of the Alliance, 1779-1780.

736a. An Heroic Congratulation, Addressed to the Hon. Augustus Keppel, Admiral of the Blue, on his Being Fully Acquitted of the Five Malicious Charges Exhibited Against Him by Sir Hugh Palliser. To which is Annexed "An Address to the Public Containing the Five Charges...." London: J. Dodsley, 1779. 32p.

737. Hewitt, M. J. "The West Indies in the American Revolution." Unpublished Ph.D. Dissertation, Oxford University, 1938.

738. Hill, Frederick S. The "Lucky Little Enterprise" and Her Successors in the United States Navy, 1776-1900. Boston, 1900. 26p.

739. -----. Twenty-six Historic Ships; the Story of Certain Famous Vessels of War and of Their Successors in the Navies of the United States and Confederate States of America, from 1775 to 1902. New York: Putnam, 1903. 515p.
Features Bon Homme Richard.

740. Hoadly, Charles J., ed. Public Records of the State of Connecticut (1776-1796) ... With the Journal of the Council of Safety (1775-1783). 3 vols.; Hartford: Case, Lockwood & Brainard, 1894-1922.

741. Hood, Alexander N., jt. author. See Bridport, Alexander N., no. 253.

742. Hood, Dorothy. The Admirals Hood. London: Hutchinson, 1942. 255p.

742a. Hood, Samuel. Letters Written by Sir Samuel Hood

Horn, D. B.

(Viscount Hood) in 1781-2-3, Illustrated by Extracts from Logs and Public Records. Edited by David Hannay. Navy Records Society Publications, v. 3. London: The Society, 1895. 170p.

743. Horn, D. B. and M. Ransome, eds. English Historical Documents, 1714-1783. Vol. X of English Historical Documents, D. C. Douglas, General Editor. London: Eyre & Spottiswoode, 1953--. 972p.
This volume contains excerpts from naval commanders of Britain on events during the Revolution.

744. Hornor, W. M., Jr. "Obstructions of the Hudson River During the Revolution." American Collector, II (September 1926), 436-445.

744a. Hoste, William. Memoirs and Letters of Captain Sir William Hoste. 2 vols.; London: R. Bentley, 1833.

745. Hough, Franklin B. The Siege of Charleston by the British Fleet and Army Under the Command of Admiral Arbuthnot and Sir Henry Clinton, which Terminated with the Surrender of that Place on the 12th of May 1780. Albany: J. Munsell, 1867. 224p.

746. -----. The Siege of Savannah by the Combined American and French Forces, under the Command of Gen. Lincoln and the Count d'Estaing, in the Autumn of 1779. Albany: J. Munsell, 1866. 187p.

747. Howard, George E. Preliminaries of the Revolution, 1763-1775. Vol. VI of The American Nation: A History. New York: Harper, 1907. 359p.

748. Howard, James L. Seth Harding, Mariner; A Naval Picture of the Revolution. New Haven: Yale University Press, 1930. 301p.

749. Howe, Archibald M., ed. See Campbell, Archibald, no. 291.

750. Howe, Octavious T. "Beverly Privateers in the American Revolution." Massachusetts Historical Society Publications, XXIV (1923), 318-435.
Features a list of officers and vessels.

751. -----. "Massachusetts on the Seas in the War of the

Revolution (1775-1783)." In Albert B. Hart, ed. Commonwealth History of Massachusetts: Colony, Province, and State. 5 vols.; New York: States History Company, 1927-1930. III, 30-63.

752. [Howe, Richard.] Reflections on a Pamphlet Entitled "A Letter to the Right Honble Lord Vict H--e." Edited, with an Introduction, by Gerald S. Brown, from the Original Manuscript in the William L. Clements Library. Ann Arbor: University of Michigan Press, 1959. 39p.

753. Howland, Henry R. "A British Privateer in the American Revolution." American Historical Review, VII (January 1902), 286-303.
Captain George Dean and the Vengeance.

754. Hoyt, William D. "'Letters Taken in Prizes,' 1778-1780." American Neptune, V (April 1945), 111-114.
British official, business and personal papers taken by Continental privateers.

755. Hozey, Peleg. "Privateer Sloop Independent; a Journal Kept by Peleg Hozey, Master." Rhode Island Historical Society Collections, XXXI (1938), 82-89, 122-123.
Dated 24 July-5 September, 1776.

756. Hubbard, Timothy W. "The Battle of Valcour Island: Benedict Arnold as Hero." American Heritage, XVII (October 1966), 8-11, 87-91.

757. Hudson, Edward A. and Arthur Herbert. "James Lind: His Contributions to Shipboard Sanitation." Journal of the History of Medicine and Allied Sciences, XI (January 1956), 1-12.

758. Huhner, Leon. "Jews Interested in Privateering in America During the Eighteenth Century." American Jewish Historical Society Publications, XXIII (1915), 163-176.
The War of Independence included.

759. Hulton, Ann. Letters of a Loyalist Lady: Being the Letters of Ann Hulton, Sister of Henry Hulton, Commissioner of Customs at Boston, 1767-1776.

Cambridge: Harvard University Press, 1927. 126p. Rpr. 1971.

760. Hunt, Galliard, jt. editor. See United States, Continental Congress, no. 1489.

761. Hunt, Livingston. "The British Naval Waterloo of the Chesapeake." Harvard Graduate Magazine, XXXVIII (March 1930), 272-281.

762. [Hutchinson, James.] "A Fragment of History." Edited by William B. Clark. The Minute Man, XXXIX, SL (February 1949-February 1950), nos. 1-4, 1.
    Diary of a surgeon returning to Philadelphia from France aboard the Salley with dispatches for the Continental Congress. Dated 26 February-16 March, 1777.

763. Hutchinson, William. A Treatise on Naval Architecture. Annapolis: U.S. Naval Institute, 1969. 303p.
    Reprint of the 1794 edition; based on the author's twenty years (1770's and 1780's) as Dock Master at Liverpool.

764. Ingalsbe, Grenville M. Benedict Arnold: The Heroic Years. Hudson Falls, N.Y.: The Author, 1913. 20p.

765. Inman, George, Comp. "Losses of the Military and Naval Forces Engaged in the War of the American Revolution." Pennsylvania Magazine of History and Biography, XXVII (April 1903), 176-205.

766. Institute Français de Washington, ed. See Washington, George, no. 1536.

767. The Interesting Life, Travels, Voyages, and Daring Engagements of the Celebrated Paul Jones. To which is Added a Song Written on the Engagement between the Good Man Richard and the Serapis. New York: G. Sinclair, 1809. 35p.
    Three more editions, with various pagination, in 1817, 1823, and 1828.

768. Jackson, George, ed. See Keppel, Augustus K., no. 820.

769. -----., ed. See Pallister, Hugh, no. 1169.

770. Jackson, Henry. "Letter of Colonel Henry Jackson to the Massachusetts Council." Collections and Proceedings of the Maine Historical Society, 2nd Series VI (1895), 299-302.

771. Jackson, T. B. "Howe." In John K. Laughton, ed. From Howard to Nelson: Twelve Sailors. London: Lawrence and Bullen, 1899. p. 321-358.

772. [James, Bartholomew.] Journal of Rear Admiral Bartholomew James, 1752-1828. Edited by John K. Laughton, with the assistance of James Y. F. Sullivan, ... James' Great Grandson. Publications of the Navy Records Society, v. 6. London: The Society, 1896. 402p.
   As a young officer, James saw service in the Revolution in New York, the West Indies, and the Battle of Chesapeake Bay.

773. James, James A. Oliver Pollock: The Life and Times of an Unknown Patriot. New York: D. Appleton-Century, 1937. 376p.
   Continental naval agent at New Orleans.

774. James, W. R. W. "Coast Fortresses During the American War of Independence." Royal United Service Institute Journal, LIX (August 1914), 75-100.

775. James, William M. The British Navy in Adversity: A Study of the War of American Independence. London: Longmans, Green, 1926. 459p. Rpr. 1970.
   Includes administration as well as operations.

776. -----. Old Oak: The Life of John Jervis, Earl of St. Vincent. New York: Longmans, Green, 1950. 230p.
   Some data on his career during the American Revolution.

777. "James River Naval Office, Manifest Book, 1774-1775." In U.S. Navy Department, Naval History Division. Naval Documents of the American Revolution. Edited by William B. Clark, et al. Washington: U.S. Government Printing Office, 1964--. I, 1387-1394.

778. Jameson, J. Franklin. "St. Eustatius in the American Revolution." American Historical Review, VIII (July 1903), 683-708.

779. Jeffery, Walter, jt. author. See Becke, Louis, no. 120.

780. Jenkins, C. W. "Combined Operations. Revolutionary War--Yorktown." Coast Artillery Journal, LXXII (April 1930), 315-333.

781. Jennett, Richard P. "Arnold on Champlain." Infantry, LIV (September-October 1964), 24-27.

782. Jenrich, Charles H. "The Mantle of Valor." Rudder, LXXIII (June 1957), 9-13.
John Barry.

783. -----. "The Old Jersey Prison Ship." United States Naval Institute Proceedings, LXXXIX (February 1963), 168-171.

784. Jensen, Arthur L. The Maritime Commerce of Colonial Philadelphia. Madison: State Historical Society of Wisconsin for the Dept. of History, University of Wisconsin, 1963. 312p.

785. [Jervis, John.] "Letters of Sir John Jervis to Sir Henry Clinton, 1774-1782." Edited by Marie M. Hatch. American Neptune, VII (April 1947), 87-106.

786. "John Paul Jones as a Citizen of Virginia." Virginia Magazine of History and Biography, VII (January 1900), 286-293.
In Fredricksburg.

787. Johnson, Allen and Dumas Malone, eds. The Dictionary of American Biography. 20 vols.; New York: Scribner, 1930.
A basic source for biographies of Continental naval officers.

788. Johnson, Amandus, trans. See Tournquist, Carl G., no. 1469.

789. Johnson, Cecil. British West Florida, 1763-1783.

New Haven: Yale University Press, 1943. 258p.

790. Johnson, Gerald W. <u>The First Captain: The Story of John Paul Jones.</u> New York: Coward-McCann, 1947. 312p.

790a. Johnson, R. F. <u>The Royal George.</u> London: Knight, 1971. 201p.

791. Johnston, Ruth Y. "American Privateers in French Ports, 1776-1778." <u>Pennsylvania Magazine of History and Biography,</u> LIII (October 1929), 352-374.

792. Jones, Charles C., ed. <u>The Siege of Savannah in 1779, as Described in Two Contemporaneous Journals of French Officers in the Fleet of Count d'Estaing.</u> Albany: J. Munsell, 1874. 77p.
Journalists unknown.

793. Jones, Charles H. <u>Captain Gustavus Conyngham, a Sketch of the Service He Rendered to the Cause of American Independence.</u> Philadelphia: The Pennsylvania Society of the Sons of the Revolution, 1903. 32p.

794. Jones, G. "An Early Amphibious Operation: Danbury, 1777." <u>Journal of the Society for Army Historical Research,</u> XLVI (1968), 129-131.
A successful coastal raid by elements of the British army and fleet.

795. Jones, John. <u>Plain Concise Practical Remarks, On the Treatment of Wounds and Fractures: To Which is Added an Appendix on Camp and Military Hospitals; Principally Designed for the Young Military and Naval Surgeons of North America.</u> Philadelphia, 1776. 118p. Rpr. 1971.
A handbook for medical personnel.

796. Jones, John P. <u>An Account of the Celebrated Commodore Paul Jones: Translated from a Manuscript Written by Himself.</u> Philadelphia: Peter K. Wagner, 1806. 37p.
An American translation of his French memoirs.

797. -----. <u>Battle Between the Bon Homme Richard and the Serapis: Commodore Jones's Report to Congress</u>

[Jones, John P.]

through Dr. [Benjamin] Franklin. Old South Leaflets, v. 7, no. 152. [Boston: Directors of the Old South Work, 1904.] 28p.

Contains Jones's advice on the organization of the Continental Navy and a passage from Buell's Jones.

798. [Jones, John P.] Great Sovereigns, Heroes, and Pioneers: Admiral John Paul Jones. The First and Most Fascinating Naval Hero: His Remarkable Deeds During the Revolutionary War; Grand Commemoration, a Fitting Tribute to his Memory. Compiled from his Original Journals and Correspondence, and the U. S. Naval War Records. New York: Werner, 1910. 401p.

799. -----. Letter of John Paul Jones: Facsimile of Letter Written Aboard the Ranger, February 13, 1778, While at Anchor in Quiberon Bay, Arranging for the First National Salute Ever Given the American Flag in Europe. [Boston: The Bibliophile Society] 1903. 1p.

800. -----. "Letter of John Paul Jones to Joseph Hewes, May 19, 1776." United States Naval Institute Proceedings, LIV (July 1928), 632-633.

801. -----. "Letters by Paul Jones: Glimpses of the American Navy in the Revolution." United Service, New Series XIV (July 1895), 90-98.

802. -----. Letters of John Paul Jones, Printed from the Unpublished Originals in Mr. W. K. Bixby's Collection, with Introductory Remarks by General Horace Porter and Franklin B. Sanborn. Boston: Printed Exclusively for Members of the Bibliophile Society [New York: De Vinne Press] 1905. 123p.

General Horace's piece "The Recovery of the Body of John Paul Jones," p. 57-123.

803. -----. Life and Correspondence of John Paul Jones, Including his Narrative of the Campaign of the Liman. From Original Letters and Manuscripts in the Possession of Miss Janette Taylor. New York: D. Fanshaw, 1830. 555p.

804. -----. Life of Rear-Admiral John Paul Jones, Chevalier of the Military Order of Merit, and of the

Russian Order of St. Anne, etc. etc. Comp. from His Original Journals and Correspondence including an Account of his Services in the American Revolution and in the War Between the Russians and Turks in the Black Sea. [Edited by Benjamin Walker.] Illustrated with Numerous Engravings from Original Drawings by James Hamilton. Philadelphia: Walker & Gillis, 1845. 399p.
Subsequent editions published in 1846, 1851, 1867, and 1883.

805. Jones, John Paul. Memoires de Paul Jones, ou Il Expose Ses Principaux Services, et Rappelle ce Qui Lui Est Arrive de Plus Remarquable Particutierement en Europe, Ecrits par Lui-meme en Englais, et Tranduits Sous Ses Yeux par le Citoyen [Benoit] Andre. Paris: Chez Louis, AN VI, 1798. 244p.

806. -----. "Memoires de Paul Jones...." English Translation. Niles Weekly Register, II (1812), 230-231, 249-251, 277-278, 296-298, 317-318, 330-331.

807. -----. Memoirs of Rear-Admiral Paul Jones. Now First Compiled from His Original Journals and Correspondence; Including an Account of His Services Under Prince Potemkin. 2 vols.; Edinburgh: Oliver & Boyd, 1830.
A second edition, with further details on his Russian service, was published in London in 1843.

808. -----. "Paul Jones and Lord Selkirk's Plate. From a Correspondent in Paris, London Times, March 26, 1894." United States Naval Institute Proceedings, XX (1894), 463-465.

809. Jones, Thomas. History of New York During the Revolutionary War and of the Leading Events in the Other Colonies at that Period. Edited by Edward Floyd de Lancey. New York Historical Society. The John D. Jones Fund Series of Histories and Memoirs. 2 vols.; New York: The Society, 1879. Rpr. 1968.

810. Jones, William R. and Joseph G. Branch. John Paul Jones and His Ancestry. Together with his Last Days. Chicago: The Authors, 1927. 284p.

811. "Journal of a Cruise in 1777 in the Privateer

Brig Oliver Cromwell." Essex Institute Historical Collections, XLV (July 1909), 245-255.

812. "Journal of an Officer in the Naval Army in America, in 1781 and 1782." In John D. G. Shea, ed. The Operations of the French Fleet under the Count de Grasse in 1781-2, as Described in Two Contemporaneous Journals. Bradford Club Series, no. 3. New York: The Club, 1864. p. 136-185. Rpr. 1971.
Possibly written by Admiral De Grasse.

813. Kain, C. Henry. The Military and Naval Operations on the Delaware in 1777, written for the City Historical Society of Philadelphia. Publication of the City Historical Society of Philadelphia, no. 7. Philadelphia: Printed for the Society, 1910. 203p.

814. Keevil, John J. Medicine and the Navy, 1220-1900. 4 vols.; Edinburgh: E. & S. Livingstone, 1957-1963.
The third volume, on the Eighteenth Century, was completed by Christopher Lloyd and Jack L. S. Coulter after the author's death.

815. Keim, De B Randolph, ed. See United States, Congress, Senate, no. 1486.

815a. Keith, George Elphinstone, Lord. The Keith Papers: Selected from the Letters and Papers of Admiral Viscount Keith. Edited by W. G. Perrin and Christopher Lloyd. Naval Records Society Publications, nos. 62, 90, 96. 3 vols.; London: Naval Records Society, 1927-1964.
Keith was involved in several actions on the American coast during the conflict.

816. [Kelly, Samuel.] Samuel Kelley: an Eighteenth Century Seaman. Edited by Crosbie Garstin. London: Cape, 1925. 320p.
A British merchant sailor on the Atlantic crossings during the Revolution.

817. Kendall, Roger and John S. Rowe. "The Man-of-War Ranger." Nautical Research Journal, XI (Fall-Winter 1960), 93, 129.

818. Kepner, Frances R., ed. See Simpson, James, no. 1364.

819. Keppel, Augustus K. An Authentic and Impartial Copy of the Trial of the Hon. Augustus Keppel, Admiral of the Blue, Held at Portsmouth on the 7th of January 1779 and Continued by Several Adjournments to the 11th Day of February 1779. Taken in Short Hand by a Person who Attended the Whole Trial and Printed by the Desire of a Society of Gentlemen, with Several Interesting Papers. Portsmouth: Sold in London by Wheldon, 1779. 415p.

His courtmartial for "misconduct and neglect of duty" at the July 27-28, 1778 Battle of Ushant.

820. -----. Minutes of the Proceedings at a Court-Martial, Assembled for the Trial of the Honourable Admiral Augustus Keppel, on a Charge Exhibited Against him by Vice-Admiral Sir Hugh Pallister, Baronet. As Taken by George Jackson; Published by Order of the Right Honourable the Lords Commissioners of the Admiralty. With an Appendix Containing all the Letters and Papers that have any Relation to the Trial. London: W. Strahan, 1779. 182p.

821. -----. The Proceedings at Large of the Court-Martial, on the Trial of the Honourable Augustus Keppel, Admiral of the Blue, Held on board His Majesty's Ship Britannian, on Thursday, January 7th, 1779. And Adjourned to the House of the Governor of Portsmouth, and Held there till Thursday, February 11th, When the Admiral was Honourably Acquitted. Taken in Short Hand, by W. Blanchard, for the Admiral and Published by his Permission. London: J. Almon, 1779. 184p.

822. Keppel, Thomas R. Life of Augustus, Viscount Keppel, Admiral of the White, and First Lord of the Admiralty, in 1782-3. 2 vols.; London: H. Colburn, 1842.

823. Kerallain, R. de. "Bougainville a l'Armee du Comte de Grasse, Guerre de l'Amerique, 1781-1783." Journal de la Societe des Americanistes de Paris, nsXX (1928), 1-70.

The noted French explorer's commanded part of the admiral's fleet at the Battle of the Saints.

824. Kerguelen-Tremarec, Yves J. de. Relation des Combats et des Evenements de la Guerre Maritime de

Kerr, W. M.

1778 entre la France et l'Angleterre, melee de Reflexions sur les Manoeuvres des Generaux.... Paris: Impraimerie de Patris, 1796. 403p.

825. Kerr, W. M., jt. author. See Pleadwell, F. L., no. 1228.

826. Kerr, Wilfred B. Bermuda and the American Revolution, 1760-1783. Princeton: Princeton University Press, 1936. 142p.

827. -----. The Maritime Provinces of British North America and the American Revolution. Sackville, N.B., Can.: Busy East Press, 1941. 172p.

828. Kidder, Frederic, ed. See Allan, John, no. 38.

829. [Kilby, John.] "Narrative of John Kilby, Quarter-Gunner of the United States of the U.S. Ship Bonhomme Richard, Under John Paul Jones." With an Introduction and Notes by Augustus C. Buell. Scribners Monthly, XXXVIII (July 1905), 23-41.

830. King, C. H.M.S.: His Majesty's Ships and Their Forbears. London: Studio Publications, 1940. 328p.

831. King, G. H. The Gibralter of the West Indies: A Chapter from British Imperial History. St. Kitts: St. Kitts Printery, n.d. 22p.
Capture of St. Kitts by the French in 1782.

832. Kirby, Percival R. The True Story of the Grosvenor East Indiaman, Wrecked on the Coast of Pondoland, South Africa, on 4 August 1782. New York: Oxford University Press, 1960. 266p.

833. Kite, Elizabeth S. "French 'Secret Aid': Precursor to the French American Alliance, 1776-1777." French American Review, I (April-June 1948), 143-152.

834. -----. "Lafayette and His Companions on the Victoire." American Catholic Historical Record, XLV (March, December 1934), 1-32, 275-311.

835. Kleber, Louis C. "Jones Raids Britain." History

Today, XIX (April 1969), 277-82.

836. Kline, Sherman J. "John Paul Jones--Man of Destiny." Americana, XXI (July 1927), 284-414.

837. Klingaman, David C. "The Development of the Coastwise Trade in Virginia in the Late Colonial Period." Virginia Magazine of History and Biography, LXXVII (January 1969), 26-45.

838. Klotz, Edwin F. Los Corsarios Americanos y España (1776-1786). Editato en Colaboración con Fundación del Amo, de California. Madrid: Seminario de Estudias Americanistas, Universidad de Madrid, 1959. 125p.

839. Knapp, Samuel L. "The United States Navy from the Beginning to 1828." In his Lectures on American Literature, with Remarks on Some Passages of American History. New York: E. Bliss, 1829. p. 266-285.

840. Knight, Russel W., jt. author. See Smith, Philip C. F., no. 1381.

841. Knowles, Charles H. Observations on Naval Tactics and on the Claims of Mr. Clerk of Eldin, etc. London, 1830.
    Gives credit for Rodney's 1783 victory to the French!

842. Knox, Dudley W. "D'Estaing's Fleet Revealed." United States Naval Institute Proceedings, LXI (February 1935), 161-168.

843. -----. A History of the United States Navy. With a foreword by Chester W. Nimitz. New ed. New York: G. P. Putnam's Sons, 1948. 704p.

844. -----. The Naval Genius of George Washington. Boston: Houghton, Mifflin, 1932. 138p.
    Demonstrates the strategic use of seapower made by the American general.

845. -----. "Navies in the American Revolution: The Influence of Sea Power on Military Operations." Army Ordnance, XV (January-February 1935), 213-216.

846. Koke, Richard J. "Forcing the Hudson River Passage, October 9, 1776." New York Historical Society Quarterly, XXXVI (October 1954), 458-466.
The Royal Navy moves upstream.

847. -----. "The Struggle for the Hudson: The British Naval Expedition Under Captain Hyde Parker and Captain James Wallace, July 12-August 18, 1776." New York Historical Society Quarterly, XL (April 1956), 114-175.

848. Konetzke, Richard. "Die Grosse Belagerung von Gibraltar in den Jahren 1779 bis 1783." Ibero-Amerikanisches Archives, XV Heft 1/2 (April-July 1941), 20-26.
The Great Siege.

849. Kurtz, Henry J. "The Battle of Sullivan's Island." American History Illustrated, III (June 1968), 18-27.
Charleston, South Carolina, 1776.

850. Labaree, Benjamin W. The Boston Tea Party. New York: Oxford University Press, 1964. 347p.

851. -----. "Patriots and Partisans: The Merchants of Newburyport, 1764-1815." Unpublished Ph.D. Dissertation, Harvard University, 1962.
Includes those in the shipping business.

852. -----. Harvard University Studies, no. 73. Cambridge: Harvard University Press, 1962. 242p.

853. Lacour-Gayet, Georges. "La Campagne Navale de la Manche en 1775." Revue Maritime, CL (1901), 1629-1673.

854. -----. La Marine Militaire de la France Sous le Règne de Louis XVI. Paris: H. Champion, 1905. 719p.

855. Lacour-Gayet, Y. "L'Amiral de Grasse a Yorktown et le 150me Anniversaire de la Victoire Franco-Americaine de Yorktown." France-Amerique, New Series XXXII (1931), 289-297.

856. "The Lady Washington Galley." Olde Ulster, IX (October 1913), 305-309.

857. Laing, Alexander. American Ships. Annapolis: U.S. Naval Institute, 1971. 500p.
Features the story of Bushnell's Turtle.

858. Lallou, W. J. "Aid to American Colonists from Catholic France." American Catholic Historical Record, XL (March 1929), 78-82.

859. Lambert de Sainte-Croix, A. Essai sur l'Histoire de l'Administration de la Marine de la France, 1689-1792. Paris: Calmann Levy, 1892. 457p.

860. Lancaster, Bruce. The American Heritage Book of the Revolution. Editor-in-Charge Richard M. Ketchum, with an introduction by Bruce Catton. New York: American Heritage, distributed by Simon & Schuster, 1953. 394p. Rpr. 1971.

861. Lanctot, Gustave. Canada and the American Revolution, 1774-1783. Translated by Margaret Cameron. Cambridge, Mass.: Harvard University Press, 1967. 321p.

862. Landais, Peter. Charges and Proofs Respecting the Conduct of Peter Landais. New York: Francis Childs, Jr., 1787. 18p.
Defense of the weird skipper of the Alliance who fired into the Bonhomme Richard while she fought the Serapis.

863. -----. Memorial to Justify Peter Landais's Conduct During the Late War. Boston: P. Edes, 1784. 52p.

864. -----. Second Part of the Memorial to Justify Peter Landais's Conduct During the Late War. New York: Samuel Louden, pr., [1787?] 52p.

865. Landers, H. L., author. See United States, Army, War College, no. 1482.

866. Lapayrouse Bonfils, Comte de. Histoire de la Marine Française. 3 vols.; Paris: Chez Dentu, 1845.

867. La Renclere, Charles G. M. B. de. Histoire de la Marine Française. 6 vols.; Paris: E. Plon, Nourrit, 1809-1912.

Larrabee, Harold A.

History of the French navy, including the period of the American Revolution.

868. Larrabee, Harold A. Decision at the Chesapeake. New York: Potter, 1964. 317p.
The British/French naval battles and the Yorktown campaign.

869. -----. "A Near Thing at Yorktown." American Heritage, XII (October 1961), 56-64, 69-73.
An overview of the siege and fleet operations.

870. Larter, Harry C., Jr. "The Lauzun Legion, French Navy, 1780-1783." Military Collector and Historian, III (June 1951), 40-42.

871. Lasseray, Andre. Les Francais Sous les Treize Etoiles (1775-1783). 2 vols.; Macon: Imprimerie Protat Freres; se Trouve a Paris chez D. Janvier, 1935.
The greatest part of the work is devoted to biographical studies, with emphasis on Revolutionary service.

872. Lassiter, Francis R. Arnold's Invasion of Virginia, 1781. New York: Longmans, Green and Company, 1901. 36p.
A brief account of the attack which destroyed most of the Virginia State Navy.

873. Lathrop, Constance. "A Sponsor of the American Navy--Benjamin Franklin." United States Naval Institute Proceedings, LIV (October 1928), 31-32.
A segment of his French activities.

874. Laughton, John K. "Rodney and the Navy of the Eighteenth Century." Edinburgh Review, XC (January 1892), 166-200.

875. -----. Studies in Naval History: Biographies. London: Longmans, 1887. 469p.
Lengthy pieces on John Paul Jones and the Baille de Suffren included. Rpr. 1970.

876. -----., ed. See Barham, Charles M., no. 92.

877. -----., ed. See Duncan, Henry, no. 470.

878. -----., ed. See Gardner, James A., no. 614.

879. -----., ed. See James, Bartholomew, no. 772.

880. Lauzun, Armand Louis De Gontaut, Duc de. "Narrative of the Duke de Lauzun." American Historical Magazine, II (July 1907), 292-298.

881. -----., "Narrative of the Duke de Lauzun." Magazine of American History, VI (January 1881), 51-53.

882. -----. Memoirs du Duc de Lauzun. Paris: Poulet-Malassis et de Broise, 1858. 409p. Rpr. 1971.

883. La Varende, Jean de. Suffren et ses Ennemis. Paris, Editions de Paris, 1948. 336p.

884. -----. Suffren et ses Ennemis. Paris: Flammarion, 1967. 315p.

885. Lavisse, E., ed. Histoire de France Depuis les Origines Jusqu'a la Revolution. 9 vols. in 18.; Paris: Hachette, 1900-1911.

886. Lawrence, Alexander A. Storm Over Savannah: The Story of Count D'Estaing and the Siege of the Town in 1779. Athens: University of Georgia Press, 1951. 220p.
The operation was a failure.

887. Leary, Lewis G. That Rascal Freneau; a Study in Literary Failure. 2d ed. New York: Octagon Books, 1964. 501p.
A study of the literary gifts of the "Poet of the Revolution."

888. Leavitt, John F. "Shipwrights' Tools During the Revolution." In U.S. Navy Department, Naval History Division. Naval Documents of the American Revolution. Edited by William B. Clark, et al. Washington: U.S. Government Printing Office, 1964--. V, 1323-1337.

889. Leavitt, Walter C. "Hannah: Copied from Letters from Mr. Walter C. Leavitt to the Addison Gallery." Mariner, IX (October 1935), 100-102.
Washington's 1775 schooner.

890. Leavitt, William. "Materials for the History of Shipbuilding in Salem [Massachusetts]." Essex Institute Historical Collections, VI (1864), 136-140, 171-175, 226-227, 252-255; VII (1865), 207-213.
Many accounts of privateers of the Revolution.

891. Le Boucher, Odet Julien. Histoire de la Derniere Guerre, Entre la Grande-Bretagne et les Etats-Unis de l'Amerique, la France, l'Espagne et la Hollande. Paris: Brocas, 1787. 358p.

892. Lecky, Halton S. The King's Ships [Aboukir to Jupiter.] 3 vols.; London: H. Muirhead, 1913-1914.
An alphabetical list of ships histories on the order of The Dictionary of American Naval Fighting Ships.

893. Lee, F. D. and J. L. Agnew. Historical Record of the City of Savannah. Savannah, Ga.: J. H. Estill, 1869. 200p.

894. Lee, Henry. Memoirs of the War in the Southern Department of the United States. A new ed., with Revisions, and a Biography of the Author, by Robert E. Lee. New York: University Publishing Co., 1869. 620p. Rpr. 1969.

895. Lee, Jonathan. The Fate of the Grosvenor. London: Methuen, 1938. 332p.

896. [Lee, Richard Henry.] The Letters of Richard Henry Lee. Edited by James C. Ballagh. 2 vols.; New York: Macmillan, 1911-1914.

897. Lee, Richard H. Memoir of the Life of Richard Henry Lee and His Correspondence with the Most Distinguished Men in America and Europe, Illustrative of Their Characters, and of the Events of the American Revolution. By His Grandson Richard H. Lee of Leesburg, Virginia. 2 vols.; Philadelphia: H. C. Cary & I. Lea, 1825.

898. Lee, Sidney, jt. editor. See Stephen, Leslie, no. 1408.

899. [Lee, William.] Letters of William Lee, Sheriff and Alderman of London; Commercial Agent of the

Continental Congress in France, and Minister to the Courts of Vienna and Berlin, 1766-1783. Edited by Worthington C. Ford. 3 vols.; Brooklyn: Historical Printing Club, 1891. Rpr. 1970.

900. Leiby, Adrian C. The Revolutionary War in the Hackensack Valley: The Jersey Dutch and the Neutral Ground, 1775-1783. New Brunswick, N.J.: Rutgers University Press, 1962. 329p.
The whale-boat raids are included.

901. Lemisch, Jesse. "Jack Tar in the Streets: Merchant Seamen in the Politics of Revolutionary America." William and Mary Quarterly, 3rd Series XXV (July 1968), 371-407.

902. Leroy, Perry E. "Sir Guy Carleton as a Military Leader during the American Invasion and Repulse in Canada, 1775-1776." Unpublished Ph.D. Dissertation, Ohio State University, 1960.
Comments on the fleet built to oppose Arnold on Lake Champlain.

902a. Letter from an Officer of the Naval Army of France to the Hon. Admiral Keppel, Dated on Board a French Squadron off Ushant, 9th of August, 1778. With an Engraved Plan of the Evolutions of the Fleets in the Engagement off Ushant. Translated from the Original Printed at Breast, with Notes. London, 1778. 36p.

903. Lewis, Charles L. Admiral De Grasse and American Independence. Annapolis: United States Naval Institute, 1945. 403p.

904. -----. Famous American Marines; an Account of the Corps: The Exploits of Officers and Men on Land, by Air and Sea, from the Decks of the Bonhomme Richard to the Summit of Mount Surivachi. Boston: Page, 1950. 375p.
Includes a biography of the noted Continental Marine, Samuel Nicholas.

905. -----. "John Paul Jones and the Beginning of Our Navy." In his Famous American Naval Officers. Boston: Page, 1924. p. 3-35.

906. Life and Adventures of Paul Jones, the English Pirate. London: E. Lloyd, n. d. 12p.

907. "Life of Commodore [Alexander] Murray." Portfolio, 3rd Series III (April 1814), 399-409.
After commanding a privateer, served as a lieutenant on the Trumbell and Alliance.

908. "Life of Commodore [Richard] Dale." Portfolio, 3rd Series III (June 1814), 499-515.

909. "Life of Virginia Navy Officers, Sailors, and Marines." Virginia Magazine of History and Biography, I (July 1893), 64-75.
In the Revolution.

910. The Life, Travels, Voyages and Daring Engagements of Paul Jones: Containing Anecdotes of Undaunted Courage. Printed for the Benefit of William Earl, who Lost a Limb on board the Goodman Richard. Boston: Printed by N. Coverly, [181-?] 48p.

911. Life, Voyages, and Sea Battles of That Celebrated Pirate, Commodore Paul Jones. Accurately Compiled from Authentic Documents. New Edition. Bradford, Yorkshire: Walker and Scarlett [1825?] 24p.

912. Lincoln, C. H. "John Paul Jones and Our First Triumphs on the Sea." Review of Reviews, XXXII (July 1905), 39-42.

913. Lincoln Co., Me. Citizens. "Settlements in Maine After the Penobscot Expedition." Collections and Proceedings of the Maine Historical Society, 2nd Series VII (1896), 433-435.

914. Lind, James. A Treatise on the Scurvey; In Three Parts. 3rd ed., enl. and improved. London: S. Crowder, 1772. 559p.

915. Lindsay, Colin. "Narrative of the Occupation and Defence of the Island of St. Lucie, 1779." In Alexander W. Lindsay, ed. Lives of the Lindsays; or, A Memoir of the House of Crawford and Balcarres. 3 vols.; London: J. Murray, 1849. III, 195-235.

915a. Lingel, Robert. "The Atlantic Neptune." New York Public Library Bulletin, XL (1936), 571-603.
On the J.F.W. Desbarres charts of the North American coast used by the Royal Navy during the Revolution.

916. Linzee, John W. "Captain John Linzee of His Majesty's Navy." Massachusetts Magazine, III (April 1910), 143-144.
A biographical sketch of the skipper of HMS Falcon which fired on Bunker Hill on June 17, 1775.

917. Lippincott, Bertram. Indians, Privateers and High Society. A Rhode Island Sampler. Philadelphia: Lippincott, 1961. 301p.

918. Lippitt, Charles W. "The Battle of Rhode Island." Newport Historical Society Bulletin, XVIII (October 1915), 1-14.

919. "List of Nantucket Men who Served Under John Paul Jones During the Revolutionary War." In Nantucket Historical Association. Proceedings of the Seventh Annual Meeting at Nantucket, Massachusetts, July 24, 1901. Nantucket: The Society, 1901. 23p.

920. Little, L. "Narrative of An American Sea Captain." Journal of American History, XIII (April-June 1910), 217-252.
During the Revolution.

921. Lloyd, Christopher. "Armed Forces and the Art of War: Part I, Navies." In A. Goodwin, ed. The American and French Revolutions, 1763-1793. Vol. VIII of The Cambridge Modern History. Cambridge, Eng.: Cambridge University Press, 1957--. p. 174-190.
Excellent summary of the American Revolution.

922. -----. The Navy and the Nation: A History of Naval Life and Policy. Rev. ed. London: Cresset, 1961. 314p.

923. -----. "Sir George Rodney: Lucky Admiral." In George A. Billias, ed. George Washington's Opponents: British Generals and Admirals in the American Revolution. New York: Morrow,

[Lloyd, Henry]

1969. p. 327-354.

924. -----, comp. The Health of Seamen: Selections from the Works of Dr. James Lind, Sir Gilbert Blane, and Dr. Thomas Trotter. Publications of the Navy Records Society, v. 107. London: Printed for the Navy Records Society, 1965. 320p.

925. -----., jt. author. See Keevil, John J., no. 814.

926. -----., jt. editor. See Trevenen, James, no. 1472.

926a. -----., jt. ed. See Keith, George Elphinstone, no. 815a.

927. [Lloyd, Henry.] "Invasion and the Means to Defeat It in 1779." Edited by K. N. Colvile. Army Quarterly, XLI (October 1940), 145-147.

928. Lloyd, Malcolm. "The Taking of the Bahamas by the Continental Navy in 1776." Pennsylvania Magazine of History and Biography, XLIX (October 1925), 349-366.

929. Loir, Maurice. La Marine Royale en 1789. Paris: Armand Colin, 1892. 319p.
Offers some comments on its merits during the early 1780's.

930. Lomenie, Louis L. de. Beaumarchais and His Times. Trans. by Henry S. Edwards. 4 vols.; London: Addey, 1856.

930a. Long, Jane T. "Naval Heroes of the Revolution." American Monthly Magazine, XIII (October 1898), 338-347.
Colonial champions.

931. Longfellow, David. "Thunder at Machas [Maine]." DAR Magazine, C (October 1966), 690-693.

932. Lord, Alice F. "Commodore Samuel Tucker--Hero of the Early American Navy." Journal of American History, III (1911), 435-440.

933. Lorenz, Lincoln. The Admiral and the Empress: John Paul Jones and Catherine the Great. New

York: Bookman Associates, 1954. 194p.
Brief mention of his Revolutionary service.

934. -----. "The Bicentennial of John Paul Jones." United States Naval Institute Proceedings, LXXIII (July 1947), 767-777.

935. -----. John Paul Jones, Fighter for Freedom and Glory. Annapolis: United States Naval Institute, 1948. 846p.

936. "Loss of the Ship Randolph, 1778." South Carolina Historical and Genealogical Magazine, X (July 1909), 171-173.

937. Lossing, Benson J. "John Paul Jones." Harper's New Monthly Magazine, XI (July 1855), 145-170.

938. -----. "Our French Allies." Harper's New Monthly Magazine, XLII (April 1871), 753-763.
Including the admirals and seamen.

939. -----. The Pictorial Field Book of the Revolution. 2 vols.; New York: Harper, 1851-1852. Rpr. 1969.

940. [Lostanges, Arnaud Louis Charles Rose de.] Relation du Combat de la Frégate Française la Surveillante, contre la Frégate Anglaise le Québec. Paris: F. Didot, Imprimeur du Roi, 1817. 68p.

941. Loture, Robert de. Washington Nous Voici! La France au Secours de l'Independence Americaine. Preface de M. Louis Madelin. Paris: Hachette, 1934. 245p.

942. Louis XVI, King of France. Letter du Roi a M. l'Amiral Concernant le Jugement des Prises Faites Par les Corsaires que les Etats-Unis d'Amerique Arment dans les Ports de France. 10 Aout, 1780. Paris: De l'Imprimerie Royale, 1780. 1l.

943. -----. Ordonnance ... Concernant Les Prises Faite Par Les Vaisseaux ... de sa Majesté. Du 28 Mars 1778. Paris, 1778. 1p.
Revised at various times to 1783.

944. [Loundes, Rawlins.] "Account of the Loss of the

Randolph, as given in a Letter from Rawlins Loundes to Henry Laurens." South Carolina Historical Magazine X (July 1909), 171-173.

945. Loughrey, Mary E. France and Rhode Island, 1686-1800. New York: Kings Crown Press, 1944. 186p.
Includes the activities of the French fleet under D'Estaing.

946. Lovejoy, David S. Rhode Island Politics and the American Revolution, 1760-1776. Brown University Studies, v. 23. Providence: Brown University Press, 1958. 256p.
Data on H. M. S. Gaspee included.

947. -----. "Rights Imply Equality: The Case Against Admiralty Jurisdiction in America, 1764-1776." William and Mary Quarterly, 3rd Series XVI (October 1959), 459-482.

948. Lovell, Solomon. "Original Journal of General Solomon Lovell Kept During the Penobscot Expedition, 1779; with a Sketch of his Life by Gilbert Nash." Weymouth Historical Society Papers, I (1881), 14-105.

949. Low, Charles R. The Great Battles of the British Navy. New York: G. Routledge, 1872. 496p.

950. -----. History of the Indian [British] Navy. 2 vols.; London: R. Bentley, 1877.

951. Lundeberg, Philip K. The Continental Gunboat Philadelphia and the Northern Campaign of 1776. Smithsonian Publication, 4651. Washington, D. C.: Smithsonian Institution, 1966. Unpaged.

952. McCarty, William, comp. Songs, Odes, and Other Poems, on National Subjects. 3 vols.; Philadelphia: The Author, 1842.
Vol. II, Naval ..., deals mainly with the Revolution.

953. McCaw, Walter D. "Captain John Harris of the Virginia Navy: A Prisoner of War in England, 1777-1779." Virginia Magazine of History and Biography, XXII (April 1914), 160-172.

954. McClellan, Edwin N. "American Marines in the Revolution." United States Naval Institute Proceedings, XLIX (June 1923), 957-963.

955. -----. "The First American Flag to Fly Over Foreign Soil." Marine Corps Gazette, XVIII (May 1933), 3-5.
    Role of the marines in the March 3, 1776 attack on Nassau.

955a. -----. "Marine Officers of the Revolution." DAR Magazine LXVI (September 1932), 560-68.

956. -----. "Natal Day of the American Navy and Marines." DAR Magazine LXVIII (August 1934), 470-72.
    Role of the Enterprize, 3 May-1 July 1775 whose pay-roll offers "convincing information" that 3 May 1775 is the "earliest date of the American navy and marines."

956a. -----. "The Navy at the Battles of Trenton and Princeton." United States Naval Institute Proceedings, XLIX (November 1923), 1848-1855.

957. McClellan, William S. Smuggling in the American Colonies at the Outbreak of the Revolution, with Special Reference to the West India Trade. David A. Wells Prize Essays, no. 3. New York: Printed for the Department of Political Science of Williams College by Moffat, Yard and Company, 1912. 105p.

958. McCowen, George S., Jr. The British Occupation of Charleston, 1780-82. Tricentennial Studies, no. 5. Columbia: University of South Carolina Press, 1972. 169p.

959. McCusher, John J., Jr. "The American Invasion of Nassau in the Bahamas." American Neptune, XXV (July 1965), 189-217.

960. -----. "The Continental Ship Alfred." Nautical Research Journal, XIII (Autumn 1965), 37-68.

961. -----. "The Tonnage of the Continental Ship Alfred." Pennsylvania Magazine of History and Biography, XC (July 1966), 227-235.

962. McGuffie, Tom H. The Siege of Gibraltar, 1779-1783. Philadelphia: Dufour, 1965. 208p.

963. Machias, Maine. Bicentennial Corporation. Machias Bicentennial--August 2-10. Machias, Me. Np., 1963.
    Much on the "Lexington of the Sea."

964. McIlwaine, H. R., ed. Journals of the Council of the State of Virginia, 1776-1781. 2 vols.; Richmond: Virginia State Library, 1931.

965. Macintyre, Donald G. F. W. Admiral Rodney. New York: Norton, 1963. 280p.

966. McKay, R. H., Jr. "Elias Hasket Derby, Merchant of Salem, Massachusetts, 1739-1799." Unpublished Ph.D. Dissertation, Clark University, 1961.
    Includes his Revolutionary activities.

967. Mackenzie, Alexander S. The Life of Paul Jones. 2 vols.; New York: Harper, 1845.

968. Mackesy, Piers. "British Strategy in the War of American Independence." Yale Review, LII (Summer 1963), 539-557.
    Includes their naval strategy.

969. -----. The War for America, 1775-1783. Cambridge: Harvard University Press, 1964. 565p.
    Very good on naval aspects.

970. McLarty, R. N. "The Expedition of Major General John Vaughan to the Lesser Antilles, 1779-1781." Unpublished Ph.D. Dissertation, University of Michigan, 1951.

971. Maclay, Edgar S. A History of American Privateers. New York: Appleton, 1899. 519p.

972. -----. "How Our Infant Navy Strangled a War Horror." United States Naval Institute Proceedings, XLV (December 1919), 2041-2048.
    The capture of the ship Nancy by the Colonial warship Lee put an end to the smuggling of 50 "town burning machines" by the Tories.

973. -----. "John Paul Jones' Fellow Officers," Magazine of History, I (May 1905), p. 301-305.

973a. -----. "Our Sea Forces of the Revolution." DAR Magazine, XLIX (1916), 85-96, 149-161, 227-237.

974. -----. "A Sea Fight Long Forgot." Magazine of History with Notes and Queries, XI (March 1910), 150-154.
A battle between a single Continental ship and one or more British vessels off the coast of France on September 9, 1780 commemorated and described only upon a single headstone at Rochester Cemetery, Plymouth County, Mass.

975. -----. "A Sea View of Our Revolution." United States Naval Institute Proceedings, XXXVII (March 1911), 219-237.

976. McMaster, Gilbert T. "Signal Codes Used by Our Revolutionary Commanders for the Convoy of Merchantmen." United States Naval Institute Proceedings, XXXVIII (September 1912), 1041-1043.

977. MacMechan, A. "William Greenwood and the Ship Flying Fish." Universal Magazine, XIII (February 1914), 93-104.
During the Revolution.

977a. Maconochie, Charles C. "From the Outposts, 1775--the Defence of St. Johns [Canada]." Blackwood's Magazine, CXCV (1914), 563-572.
Captured by Benedict Arnold.

978. Mahan, Alfred T. The Influence of Sea Power on History, 1660-1783. Boston: Little, Brown, 1890. 557p.

979. -----. "John Paul Jones in the Revolution." Scribner's Magazine, XXIV (July-August 1898), 22-36, 204-219.
Still one of the best essays.

980. -----. Major Operations of the Navies in the War of Independence. Boston: Little, Brown, 1913. 280p. Rpr. 1968.
More attention paid to activities of British,

French, and Spanish than to Americans.

981. -----. "Major Operations of the Royal Navy, 1762-1783." In William L. Clowes, ed. The Royal Navy: A History from the Earliest Times to the Present. 7 vols.; Boston: Little, Brown, 1897-1903. III, 353-564.

982. -----. "The Naval Campaign of 1776 on Lake Champlain." Scribners Magazine, XXIII (February 1898), 147-160.

983. -----. Types of Naval Officers Drawn from the History of the British Navy. Boston: Little Brown, 1901. 500p.
Features lengthy biographies of Howe and Rodney.

983a. Maida, Stewart A. "The Turtle and the Nautilus." Bureau of Ships Journal, V (July 1956), 15-16.
One craft invented by David Bushnell in 1775.

983b. Main, Charlotte M. "John Paul Jones." American Monthly Magazine, XXV (September 1904), 653-660.

984. ----- ----- -----. XXVII (August 1905), 343-348.

985. Majet, Horace S. "The Navy's Forgotten Hero." United States Naval Institute Proceedings, LXIII (March 1937), 347-354.
Abraham Whipple.

986. Makinson, D. H. "Barbadoes: A Study in North America-West Indian Relations, 1739-1789." Unpublished Ph.D. Dissertation, Iowa State University, 1962.

987. Mallory, William E. "A Suitable Tomb for John Paul Jones." United States Naval Institute Proceedings, XLVI (June 1920), 899-902.

988. Malo, Henri. "American Privateers at Dunkerque." Trans. from the French by Stewart L. Mims. United States Naval Institute Proceedings, XXXVII (September 1911), 933-993.

989. -----. Les Derniers Corsaires Dunkerque (1715-1815). Paris: Emile-Paul Frères, 1925. 292p.

990. Malone, Dumas, jt. editor. See Johnson, Allen, no. 787.

991. Malone, Joseph J. Pine Trees and Politics: The Naval Stores and Forest Policy in Colonial New England, 1691-1775. Seattle: University of Washington Press, 1964. 219p.

991a. "A Map of the Colony of Rhode Island: With the Adjacent Parts of Connecticut, Massachusetts Bay, etc." London Magazine, XLVII (1778), 513.

992. Maps, James. "The Battle of Ushant--and After." United States Naval Institute Proceedings, XC (March 1964), 80-87.
Between the British and French during the American Revolution.

993. Marchus, Geoffrey J. The Formative Centuries. Vol. I of The Naval History of England. Boston: Little, Brown, 1961. 485p.
Covers the period to 1783.

994. Marie, Rene. "D'Estaing aux Antilles." Revue Maritime, XXXIII (1921), 735+.

995. Mariner's Museum, Newport News, Va. Naval Actions of the American Revolution. Annapolis: U.S. Naval Institute, 1956. 32p.

996. Marion, Henri. John Paul Jones' Last Cruise and Final Resting Place the United States Naval Academy. Washington: G. E. Howard, 1906. 67p.

997. Marsh, Philip. "Philip Freneau, Our Sailor Poet." American Neptune, VI (April 1946), 115-120.

998. Martelli, George. Jemmy Twitcher: a Life of the Fourth Earl of Sandwich, 1718-1792. London: Cape, 1962. 292p.

999. Martin, Asa E. "American Privateers and the West India Trade, 1776-1777." American Historical Review, XXXIX (July 1934), 700-706.

1000. Martin, Frederick. The History of Lloyd's and of Marine Insurance in Great Britain: With an Ap-

pendix Containing Statistics Relating to Marine Insurance. London: Macmillan, 1876. 416p.
Rates skyrocketed during the Revolution as English merchantmen were prized by the Americans.

1001. Martin, Gaston. "Commercial Relations Between Nantes and the American Colonies During the War for Independence." Journal of Economic and Business History, IV (August 1932): Supplement, 812-829.

1002. [Martin, Thomas Byam.] Letters and Papers of Admiral of the Fleet Sir Thomas Byam Martin, GCB. Edited by Richard Vesey Hamilton. Publications of the Navy Records Society, v. 12, 19, 24. 3 vols.; London: The Society, 1898-1903.

1003. Martingale, A. "John Paul Jones." United States Naval Institute Proceedings, LXV (October 1933), 1495-1496.
Taken from The Naval and Military Record of July 19, 1933.

1004. "The Maryland Ship Defence--Estimated Cost, Dimensions, Inventory." In U.S. Navy Department, Naval History Division. Naval Documents of the American Revolution. Edited by William B. Clark, et al. Washington: U.S. Government Printing Office, 1964--. III, 1371-1375.

1005. Masefield, John. Sea Life in Nelson's Time. London: Methuen & Co., 1905. 218p.

1006. Mason, Bernard. "Entrepreneurial Activity in New York During the American Revolution." Business History Review, XL (June 1966), 190-212.
Some discussion of privateering.

1007. Mason, George C. "The British Fleet in Rhode Island." Rhode Island Historical Society Collections, VII (1885), 299-325.
During the Revolution.

1007a. Mason, W. Ode to the Naval Officers of Great Britain. Written Immediately After the Trial of Admiral Keppel, February 1779. London: T. Cadell,

1779. 8p.

1008. Massachusetts. General Court. Proceedings of the General Assembly and of the Council, of the State of Massachusetts Bay, relating to the Penobscot Expedition; and orders of the Continental Navy-Board to the Commander of Naval Forces. Together with a Report of the Committee to Enquire into the Cause of the Failure of Said Expedition. Boston: J. Gill, 1780. 29p.

1009. Massachusetts Soldiers and Sailors of the Revolutionary War. 17 vols.; Boston: Wright and Potter, 1896-1908.

1010. Massey, Edouard R., ed. See Roberneir, J. P. S., no. 1279.

1011. Matthewman, Luke. "Narrative of Lieut. Luke Matthewman of the Revolutionary Navy." Magazine of American History, II (March 1878), 175-185. Reprinted from the New York Packet, 1878.

1012. Matthews, John. Twenty-One Plans, with Explanations, of Different Actions in the West Indies, During the Late War, by an Officer of the Royal Navy, who was Present. Chester, Eng.: J. Fletcher, 1784.
Maps and charts of the British and French encounters of 1779, 1781, and 1782.

1013. Mattox, A. H. A History of the Cincinnati Society of Ex-Army and Navy Officers, with the Name, Army [and Navy] Record, and Rank of the Members. Alphabetically Arranged. Cincinnati: P. G. Thomson, 1880. 214p.

1014. Maurer, Maurer. "Coppered Bottoms for the Royal Navy: A Factor in the Maritime War of 1778-1783." Military Affairs, XIV (April 1950), 57-61.

1015. May, W. E. "His Majesty's Ships on the Carolina Station." South Carolina Historical Magazine, L (July 1970), 162-169.
Ends with 1774.

1016. Mayo, Laurence S. John Langdon of New Hampshire.

Mead, Hilary P.

    Concord: The Rumford Press, 1937. 303p.
    An original member of the 1775 Marine Committee.

1017. Mead, Hilary P. "Some Remarks on Squadronal Colours and Ships Distinguishing Vanes." Mariner's Mirror, XXIII (October 1937), 502-503.

1018. Meany, William B. Commodore John Barry, the Father of the American Navy: A Survey of Extra-Ordinary Episodes in his Naval Career. New York: Harper, 1911. 74p.

1019. Melville, Phillips. "Eleven Guns for the 'Grand Union.'" American Heritage, IX (October 1958), 58-64.
    At St. Eustatius.

1020. "Memoirs of the Public Services of Admiral Sir Charles M. Pole, Bart." Naval Chronicle, XXI (January-July 1809), 265-95.

1021. "Memoirs of the Public Services of Captain Hugh Downman." Naval Chronicle, XXI (January-July 1809), 1-10.

1022. "Memoirs of the Public Services of Captain Nicholas Tomlinson." Naval Chronicle, XXV (January-July 1811), 89-128.
    As a Midshipman, commanded the gunboat part of Arnold's campaign on Virginia waters in 1781.

1023. "Memoirs of the Public Services of Captain William Henry Jervis." Naval Chronicle, XX (July-December 1808), 1-14.

1024. "Memoirs of the Public Services of James Athol Wood, Knt." Naval Chronicle, XXIV (July-December 1810), 177-94.

1025. "Memoirs of the Public Services of the Late Captain Henry Inman." Naval Chronicle, XXV (January-July 1811), 1-18.

1026. "Memoirs of the Public Services of the Late Captain John Shortland." Naval Chronicle, XXIV (July-December 1810), 1-21.

1027. "Memoirs of the Public Services of the Late Captain John Turnor." Naval Chronicle, XXIV (July-December 1810), 441-48.

1028. "Memoirs of the Public Services of the Late Captain Sir Andrew Snape Douglas, Knt." Naval Chronicle, XXV (January-July 1811), 353-82.

1029. "Memoirs of the Public Services of the Late Marriot Arbuthnot, Esq." Naval Chronicle, XXIII (January-July 1810), 265-76.

1030. "Memoirs of the Public Services of the Late Right Honourable Molyneux Shuldham, Lord." Naval Chronicle, XXIII (January-July 1810), 441-47.

1031. "Memoirs of the Public Services of the Late Sir Charles Saxton, Bart." Naval Chronicle, XX (July-December 1808), 425-429.

1032. "Memoirs of the Public Services of the Late Sir Joshua Rowley, Bart." Naval Chronicle, XXIV (July-December 1810), 89-98.

1033. "Memoirs of the Public Services of the Late Sir Richard Pearson, Knt." Naval Chronicle, XXIV (July-December 1810), 353-61.

1034. "Memoirs of the Public Services of the Late Sir Thomas Troubridge, Bart." Naval Chronicle, XXIII (January-July 1810), 1-29; XXXVIII (July-December 1817), 353-58.

1035. Mempstead, Stephen, Sr. "Attempt to Burn the British Frigates in the North [Hudson] River, in July 1776, by One of the Party." Historical Magazine, X (1866), Supplement IV, 84-87.

1036. Meng, John J. D'Estaing's American Expedition, 1778-1779. Franco-American Pamphlet Series, no. 8. New York: American Society of the French Legion of Honor, 1936. 12p.

1037. -----. "The Franco-American Alliance of 1778 and its Contribution to the Cause of American Independence." American Catholic Historical Record, XL (December 1929), 311-346.

1038. Menkman, W. R. "Het Voorspel der Verovering van St. Eustatius in 1781." West-Indische Gids, XV Jaarg., no. 10 (1934) 321-337; no. 11, 353-370.

1039. "Merchantmen Permitted to Sail from Rhode Island, March-May 1776." In U.S. Navy Department, Naval History Division. Naval Documents of the American Revolution. Edited by William B. Clark, et al. Washington: U.S. Government Printing Office, 1964--. IV, 1479-1483.

1040. Merlant, Joachim. Soldiers and Sailors of France in the American War for Independence. Authorized ed., Translated from the French by Mary Bushnell Coleman. New York: Scribner, 1920. 213p.

1041. Meserve, John B. "A Privateersman [William C. Meserve] of the Revolution." Granite Monthly, LIX (May 1927), 135-143.

1042. -----. "Sailors of the Revolution." National Republic, XVIII (January 1931), 30.

1043. Middlebrook, Louis F. Captain Gideon Olmstead, Connecticut Privateersman, Revolutionary War. Salem, Mass.: Newcomb & Gauss, 1933. 172p.

1044. -----. Exploits of the Connecticut Ship "Defense," Commanded by Captain Samuel Smedley of Fairfield, Ct., Revolutionary War. Hartford: Private, 1922. 33p.

1045. -----. The Frigate South Carolina: A Famous Revolutionary War Ship. Essex, Mass.: Essex Institute, 1929. 2p.

1046. -----. History of Maritime Connecticut during the American Revolution, 1775-1783. 2 vols.; Salem, Mass.: The Essex Institute, 1925.

1047. -----. The Last Cruise of the "Oliver Cromwell," 1779. Publication of the Marine Historical Association, v. 1. Mystic, Conn.: Marine Historical Association, Inc., 1931. 52p.

1048. Miles, A. H. "Naval Views of the Yorktown Campaign." United States Naval Institute Proceedings,

LVII (October 1931), 1303-1312.

1049. -----. "Sea Power and the Yorktown Campaign."
United States Naval Institute Proceedings, LIII (November 1927), 1169-1184.

1050. Miller, Frank B. Soldiers and Sailors of the Plantation of Lower St. George Maine, who Served in the War for American Independence. Rockland, Me., 1931. 66p.

1051. Miller, William D. "The Capture of His Majesty's Ship Syren." Rhode Island Historical Society Collections, XVII (January 1924), 24-28.
Off Point Judith, November 6, 1777.

1052. Mims, Stewart L., trans. See Malo, Henri, no. 990.

1053. [Montagu, John and Andrew S. Hamond.] "The Admiral and the Captain: Letters Between Rear Admiral John Montagu and Captain Andrew Hamond Illustrating Problems Faced by the Royal Navy in North American Waters in 1772." Edited by William H. Moomaw. John P. Branch Historical Papers, New Series IV (December 1955), 23-43.
Some data on the Gaspee affair.

1054. -----. "Letter of Admiral John Montagu, 1775." Magazine of History, XVI (January 1913), 35-36.

1055. Montross, Lynn. "Francois Louis de Fleury, Fort Mifflin, 1777, Stony Point, 1779." Revue Historique de l'Armee, XIII (1957), 21-29.
The French officer who gallantly aided the Americans against the British fleet in the Delaware.

1056. -----. The Reluctant Rebels: The Story of the Continental Congress, 1774-1789. New York: Harper, 1950. 467p. Rpr. 1970.
Naval business included.

1057. Moomaw, William H. "The British Leave Colonial Virginia." Virginia Magazine of History and Biography, LXVI (April 1958), 147-160.

1058. -----. "The Denouement of General Howe's Campaign

of 1777." English Historical Review, LXXIX (July 1964), 498-512.

On the General's decision to attack Philadelphia via Chesapeake Bay; much on the role of the Royal Navy in the decision.

1059. -----. "The Naval Career of Captain [Andrew Snape] Hamond, 1775-1779." Unpublished Ph.D. Dissertation, University of Virginia, 1955.

Commander of H.M.S. Roebuck.

1060. -----., ed. See Montagu, John, no. 1053.

1061. Moore, Frank, ed. The Diary of the Revolution. A Centennial Volume, Embracing the Current Events in Our Country's History from 1775 to 1781 as Described by American, British, and Tory Contemporaries. Compiled from the Journals, Documents, Private Records, Correspondence, etc., of that Period, Framing an Interesting, Impartial, and Valuable Collection of Revolutionary Literature. Hartford: J. B. Burr, 1875. 1,084p. Rpr. 1969.

1062. -----., trans. See Estaing, Charles Hector, Comte de, no. 502.

1063. Moorhouse, E. Hallam, ed. Letters of the English Seamen, 1587-1808. London: Chapman & Hall, 1910. 318p.

Papers from Keppel, Hood, Howe, and Rodney of the Revolutionary period.

1064. Moran, Charles. "Saint Eustatius, the Island that was Different." United States Naval Institute Proceedings, LXVIII (January 1942), 84-88.

In honoring the flag of the Andrew Doria; seized by Rodney in 1781.

1065. -----. "Suffren, the Apostle of Action." United States Naval Institute Proceedings, LXIV (March 1938), 315-325.

Pierre Andre de Suffren Saint-Tropez of the French Fleet in operations off Newport in August 1778. He was later sent to India.

1066. Morgan, Marshall, trans. See Berthier, Alexandre, no. 130.

1067. Morgan, William J. Captains to the Northward: The New England Captains in the Continental Navy. Barre, Mass.: Barre Gazette, 1959. 260p.
Biographies of 22 New England naval commanders.

1068. -----. "The Pivot Upon Which Everything Turned!; French Naval Superiority that Ensured Victory at Yorktown." The Iron Worker, XXVII (Spring 1958), 1-9.

1069. -----. "The Stormy Career of Captain [Hector] McNeill, Continental Navy." Military Affairs, XVI (Fall 1954), 119-122.
In 1777-1778.

1070. Morison, Samuel E. "The Arms and Seals of John Paul Jones." American Neptune, XVIII (October 1958), 301-305.

1071. -----. "The Battle that Set Us Free." Saturday Evening Post, CCXXIX (July 7, 1956), 32-33, 56-57, 59.
Battle of the Chesapeake.

1072. -----. "The Commerce of Boston on the Eve of the American Revolution." American Antiquarian Society Proceedings, ns XXXII (April 1922), 24-51.

1073. -----. John Paul Jones: A Sailor's Biography. Boston: Little Brown, 1959. 453p.
The "best" accounting to date.

1074. -----. "The Real John Paul Jones." Saturday Evening Post, CCXXXII (August 1, 1959), 26-27, 55-57.

1075. -----. "Remarks in Communicating Joseph Bartlett's Log of the Pilgrim, 1781-1782." Massachusetts Historical Society Publications, XXV (1924), 94-124.
One of the Beverly privateers.

1076. -----. "The Willie Jones-John Paul Jones Tradition." William and Mary Quarterly, 3rd Series XVI (April 1959), 198-206.
On the seaman's 1773 arrival in North Carolina.

1077. Morris, Charles. Heroes of the Navy in America. Philadelphia: Lippincott, 1907. 320p.
Short biographies of Revolutionary officers O'Brien, Nicholas Biddle, John Paul Jones.

1078. Morris, Richard B., jt. editor. See Commager, Henry S., no. 374.

1079. Morris, Robert. The Confidential Correspondence of Robert Morris, the Great Financier of the Revolution and Signer of the Declaration of Independence, Embracing Letters of the Most Vital Historical Importance from Signers of the Declaration of Independence (Many of them Written in 1776), Members of the Continental Congress, Generals, Commodores, and Other Officers and Patriots in the Revolution. To be Sold Tuesday Afternoon and Evening, Jan. 16th, 1917. Catalogue, no. 1183. Philadelphia: S. V. Henkels, 1917. 208p.

1080. -----. "The Foundation of the Navy." In The Building of the Republic, 1789-1783. Vol. II of Albert B. Hart, ed. American History as Told by Contemporaries. 5 vols.; New York: Macmillan, 1897-1929. p. 554-555.
The financier's 1776 remarks.

1081. Morrison, C. A. "The Earl of Sandwich and British Naval Administration in the War of American Independence." Unpublished Ph.D. Dissertation, Ohio State University, 1950.

1082. Morse, Sidney G. "New England Privateering in the Revolution." Unpublished Ph.D. Dissertation, Harvard University, 1941.

1083. -----. "The Ship Lord Dartmouth: American Built Merchantman of Revolutionary Days." American Neptune, IV (July 1944), 207-217.

1084. -----. "State or Continental Privateers?" American Historical Review, LII (October 1946), 68-74.

1085. -----. "The Yankee Privateersmen of 1776." New England Quarterly, XVII (March 1944), 71-86.

1086. Moultrie, William. Memoirs of the American

Revolution, so far as it Related to the States of North and South Carolina and Georgia. New York: D. Longworth, 1802. Rpr. 1968. 2 vols.
Very useful for the 1776 attack on Sullivan's Island.

1087. Mountaine, William. The Practical Sea-Gunner's Companion; or, an Introduction to the Art of Gunnery.... London: J. Mount, 1781. 127p.
As practiced in the Royal Navy during the Revolutionary period.

1088. [Moutray, John.] Minutes of the Proceedings at a Court Martial Assembled for the Trial of Capt. John Moutray, of His Majesty's Ship the Ramillies; Respecting the Cause, Circumstance, and Capture of the Convoy under his Charge, on the 9th of August [1781] Last, by the Enemy's Fleet. As Taken by Henry Parry. London: Printed for John Fielding, 1781. 170p. Rpr. 1969.

1089. Mouzon, Harold A. "Defence: A Vessel of the Navy of South Carolina." American Neptune, XIII (January 1953), 28-50.
Captured by the British and taken into their service.

1090. -----. "The Ship Prosper." South Carolina Historical Magazine, LVIX (January 1958), 1-10.
In the defense of Charleston.

1091. -----. "The Sloop Sally of Charles Town." Nautical Research Journal, IV (August 1954), 123-128.
Her service in the defense of South Carolina and Georgia in 1778.

1092. Mundy, Godfrey B. The Life and Correspondence of the Late Admiral Lord Rodney. 2 vols.; London: J. Murray, 1830.
By the sailor's son-in-law.

1093. Munro, Donald J. Commodore John Paul Jones, U.S. Navy; A Biography of Our First Great Naval Hero. New York: William-Frederick Press, 1954. 106p.

1094. Murphy, W. S. "The Irish Brigade of Spain at the

Murray, Eleanor S.

Capture of Pensacola, 1781." Florida Historical Quarterly, XXXVIII (January 1960), 216-225.

1095. Murray, Eleanor S. "The Battle of Valcour Island." Nautical Research Journal, III (September 1954), 113-115.
On Lake Champlain in 1776.

1096. Murray, Geoffrey. The Life of Admiral Collingwood. London: Hutchinson, 1936. 288p.
Served as a midshipman in the Royal Navy in American Waters during the Revolution.

1097. Murray, Oswyn A. R. "The Admiralty." Mariner's Mirror, XXIII (January-July 1937), 13-25, 129-147, 316-331; XXIV (January-October 1938), 101-104, 204-225, 329-352, 458-478.
Includes the period of the Sandwich reign.

1098. Murray, Thomas H. The O'Briens of Machias, Me., Patriots of the American Revolution. Their Services in the Cause of Liberty. A Paper Read before the American-Irish Historical Society in New York City, January 12, 1904. With a Sketch of the Clan O'Brien. Boston: The Society, 1904. 87p.
Includes Capt. Jeremiah O'Brien.

1099. Namier, Lewis B. Additions and Corrections to Sir John Fortescue's Edition of the Correspondence of King George the Third. Manchester, Eng.: Manchester University Press, 1937. 86p.

1100. Nash, Gilbert, author. See Lovell, Solomon, no. 946.

1101. National 'Cyclopedia of American Biography. New York: David White, 1892--.

1102. "Naval Actions in the American Revolution." United States Naval Institute Proceedings, LXXXI (February 1955), 204-212.
Commentary on the battle scenes in the Bailey Collection of Water Colors of American Naval Battles in the Mariners Museum.

1103. Naval Biography, Consisting of Memoirs of the Most

Distinguished Officers of the American Navy. To Which is Annexed the Life of General Pike. Cincinnati: Morgan, Williams & Co., 1815. 296p.
 Revolutionary officers include only Jones and Nicholas Biddle.

1104. "Naval Biography of James Horsburgh Esq." Naval Chronicle, XXVIII (July to December 1812), 441-451.

1105. "Naval Biography of Rear Admiral Richard Kempenfelt." Naval Chronicle, VII (January-July 1802), 365-371.
 Pioneer in Royal Navy signals; lost in collapse of Royal George.

1106. "Naval Biography of Sir David Milne, KCB." Naval Chronicle, XXXVI (July-December 1816), 353-367.

1107. "Naval Biography of Sir Thomas Graves." Naval Chronicle, VIII (July-December 1802), 353-372, 463-464.
 Captain of H.M.S. Bedford at the Battle of the Saintes; not to be confused with Admiral Lord Graves.

1108. "Naval Biography of the Late Alexander Dairymple, Esq." Naval Chronicle, XXXV (January-July 1816), 177-204.

1109. "Naval Biography of the Late James Richard Dacres, Esq." Naval Chronicle, XXVI (July-December 1811), 266-279.
 At Valcour Island.

1110. "Naval Biography of the Late Sir Charles Cotton, Bart." Naval Chronicle, XXVII (January to July 1812), 353-364.

1111. "Naval Biography of the Late Sir Edward Hughes." Naval Chronicle, IX (January-July 1803), 85-109.
 Suffren's opponent in the great battles off India.

1112. "Naval Evolutions." Fraser's Magazine, III (March 1833), 359-364.
 Supports the claim of Douglas against Clerk.

1112a. "A Naval Letter Book of the American Revolution: an Official Record of the Navy Board of the Eastern District Sitting in Boston." New York Public Library Bulletin, XXXVI (1932), 804-815.
Covers the period from October 1778 to October 1779.

1113. "Naval Tactics--Breaking the Enemy's Line." Edinburgh Review, XXVIII (April 1830), 1-38.
Supports the claim of Clerk against Douglas.

1114. Neafie, John. "Captain Peter Nafey and His Whaleboat Crew in the Revolution." New Jersey Historical Society Proceedings, New Series XIII (October 1928), 421-424.

1115. Neeser, Robert W. "Historic Ships of the Navy--Alliance." United States Naval Institute Proceedings, LIV (April 1928), 289-292.

1116. -----. "Historic Ships of the Navy--Congress." United States Naval Institute Proceedings, LXII (March 1936), 345-351.
First one built in 1775.

1117. -----. "The Ships of the United States Navy.... 1776-1915--Connecticut." United States Naval Institute Proceedings, XLII (March-April 1916), 522.
Specifically the first Connecticut, a unit of Arnold's fleet at Valcour Island.

1118. -----. "Historic Ships of the Navy--Ranger." United States Naval Institute Proceedings, LV (March 1929), 209-214.

1119. -----. A Statistical and Chronological History of the United States Navy, 1775-1907. 2 vols.; New York: Macmillan, 1909. Rpr. 1971.
Vol. 1 is a comprehensive bibliography; Vol. 2 contains chronological tables of battles and captures. Well indexed.

1120. -----. "The True Story of the America." United States Naval Institute Proceedings, XXXIV (June 1908), 573-580.
The first American ship-of-the-line intended as flagship for John Paul Jones, but given as a gift

to the French.

1121. -----., ed. See Conyngham, Gustavus, no. 381.

1122. -----., ed. See Shuldham, Molyneux S., no. 1362.

1123. [Nelson, Horatio.] The Dispatches and Letters of Vice Admiral Lord Viscount Nelson. Edited by Sir Nicholas H. Nicholas. 7 vols.; London: H. Colburn, 1845-1846.
Early volumes useful for his efforts in the West Indies in the early 1780's.

1124. "A New and Accurate Map of the Province of Georgia in North America." Universal Magazine, LXIV (1779), 168.

1125. "A New and Accurate Map of the Province of Virginia in North America." Universal Magazine, LXV (1779), 281.

1126. "A New and Accurate Plan of the Town of Boston in New England [and] A New Plan of Boston Harbor from an Actual Survey." Universal Magazine, LIV (1774), 225.

1127. New Jersey. Documents Relating to the Colonial History of the State of New Jersey. Edited by William A. Whitehead. 10 vols.; Newark: Daily Journal, 1880-1886.

1128. New York. Journals of the Provincial Congress, Provincial Convention, Council of Safety and Council of Safety of the State of New York, 1775-1776-1777. 2 vols.; Albany: T. Weed Thurlow, 1842.

1129. New York. Office of the State Comptroller. New York in the Revolution as Colony and State: A Compilation of Documents and Records from the Office of the State Comptroller. 2 vols.; Albany: J. B. Lyon, 1904.

1130. Nichols, G. E. E. "Nova Scotia Privateers." Nova Scotia Historical Society Proceedings, XIII (1908), 111-152.
In the Revolution.

1131. Nickerson, Hoffman. "Yorktown, 1781." American Mercury, XXIV (September 1931), 79-81.
Brilliant summary.

1132. Nicodeme. "Notice Historique Sur le Vaisseau le Bonhomme Richard." Revue Maritime, CLXXIII (Juin 1907), 545-554.

1133. Nicolas, Nicholas H. A History of the Royal Navy from the Earliest Time to the Wars of the French Revolution. 2 vols.; London: R. Bentley, 1847.
The American Revolution receives good coverage in Vol. II.

1134. -----., ed. See Nelson, Horatio, no. 1115.

1135. Nicolas, Paul H. Historical Record of the Royal Marine Forces. 2 vols.; London: T. & W. Boone, 1845.

1136. Nimitz, Chester W., jt. editor. See Potter, Edward B., no. 1234.

1137. Nolan, G. J. "An Unsung Patriot." National Republic, LI (May 1927), 7-8.
Bernardo de Galvez.

1138. Norris, John N., ed. See Arnold, Benedict, no. 75.

1139. Norris, Walter B. "Who is the Father of the American Navy?" Current History, XXVII (December 1927), 354-360.
Concludes it is "useless to try to make one man 'Father of the American Navy,' or one ship the First American Warship."

1140. North, Frances P. "Newport A Hundred Years Ago." Lippincott's Magazine, XXVI (September 1880), 331-362.
During the Revolution.

1141. North Carolina. The Colonial Records of North Carolina. Edited by William L. Saunders. 10 vols.; Raleigh: P. M. Hale, 1886-1890.

1142. "Note on J. M. Moreau Le Jeune's Rare Portrait of John Paul Jones." United States Naval Institute

Proceedings, LXVIII (November 1942), 1659.

1143. Nourse, Michael. "The Life of Robert Morris." Bankers Magazine, XIV (February 1860), 577+.

1144. O'Beirne, Thomas. A Candid and Impartial Narrative of the Transactions of the Fleet Under Lord [Richard] Howe. London, 1779. 58p. Rpr. 1969.

1145. -----. Considerations on the Principles of Naval Discipline and Naval Courts-Martial; in which Doctrines Lately Laid Down in the House of Commons Upon These Subjects are Examined, and the Conduct of the Courts-Martial on Admiral Keppel and Sir Hugh Pallister are Compared. London: J. Almon, 1781. 190p.
O'Beirne was a Whig.

1146. Oberholtzer, Ellis P. Robert Morris, Patriot and Financier. New York: Macmillan, 1903. 372p.
And member of the Navy Board.

1147. O'Callaghan, E. "Seven British Captures of St. Lucia." (London) United Service Journal (January 1888), 29-40.
Including the one made during the Revolution.

1148. Odelberg, William, ed. See Wachmeister, Hans F., no. 1517.

1149. The Old Empire, from the Beginnings to 1783. Vol. I of The Cambridge History of the British Empire. General Eds. J. H. Rose et al. 8 vols.; Cambridge: Cambridge University Press, 1929-1936.

1150. "Old Mill Prison, Plymouth, England." Magazine of History, XX (January 1915), 19-21.

1151. Olssom, Nils W., trans. See Wachmeister, Hans F., no. 1517.

1152. Onderdonk, Henry, Jr. Revolutionary Incidents of Suffolk and King Counties with an Account of the British Prisons and Prison-Ships at New York. New York: Leavitt, 1849. 268p. Rpr. 1970.
Contains extracts from contemporary newspapers.

1153. "An Open Letter to Captain Pringle." Bulletin of the Fort Ticonderoga Museum, I (1927-1929), 14-20.
Dated 8 June 1777, it contests his account of the Battle of Valcour Island.

1153a. "Operations in Maine in 1779, Journal Found on Board the Hunter, Continental Ship of Eighteen Guns." Historical Magazine, (February 1864), 50-54.

1154. O'Quinlivan, D. Michael, jt. author. See Thacker, Joel D., no. 1456.

1154a. Orvilliers, Louis Guillouet d'. Reponse de M. le Comte d'Orvilliers, General des Armees Navales de France, a L'Impartial Nolamed, Ancien Officier Francais a Londres. Par la Quelle ce General la Remercie d'avoir Pris la Deffense de la Verite Calomniee il luy Envoie tout le Detail du Combat Naval du 27 Juillet 1778. Londres: Societe Typographique, 1779. 46p.
The French commander's account of the Battle of Ushant.

1155. Osborn, George C. "Major-General John Campbell in British West Florida." Florida Historical Quarterly, XXVII (April 1949), 317-339.
Surrendered Pensacola to Galvez.

1156. Osler, Edward. The Life of Admiral Viscount Exmouth. New York: W. Jackson, 1835. 287p.
Edward Pellew, who as a young naval officer, fought at Valcour Island.

1157. -----., author. See Barton, John A., no. 111.

1158. [Oswald, Richard.] Memorandum on the Folly of Invading Virginia, the Strategic Importance of Portsmouth, and the Need for Civilian Control of the Military; Written in 1781 by the British Negotiator of the First American Treaty of Peace. Edited with an essay on the author by W. Stitt Robinson, Jr. Charlottesville: University of Virginia Press, 1953. 61p.

1159. "Our Sea Forces in the Revolution." DAR Magazine, XLIX (June-August 1916), 85-96, 149-161, 227-237.

1160. Owen, Hamilton. Baltimore on the Chesapeake. New York: Doubleday, 1941. 329p.
    Accounts of Revolutionary privateering, the Maryland State Ship Defence, the Continental frigate Virginia.

1161. -----. "Maryland's First Warship." Maryland Historical Magazine, XXXVIII (September 1943), 199-204.
    The state ship Defence of the Revolution.

1162. Owen, John H. "The [British] Navy and the Capture of St. Lucia, 1778." Fighting Forces, II (April 1925), 42-54.

1163. -----., jt. editor. See Sandwich, John M., 4th Earl of, no. 1325.

1164. Padgett, James A., ed. See Farmer, Robert, no. 518.

1165. Paine, Ralph D. Joshua Barney, a Forgotten Hero of Blue Water. New York: Century, 1924. 410p.

1166. -----. "Privateersmen of '76." Outing Magazine, LI (March 1908), 709-171.
    From Salem Massachusetts.

1167. -----. The Ships and Sailors of Old Salem; the Record of a Brilliant Era in American Achievement. New York: Outing Publishing, 1909. 693p.
    Contains extracts from logs and journals of sailors and privateersmen, 1776-1800.

1168. Pallister, Hugh. The Defence of Vice Admiral Hugh Pallister, Bart., at the Court-Martial Lately Held Upon Him, with the Court's Sentence. London: T. Cadell, 1779. 71p.

1169. -----. Minutes of the Proceedings at a Court-Martial Assembled for the Trial of Vice Admiral Hugh Pallister, Bart., as Taken by George Jackson. London: W. Strahan, 1779. 95p.

1169a. Palmer, Dave R. The River and the Rock: The History of Fortress West Point, 1775-1783. West Point Military Library. New York: Greenwood, 1969. 395p.
Features attacks upon the post and vicinity by elements of the Royal Navy.

1170. Palmer, Peter S. History of Lake Champlain, from Its First Exploration by the French in 1609 to the Close of the Year 1814. Munsell's Series in Local American History, v. 4. Albany: J. Munsell, 1866. 276p.
Includes operations around Valcour Island.

1171. Palmer, William P. "The Virginia Navy of the Revolution." Southern Literary Messenger, XXIV (January-April 1857), 237-256, 222-236, 258-269, 271-283.
Reprinted in the Researcher, I (October 1926, January-July 1927), 9-16, 62-76, 129-136, 197-203; II (October 1927), 3-14. The author was later a surgeon in the Confederate States Navy.

1172. Panikkar, Kavalam M. India and the Indian Ocean: an Essay on the Influence of Sea Power on Indian History. London: Allen, 1945. 110p.
Suffren's activities featured.

1173. Paris, W. Francklyn. "The Navy of Provence in the American War of Independence." Legion d'Honneur, II (1932), 233-238.

1174. Parker, Foxhall A., "The First Sea-Fight of the Revolution: The Capture of the Margaretta." Magazine of American History, I (April, 1877), p. 209-221.

1175. Parker, Thomas D. "The Romance of Joshua Barney." United States Naval Institute Proceedings, XLII (July-August 1916), 1237-1250.

1176. Parker, William D., author. See United States, Marine Corps, no. 1492.

1177. Parker, William M. "Rodney and His Naval Physician." Army Quarterly, LXII (April 1941), 150-165.
Dr. Gilbert Blane.

1178. Parkinson, Cyril N. Edward Pellow, Viscount Exmouth, Admiral of the Red. London: Methuen and Co., Ltd., 1934. 478p.
Chpt. II describes his adventures at Valcour Island.

1179. -----. The Rise of the Port of Liverpool. Liverpool, Eng.: University Press, 1952. 163p.

1180. Parramore, Thomas C. "The Great Escape from Forten Gaol: An Incident of the Revolution." North Carolina Historical Review, XLV (Autumn 1968), 349-356.

1181. "Particulars of the Actions of April 9 and 12 [1782]." The Scots Magazine, XLIII (June 1782), 285+.
Between the French and British fleets.

1182. Parry, Henry, ed. See Moutray, John, no. 1088.

1183. Pasley, Louisa M. (Sabine). "Memoirs of Admiral Sir Thomas Sabine Pasley, 1734-1808." In her Memoir of Admiral Sir Thomas Sabine Pasley [1808-1884]. London: Edward Arnold, 1900. p. 327-332.
Reprinted in the European Magazine, September 1905.

1184. Pasley, Rodney M. S., ed. See Pasley, Thomas, no. 1185.

1185. [Pasley, Thomas.] Private Sea Journals, 1778-1782, Kept by Admiral Sir Thomas Pasley, Bart., When in Command of H.M. Ships Glasgow (20), Sybil (28), and Jupiter. Edited with an Introduction by his Great-Great-Great-Grandson Rodney M. S. Pasley. London: J. M. Dent, 1931. 319p.

1186. Pattee, Fred L., ed. See Freneau, Philip, no. 583.

1187. Patterson, Alfred T. The Other Armada; the Franco-Spanish Attempt to Invade Britain in 1779. Manchester: Manchester University Press, 1960. 247p.
The Bonhomme Richard squadron was originally slated as a diversion for this effort?

1188. Patton, Jacob H. "The Campaign of the Allies, 1781." Magazine of American History, VII (October 1881), 241-266.
Includes the French Navy at Yorktown.

1189. Paul Jones. [Amsterdam, 1780?] 94p.
A chapbook of popular songs.

1190. "Paul Jones." In Burton E. Stevenson, ed. Poems of American History. Boston: Houghton, Mifflin, 1936. p. 222-223.
One of many 1779 poems celebrating the victory of the Bonhomme Richard.

1191. "Paul Jones." In Burton E. Stevenson, ed. Poems of American History. Boston: Houghton, Mifflin, 1936. p. 224-225.
A poem of 1779.

1192. "Paul Jones." In Sketches of the Lives of Remarkable and Celebrated Characters, etc. Paisley, Scotland: W. Falconer, 1804. p. 79-114.

1193. Paul Jones, or the Fife Coast Garland; a Heroical Poem. Edinburgh: Private, 1779. 37p.
A satire in poetry.

1194. Paul-Jones ou Propheties sur l'Amerique, l'Angleterre, la France, l'Espagne, la Hollande, etc. Par Paul Jones, Corsaire, Prophete & Sorcier Comme il n'en Fut Jamis. Y Joint le Revue dun Suisse sur la Revolution de l'Amerique l'an V [Basle, 1781?] 120p.

1195. Paullin, Charles O. "The Administration of the Continental Navy of the American Revolution." United States Naval Institute Proceedings, XXXI (September 1905), 625-675.
An excellent essay still among the best available.

1196. -----. "The Administration of the Massachusetts and Virginia Navies of the American Revolution." United States Naval Institute Proceedings, XXXII (March 1906), 131-164.

1197. -----. "Classes of Operations of the Continental

Navy of the American Revolution." United States Naval Institute Proceedings, XXI (May 1905), 153-164.

1198. -----. "The Condition of the Continental Naval Service." United States Naval Institute Proceedings, XXXII (June 1906), 585-595.

1199. -----. "Connecticut Navy of the American Revolution." New England Magazine, New Series XXXV (February 1907), 714-725.

1200. -----. Diplomatic Negotiations of American Naval Officers, 1778-1883. Baltimore: Johns Hopkins University Press, 1912. 380p. Rpr. 1970.

1201. -----. "A Forgotten Rival of John Paul Jones." Army and Navy Life, XIII (July 1908), 65-71. P. Landais.

1202. -----. "Massachusetts Navy of the American Revolution." New England Magazine, New Series XXV (January 1907), 571-578.

1203. -----. "Naval Administration of the Southern States during the Revolution." Sewanee Review, X (October 1902), 418-428.

1204. -----. The Navy of the American Revolution: Its Policy and Its Administration. Cleveland: Burrow Bros., 1906. 549p. Rpr. 1970.

1205. -----. "Origin of the Continental Navy." United States Naval Institute Proceedings, LIII (November 1927), 1158-1159.

1206. -----., ed. Out-letters of the Continental Marine Committee and Board of Admiralty, August 1776-September 1780. Publications of the Naval History Society, v. 4. 2 vols.; New York: Naval Historical Society, 1914.

1207. -----. Paullin's History of Naval Administration, 1775-1911; A Collection of Articles from the United States Naval Institute Proceedings. Annapolis: U.S. Naval Institute, 1968. 485p.

1208. -----. "A Report of John Paul Jones, Master of the Ship John." United States Naval Institute Proceedings, XLII (March-April 1916), 523-524.

1209. -----. "When Was Our Navy Founded?" United States Naval Institute Proceedings, XXXVI (May 1910), 255-262.

1210. [Pausch, Georg.] Journal of Captain Pausch, Chief of the Hanau Artillery during the Burgoyne Campaign. Trans. and Annotated by William L. Stone. Intro. by Edward J. Lowell. Munsell's Historical Series, no. 4. Albany: J. Nunsell's Sons, 1886. 185p. Rpr. 1971.
Includes naval activity on Lake Champlain, 1776.

1211. Peabody, Robert E. "The Naval Career of Captain John Manley of Marblehead." Essex Institute Historical Collections, XLV (January 1909), 1-27.

1211a. Pearson, Michael. Those Damned Rebels: The American Revolution as Seen Through British Eyes. New York: Putnam, 1972. 446p.
Includes reports by English admirals of blockade and naval activities.

1212. Pease, J. W. "Adventures of Captain S. Hoyt and the Beginnings of Trade with Foreign Lands." Journal of American History, II (January-March 1908), 64-73.
Some adventures took place during the Revolution.

1213. Peathie, D. C. "Invincible John Paul Jones, United States Navy." Reader's Digest, LXVI (May 1955), 125-129.

1214. Peckham, Howard H. The War for Independence, a Military History. Chicago: University of Chicago Press, 1958. 226p.

1215. Pell, John. "Philip Skene of Skenesborough." Proceedings of the New York State Historical Association, XXVI (1928), 27-44.

1216. -----. "The Revenge." Bulletin of the Fort

Ticonderoga Museum, I (1927-1929), 6-13, 16-17.
Valcour Island.

1217. Pennsylvania. Navy Board. "List of Officers and Men of the Pennsylvania Navy, 1775-1781." Pennsylvania Archives, 2nd Series I (1876), 327-359.

1218. Pennypacker, Samuel W. "The High Water Mark of the British Invasion." Pennsylvania Magazine of History and Biography, XXXI (October 1907), 393-405.

1219. Penrose, John. Lives of Vice Admiral Sir Charles Vinicombe Penrose, K.C.B., and Captain James Trevenen. London: Murray, 1850. 301p.

1220. Perkins, James B. France in the American Revolution. Boston: Houghton, Mifflin, 1911. 544p. Rpr. 1969.

1221. Pernoud, Regine, ed. See Suffren Saint Tropez, Pierre Andre de, no. 1439.

1222. Perry, James M. "Disaster on the Delaware." United States Naval Institute Proceedings, LXXXVIII (January 1962), 84-91.
Defeat of the Pennsylvania galleys by the British en route to take Forts Mifflin and Mercer in 1777.

1223. Peterson, Charles J. History of the US Navy and Biographical Sketches of American Naval Heroes from the Formation of the Navy to the Close of the Mexican War. Philadelphia: J & J L Gihon, 1852. 611p.

1224. Peterson, Harold L. "John Paul Jones' Corselet." Military Collector and Historian, IV (March 1952), 16-17.
His body armor.

1225. Pfister, A., ed. See Seume, J. G., no. 345.

1226. Phillips, James D. "Salem Revolutionary Privateers Condemned at Jamaica." Essex Institute Historical Collections, LXXVI (January 1940), 46-55.

1227. Pike, R. E. "The Story of the Lost Corpse."

Pleadwell, F. L. 133

American Heritage, V (Summer 1954), 14-15.
John Paul Jones.

1228. Pleadwell, F. L. and W. M. Kerr. "Lewis Heermann, Surgeon in the United States Navy." Annals of Medical History, V (June 1923), 113-145.
1779-1833.

1229. Pool, Bernard. "Lord Barham: A Great Naval Administrator." History Today, XV (May 1965), 347-354.

1230. -----. Navy Board Contracts, 1660-1832; Contract Administration Under the Navy Board. Hamden, Conn.: Archon Books, 1966. 158p.

1231. Pope, Jennie B., jt. author. See Albion, Robert G., no. 24.

1232. Pope, Joshua L. An Account of the First Naval Battle of the Revolution. New Bedford, Mass.: Printed by the New Bedford Chapter, Sons of the American Revolution [1930?] 6p.

1233. Porter, Horace. "Recovery of the Body of John Paul Jones." Century Illustrated Magazine, LXX (October 1905), 927-955.
Results of a search which the General led.

1234. Potter, Edward B. and Chester W. Nimitz, eds. Sea Power: A Naval History. Englewood Cliffs, New Jersey: Prentice-Hall, 1960. 932p.

1235. -----. The Naval Academy Illustrated History of the United States Navy. New York: Crowell, 1971. 299p.
Also the Continental Navy.

1236. Powell, M. X. "A Few French Soldiers to Whom We Owe Much." Newport Historical Society Bulletin, IX (October 1921), 1-19.

1237. Power, D. J. W. "Abraham Parsons: Mariner and Merchant." Mariner's Mirror, XLII (April 1956), 94-100.
Descriptions of his dangerous 1773-1779 voyages to India and the Middle East.

1237a. Powers, Stephen T. "The Decline and Extinction of American Naval Power, 1781-1787." Unpublished Ph.D. Dissertation, Notre Dame University, 1965.

1238. Pratt, Winthrop, Jr. "Washington's Cruisers." Nautical Research Journal, VII (July-August 1955), 104-108.

1239. Preble, George H. "Commodore John Barry, Senior Officer of the U.S. Navy from 1783 to 1803." United Service, XII (July 1885), 518-535.
   Some attention paid to his Revolutionary War activities.

1240. -----. A Complete List of the Vessels of the United States Navy From 1779-1874, Together With Tables Showing the Personnel of the US Navy and Naval Expenditures, etc. Washington: 1874. 33p.
   Appendix to Mercantile Navy List of 1874.

1241. -----. "Esek Hopkins, the First Commander-in-Chief of the American Navy, 1775." United Service, XII (February-March, 1885), 137-146, 300-317.

1241a. -----. "The First Signals Used by an American Fleet: The St. George Ensign and the Rattlesnake Standard." Historical Magazine, 2nd Series II (December 1867), 359-360.

1242. -----. Vessels of War Built at Portsmouth, New Hampshire, 1690-1868. [Boston: 1868.] 10p.
   A List, includes the America.

1243. -----., ed. See Green, Ezra, no. 658.

1244. Preston, Howard W. "Rochambeau and the French Troops in Providence in 1780-81-82." Rhode Island Historical Society Collections, XVII (1923), 1-23.
   Some mention of the French fleet.

1245. Price, Jacob M. "The Economic Growth of the Chesapeake and the European Market, 1697-1775." Journal of Economic History, XXIV (December 1964), 496-511.

1246. Prison-ship Martyrs' Monument Association. Dedication of the Prison Ship Martyrs' Monument, November 14, 1908. [New York?] Priv. print., 1908. 64p.

1247. "Privateer Junius Brutus." Essex Institute Historical Collections, I (1859), p. 111-112.

1248. Pumpelly, J. C. "Our French Allies in the Revolution." New Jersey Historical Society Proceedings, 2d Series X (1890), 145-169.

1249. Purcell, Richard J. "Captain John Barry of the American Revolution." Studies, XXIII (1934), 623-633.

1250. Purviance, Robert. Narrative of Events Which Occurred in Baltimore Town during the Revolutionary War. To Which are Appended Various Documents and Letters, the Greater Part of Which Have Never Been Heretofore Published. Baltimore: J. Robinson, 1849. 231p.

By one of the Continental naval agents assigned to that port.

1251. Quaife, Milo M. "Detroit Biographies: Commodore Alexander Grant." Burton Historical Collection Leaflets, LVII (1931), 721-736.

1252. -----. "The Royal Navy of the Upper Lakes." Burton Historical Collection Leaflets, II (1924), 49-64.

During the period 1760-1796.

1253. Quynn, Dorothy M. "The Cato and the Nautilus, Maryland Privateers." South Atlantic Quarterly, XXXVI (January 1937), 49-52.

1254. Raddal, Thomas H. Halifax, Warden of the North. London: Dent, 1948. 348p.

The prime British naval base in North America during the Revolutionary War.

1254a. Ralfe, James. The Naval Biography of Great Britain, Consisting of Historical Memoirs of Those Officers of the British Navy who Distinguished Themselves During the Reign of His Majesty George III. 4 vols.; London: Whitmore & Fenn, 1828.

1255. Rand, Edwin H. "Maine Privateers in the Revolution." New England Quarterly, XI (December 1938), 826-834.

1256. Rankin, Hugh F. "The Naval Flag of the American Revolution." William and Mary Quarterly, 3d ser., XI (July 1954), 339-353.

1257. Ransome, M., jt. editor. See Horn, D. B., no. 743.

1258. Rantoul, Robert S. The Cruise of the Quero: How We Carried the News [of Lexington and Concord] to the King; a Neglected Chapter in Local History. Salem, Mass.: Essex Institute, 1900. 30p.
By the ship of Captain John Derby. Reproduced from the Century Illustrated Magazine, LVII (September 1899), 714-721, "with considerable additions and changes."

1259. Rathbun, Frank H. "[John] Rathbun's Raid on Nassau." United States Naval Institute Proceedings, XCVI (November 1970), 40-47.
In the Providence.

1260. Rawson, Jonathan A. 1776: A Day-by-Day Story. New York: Frederick A. Stokes, 1927. 429p.

1261. "Records of the Vice-Admiralty Court at Halifax, Nova Scotia: The Condemnation of Prizes and Recaptures of the Revolution and War of 1812." Essex Institute Historical Collections, XLV (January-October 1909), 24-48, 161-184, 221-244, 309-332, XLVI (January 1910), 69-80.
The above cited pages all apply to the American Revolution.

1262. Relation de la Prise Faite par les François, sur les Anglois de l'Isle de la Dominique, Situee Entre la Martinique et la Guadeloupe, le 7 September [Sic], 1778, Suivie de l'Expedition de l'Isle Rhode Island. Laon, 1778.

1263. "Remarks on the Sea Fight of April 12 [1782]." The Gentleman's Magazine, LI (July 1782), 337+.
Lists Rodney's captures and the British officers killed.

1264. The Remembrancer; or, Impartial Repository of Public Events, 1775-1784. Edited by J. Almon. 17 vols.; London: Printed for J. Almon, 1775-1783.
Contains many official reports of naval actions.

1265. Renaut, Francis P. L'Affaire Montagu Fox, 1780-1781, d'Apres les Documents des Archives. Diplomatiques de France et d'Angleterre. Paris: Editions du Graouli, 1937. 200p.
Cloak and dagger operations concerning the British Admiralty.

1266. -----. Corsaires, Croisières, et Contrebande au Temps de la Guerre d'Amérique, 1776-1783. Paris: Editions du Graouli, 1928. 252p.

1267. -----. Le Crépuscule d'une Puissance Navale. La Marine Hollandaise de 1776 a 1783. Preface de M. Lacour-Gayet. Paris: Editions du Graouli, 1932. 266p.

1268. Repplier, Emma. "How Many Mutineers did John Paul Jones Kill?" Independant, LX (April 12, 1906), 832-834.
Aboard his merchant ship before fleeing to America.

1269. Re Riccardi, A. Guido. Lord Rodney e il suo Tempo. Roma, 1933. 203p.

1270. Restow, Walter W. "Maps of the American Revolution: A Preliminary Survey." Quarterly Journal of the Library of Congress, XXVIII (July 1971), 196-215.
Including some used by the Royal Navy.

1271. "Revolutionary Privateering." Business Historical Society Bulletin, VII (Fall 1933), 7-10.

1272. Reynolds, Helen W. "The Congress and the Montgomery, Continental Frigates built at Poughkeepsie in 1776." Dutchess County Historical Society Yearbook, XXI (1936), 99-104.
Both destroyed before launching to prevent capture by the British.

1273. Richmond, Herbert W. The [British] Navy in India,

1763-1783. London: E. Benn, Ltd., 1931. 432p.
A forgotten aspect of the British fleet during our Revolutionary period.

1274. -----. "The Hughes-Suffren Campaigns." Mariner's Mirror, XIII (July 1927), 219-237.

1275. -----. The Invasion of Britain; an Account of Plans, Attempts & Countermeasures from 1586 to 1918. London: Methuen & Co., 1941. 81p.
Includes the French attempt during the American Revolution.

1276. -----. Statesmen and Seapower. Based on the Ford Lectures Delivered in the University of Oxford in the Michaelmas Term, 1943. Oxford: The Clarendon Press, 1946. 369p.

1277. Roads, Samuel, Jr. "Privateering in the Revolution." Magazine of History, III (January 1908), 14-26.

1278. Robbins, Sally N. "Benedict Arnold in Virginia." Sons of the Revolution in the State of Virginia Magazine, II (July 1923), 15-26.
During 1781 he destroyed most of that state's navy.

1279. [Roberneir, J. P. S.] "Rhode Island in 1780 by Lieutenant J. P. S. Roberneir." Edited by Edouard R. Massey. Rhode Island Historical Society Collections, XVI (1923), 65-78.

1280. Roberts, Charles H. A Sketch of the Life of George Roberts who Fought under John Paul Jones. [Concord, N. H.] 1905. 8p.
Revised version of the article printed in the Granite Monthly, August 1905.

1280a. Robertson, A. I. "The Name of John Paul Jones." American Monthly Magazine, XV (November 1899), 535-537.
How the sailor came to choose it.

1281. Robertson, Eileen A. The Spanish Town Papers: Some Sidelights on the American War of Independence. London: Cresset Press, 1959. 199p.

Naval and privateering activities.

1282. Robertson, James, ed. "Spanish Correspondence Concerning the American Revolution." Hispanic American Historical Review, I (August 1918), 299-316.

1283. Robinson, Charles N. The British Tar in Fact and Fiction: the Poetry, Pathos, and Humour of the Sailor's Life. New York: Harper, 1909. 520p. Rpr. 1968.

1284. Robinson, Douglas H. "The Continental Frigate Confederacy." Nautical Research Journal, VIII (March-April 1956), 31-46.

1285. Robinson, W. Stitt, Jr., ed. See Oswald, Richard, no. 1158.

1286. Robison, Samuel S. A History of Naval Tactics from 1530 to 1930; the Evolution of Tactical Maxims. Annapolis: U.S. Naval Institute, 1942. 956p.
Including "the line."

1287. Robson, Eric. "The Expedition to the Southern Colonies, 1775-1776." English Historical Review, LXVI (October 1951), 535-560.

1288. Rochambeau, Eugène A. L. de Vimeur, Comte de. Yorktown. Centenaire de l'Independence des Etats-Unis d'Amérique, 1781-1881. Paris: H. Champion, 1886. 340p.

1289. Rochambeau, Jean B. D. de Vimeur, Comte de. An Account of the Operations of the French Army During the American Revolution. Translated from the French. Philadelphia: Dobson, 1817. 182p.

1290. -----. Mémoires Militaires, Historiques, et Politiques de Rochambeau, Ancien Maréchal de France, et Grand Officier de la Légion d'Honneur. 2 vols.; Paris: Fain, 1809.
Account of the American Revolution (including his relations with Admirals Barras and De Grasse) featured.

1291. -----. Memoirs of the Marshall Count de

Rochambeau. Translated by M. W. E. Wright. Paris: Belin, 1838. 114p. Rpr. 1971.
This translation, covering the Revolution, was taken from Vol. I, p. 237-329, of the 1809 French edition.

1292. -----. Relation, ou Journal des Operations du Corps Francais Sous le Commandement du Comte de Rochambeau, Lieutenant-Génèral des Armées du Roi, Dupus le 15 Août. Philadelphia: Guillaume Hampton, 1781. 15p. Rpr. 1929.
The Yorktown campaign including naval support.

1293. Roddis, Louis H. "The New York Prison Ships in the American Revolution." United States Naval Institute Proceedings, LXI (March 1935), 331-336.

1294. -----. "A Partial List of Medical Men in the Maritime Service of the Colonies during the American Revolution." Military Surgeon, LXXIX (1936), 357-358.

1295. Rodney, George B. Letter-books and Order-book of George, Lord Rodney, Admiral of the White Squadron, 1780-1782. Publications of the Naval History Society, v. 12-13. 2 vols.; New York: Printed for the Naval History Society by the New York Historical Society, 1932.

1296. -----. Letters from Sir George Brydges, now Lord Rodney, to His Majesty's Ministers, etc., etc., Relative to the Capture of St. Eustatius and its Dependencies; and Showing the State of the War in the West-Indies, at that Period. [London? 1784?] 104p.

1297. -----. Letters from Sir George Brydges, now Lord Rodney, to His Majesty's Ministers, etc., etc., Relative to the Capture of St. Eustatius and its Dependencies; and Showing the State of the War in the West Indies, at that Period. Together with a Continuation of His Lordship's Correspondence with the Governors and Admirals in the West-Indies and America during the year 1781, and Until the Time of his Leaving the Command and Sailing for England. London: A. Grant, 1789. 180p.

1298. Roelker, William and Clarkson A. Collins, III. "The Patrol of Narragansett Bay by H. M. S. Rose, Captain James Wallace." Rhode Island History, VII (January, July 1948), 12-19, 90-98; VIII (April, July 1949), 45-63, 77-83.
Contains letters from the British officer during his 1774-1776 cruise.

1299. Rogers, Bertram M. H. "The Privateering Voyages of the Tartar of Bristol." Mariner's Mirror, XVII (July 1931), 236-243.
A private British warship in the Revolution.

1300. Rogers, Ernest E., ed. Connecticut's Naval Office at New London During the American Revolution, Including the Mercantile Letter Book of Nathaniel Shaw, Jr. New London: Priv. print, 1933. 358p.
Shaw was the Continental naval agent assigned to that port.

1301. Rogers, Horatio, ed. See Hadden, James M., no. 685.

1302. Roscoe, Theodore and Fred Freeman. Picture History of the U.S. Navy, from the Old Navy to the New, 1776-1897. New York: Scribner, 1956. 384p.
Useful illustrations for the Revolutionary War.

1303. Rose, J. Holland. The Indecisiveness of Modern War and Other Essays. London: G. Bell, 1927. 204p. Rpr. 1968.
Chpt. 3, "Plans of Invasion of the British Isles"; Chpt. 4, "The Struggle for the Mediterranean in the Eighteenth Century."

1304. -----. "The Influence of Sea Power on Indian History, 1746-1802." Journal of Indian History, III (1924-1926), 188-204.
Suffern vs. Hughes examined.

1305. Ross, John. Memoirs and Correspondence of Admiral Lord [James] de Saumarez, from Original Papers in the Possession of his Family. 2 vols.; London: Bentley, 1838.
His service began as a youth during the era of the American Revolution.

1306. Rousseau, François. Règne de Charles III d'Espagne, 1759-1788. 2 vols.; Paris: Plon-Nourrit, 1907.
Franco-Spanish relations and the attempted invasion of England in 1779.

1307. Rowe, John S., jt. author. See Kendall, Roger, no. 817.

1308. Rowland, Mrs. Dunbar. "Peter Chester: Third Governor of the Province of British West Florida under British Dominion, 1770-1781." Mississippi Historical Society Publications, V (1925), 1-183.

1309. Rung, Albert M. "The Lost Grave of John Paul Jones." DAR Magazine, XCIX (March 1966), 216-218, 302, 324.

1310. Rush, M. Orwin. Spain's Final Triumph Over Great Britain in the Gulf of Mexico: the Battle of Pensacola, March 2 to May 8, 1781. Florida State University Studies, No. 48. Tallahassee: The Florida State University, 1966. 158p.

1311. Russell, Jack. Gibraltar Besieged, 1779-1783. London: Heinemann, 1965. 308p.
The War in America is linked with the defense of the "Rock," pp. 102-109.

1312. Russell, Nelson V. "Transportation and Naval Defense in the Old North West During the British Regime, 1760-1796." In A. E. R. Boak, ed. University of Michigan Historical Essays, Ann Arbor: University of Michigan Press, 1937. p. 113-139.

1313. Russell, Phillips. John Paul Jones: Man of Action. New York: [Brentano's] 1930. 314p.

1314. Rutherford, G. "Sidelights on Commodore Johnstone's Expedition to the Cape." Mariner's Mirror, XXVIII (April-July 1942), 189-212, 290-308.
The Commodore was attacked at anchor by Suffren.

1314a. -----. "The Chase and Capture of the Frigate Aigle (September 12th-14th, 1782)." Blue Peter, XV (January 1935), 82-85.

Ruttenber, Edward M.

In the Delaware River.

1315. Ruttenber, Edward M. Obstructions to the Navigation of Hudson's River, Embracing the Minutes of the Secret Committee Appointed by the Provincial Convention of New York, July 16, 1776, and other Original Documents Relating to the Subject. Together with Papers Relating to the Beacons. Munsell's Historical Series, no. 5. Albany: J. Munsell, 1860. 210p.

1316. Rutter, Owen. Red Ensign: A History of Convoy. London: Hale, 1942. 214p.

1317. Ryan, Michael J. An Address at the Commemoration of the 100th Anniversary of the Death of Commodore John Barry, Father of the American Navy. Sponsored Under the Auspices of the [Philadelphia Chapter] Knights of Columbus, September 13, 1903. Philadelphia: Bradley Brothers, 1903. 24p.

1318. Sabine, Lorenzo, ed. Biographical Sketches of Loyalists of the American Revolution. 2 vols.; Boston: Little Brown, 1864.

1319. Saint Exupery, Anais de, ed. See Saint Exupery, Georges Alexandre Cesar de, no. 1320.

1320. [Saint-Exupery, Georges Alexandre Cesar, de.] "The War Diary of Georges Alexandre Cesar de Saint-Exupery, Lieutenant in the Regiment of Sarre-Infantry." Edited by Anais de Saint Exupery. Legion d'Honneur, II (October 1931), 107-113.
A translation of that part of the young officer's journal dealing with De Grasse's operation in the Chesapeake, 1781.

1321. Salisbury, William. "John Paul Jones and His Ships: the Need for More Research." American Neptune, XXVIII (July 1968), 195-205.
On the ships, not the man.

1322. Sally, A. S., Jr., ed. See South Carolina, no. 1389.

1323. Sanborn, Nathan P. General John Glover and His Marblehead Regiment in the Revolutionary War.

A Paper Read before the Marblehead Historical Society, May 14, 1903. [Marblehead, Mass.] The Society, 1903. 56p.

1324. Sanders, Harry. "The First American Submarine." United States Naval Institute Proceedings, LXII (December 1936), 1743-1745.
 The Turtle.

1325. [Sandwich, John Montagu, 4th Earl of.] The Private Papers of John, Earl of Sandwich, First Lord of the Admiralty, 1771-1782. Edited by G. R. Barnes and J. H. Owen. Publications of the Navy Records Society. 4 vols.; London: The Society, 1932-1938.

1326. Saunders, William L., ed. See North Carolina, no. 1141.

1327. Savadge, W. R. "The West Country, and the American Colonies, 1763-1783, with Special Reference to the Merchants of Bristol." Unpublished D. Phil. Dissertation, Oxford University, 1951.

1328. Sawtell, Clement C. "Impressment of American Seamen by the British." Essex Institute Historical Collections, LXXVI (October 1940), 314-344.
 During the Revolution and War of 1812.

1329. Scharf, J. Thomas. Chronicles of Baltimore. Baltimore: Turnbull Press, 1874. 719p.

1330. -----. History of Delaware, 1609-1888. 2 vols.; Philadelphia: L. J. Richards, 1888.

1331. -----. History of Maryland. 3 vols.; Hatboro, Pa.: Tradition Press, 1967.
 Reprint of the 1879 edition. Vol. I includes some naval data on the Revolution.

1332. -----. History of Philadelphia, 1609-1884. 3 vols.; Philadelphia: L. H. Everts, 1884.

1333. Scheley, Winfield S. "John Paul Jones." New Age, V (July 1906), 57-60.
 By a noted Admiral of the Spanish-American War.

1334. "The Schooner Liberty." Researcher, II (July 1928), 123-126.

1335. Scott, James B. De Grasse à Yorktown. Paris: Les Editions Internationales, 1931. 363p. Rpr. 1970.

1336. Scott, Kenneth. "New Hampshire's Part in the Penobscot Expedition." American Neptune, VII (July 1947), 200-212.

1336a. A Seaman's Remarks on the British Ships of the Line, from the 1st of January 1756 to the 1st of January 1782. With Some Occasional Observations on the Fleet of the House of Bourbon. London, 1782. 36p.

1337. Seawell, Molly E. "John Paul Jones." In her Twelve Naval Captains: Being a Record of Certain Americans who Made Themselves Immortal. New York: Scribners, 1897. p. 1-27.

1338. -----. "Paul Jones." Century Illustrated Magazine, XLIX (April 1895), 873-893.

1339. -----. "Richard Dale." In her Twelve Naval Captains: Being a Record of Certain Americans who Made Themselves Immortal. New York: Scribners, 1897. p. 28-41.

1340. Seltz, Don C. Paul Jones, His Exploits in English Seas During 1776-1780, Contemporary Accounts Collected from English Newspapers with a Complete Bibliography. New York: Dutton, 1917. 327p.

1341. Sellers, Charles C. Benedict Arnold: the Proud Warrior. New York: Minton, Balch, 1930. 303p.

1342. Sellers, L. "Charleston Business on the Eve of the Revolution." Unpublished Ph.D. Dissertation, Columbia University, 1934.

1343. Sen, Siba Pada. The French in India, 1763-1816. Calcutta: K. L. Mukhopadhyay, 1958. 621p.
Suffern's activities highlighted.

1344. [Serle, Ambrose.] The American Journal of Ambrose Serle, Secretary to Lord [Richard] Howe, 1776-1778. Edited with an Introduction by Edward H. Tatum, Jr. Huntington Library Publications. San Marino, Calif.: The Huntington Library, 1940. 369p. Rpr. 1969.

1345. [Seume, J. G.] The Voyage of the First Hessian Army from Portsmouth to New York, 1776. Edited by A. Pfister. Heartman's Historical Series, no. 3. New York: Printed for C. F. Heartman, 1915. 31p.
Unbelievable tales of hardship suffered on the Atlantic passage.

1346. Shafroth, John F. "The Strategy of the Yorktown Campaign, 1781." United States Naval Institute Proceedings, LVII (June 1931), 721-736.

1347. Shaw, Henry I. "Penobscot Assault--1779." Military Affairs, XVII (Summer 1953), 83-94.

1348. Sheffield, William P. Rhode Island Privateers and Privateersmen. An Address Before the Rhode Island Historical Society in Providence, Feb. 7, 1882. Newport: John P. Sanborn, 1883. 65p.

1349. Shelly, F. "Demonstration Against Charleston, South Carolina, in 1779. From a Manuscript in the Abertoff Collection." Magazine of American History, XXVI (August, November 1891), 152-154, 392.

1350. Sheppard, John H. The Life of Samuel Tucker, Commodore in the American Revolution. Boston: A. Mudge, 1868. 384p.
Includes muster rolls of the ship Boston.

1351. Sherburne, Andrew. Memoirs of Andrew Sherburne: A Pensioner of the Navy of the Revolution. Written by Himself. 2nd ed., enl. and improved. Providence: H. H. Brown, 1831. 312p. Rpr. 1970.

1352. Sherburne, John H. Life and Character of the Chevalier John Paul Jones, a Captain in the Navy of the United States, During Their Revolutionary War.

New York: Wilder & Campbell, 1825. 352p.
First American edition.

1353. -----. The Life and Character of John Paul Jones, a Captain in the United States Navy, During the Civil War. 2nd ed.; New York: Adriance, Sherman, 1851. 408p.
Title misleading; Civil War referred to is the Revolutionary War.

1354. -----. The Life of Paul Jones, from Original Documents. London: J. Murray, 1825. 320p.
First English edition.

1355. Sherman, Andrew M. Life of Captain Jeremiah O'Brien, Machais, Maine, Commander of the First American Naval Flying Squadron of the War of the Revolution. Morristown, N.J.: G. W. Sherman, 1902. 247p.

1356. Sherman, Constance D. "An Account of the Scuttling of His Majesty's Armed Sloop Liberty." American Neptune, XX (October 1960), 243-249.

1357. Sherwin, Harry E. New Hampshire Helps Begin the U.S. Navy. Historical New Hampshire, v. 9. Concord: New Hampshire Historical Society, 1953. 20p.
Concerns the state-built vessels Raleigh, Ranger, and America.

1358. Sherwood, H. N. "The Attempted Seizure of the Zaffarine Islands." Mississippi Valley Historical Review, IV (December 1917), 371-373.
A naval adventure in the Mediterranean, 1777.

1359. Shipton, C. K. "Benjamin Lincoln: Old Reliable." In George A. Billias, ed. George Washington's Generals. New York: Morrow, 1964. p. 193-211.
Whose exasperation with D'Estaing after the 1779 Rhode Island fiasco almost caused a Franco-American breach.

1360. Shipton, I. "Admiral Lord [Samuel] Hood." National Review, CXXVIII (April 1947), 304-311.

1361. A Short Account of the Naval Actions of the Last War; in Order to Prove that the French Nation Never Gave Such Slender Proofs of Maritime Greatness as During that Period. By an Officer. London: Printed for J. Murray, 1788. 148p.

1362. [Shuldham, Molyneux S.] The Despatches of Molyneux Shuldham, Vice-Admiral of the Blue and Commander-in-Chief of His Britanic Majesty's Ships in North America, January-July 1776. Edited by Robert W. Neeser. Publications of the Naval History Society, v. 3. New York: Printed for the Naval History Society by the De Vinne Press, 1913. 330p.

1363. Simonds, George S. "New Light on the Campaign in Canada Under Sir Guy Carleton in 1776." U.S. Infantry Association Journal, VI (November 1907), 401-422.
 Valcour Island affair.

1364. [Simpson, James.] "A British View of the Siege of Charleston, 1776." Edited by Frances R. Kepner. Journal of Southern History, X (February 1945), 93-103.
 Text of a 1778 report to Lord George Germain.

1364a. Sinclair, Harold. "New Orleans and Another Revolution." In his The Port of New Orleans. New York: Doubleday, 1942. p. 73-88.
 The American Revolution and Oliver Pollock.

1365. Skefrett, Robert G. "Wreck of the Royal Savage Recovered." United States Naval Institute Proceedings, LXI (November 1935), 1646-1652.
 A schooner captured from British and used by Arnold on Lake Champlain, 1776.

1366. [Slade, William.] "William Slade Records Life and Death on the Prison Ship [Grosvenor]." In Danshe Dandridge, American Prisoners of the Revolution. Charlottesville, Va.: The Michie Company, 1911. p. 494-499.

1367. Slight, Julian. A Narrative of the Loss of the Royal George at Spithead, August, 1782; including Tracey's Attempt to Raise her in 1783. Portsea,

Eng.; S. Horsey, 1840. 60p.

1368. Smelser, Marshall. The Congress Founds the Navy, 1787-1798. South Bend: University of Notre Dame Press, 1959. 229p.
Useful introductory comments on the demise of the Continental Navy by 1785.

1369. -----. The Winning of Independence. Vol. I of the Quadrangle Bicentennial History of the American Revolution, Leonard W. Levy, General Editor. New York: Quadrangle Books, 1971. 448p.
Naval aspects noted.

1370. Smith, Buckingham. "Robert Farmer's Journal of the Siege of Pensacola." Magazine of History, IV (June 1860), 163-172.

1371. Smith, David B. "The Capture of the Washington." Mariner's Mirror, XX (October 1934), 420-425.
In 1775.

1372. Smith, Dorothy U. "Historic War Vessels in Lake Champlain and Lake George." In Thirty First Report of the Director of the Division of Science and the State Museum. New York State Museum Bulletin, no. 313. Albany: University of the State of New York, 1937. p. 123-136.

1373. Smith, Fitz Henry, Jr. The French at Boston During the Revolution. Boston: Priv. print, 1913. 69p.

1374. Smith, H. M., Jr. "The Yorktown Campaign." Sons of the Revolution in the State of Virginia Magazine, V (January 1937), 3-10.

1375. Smith, H. P. "The Sea Forces in Time of War." In Edward Field, ed. State of Rhode Island and Providence Plantations at the End of the Century: a History, Illustrated with Maps, Facsimilies of Old Plates, and Paintings and Photographs of Ancient Landmarks. 3 vols.; Boston: The Mason Publishing Company, 1902. I, 531-627.
The Revolutionary War included.

1376. Smith, Joseph J., Comp. Civil and Military List of

Rhode Island.... All Officers in the Revolutionary War Appointed by the Continental Congress.... and All Officers in Privateer Service during the Colonial and Revolutionary Wars. 2 vols.; Providence: Preston and Rounds, Co. 1900.

1377. Smith, M. E. C. "Machias in the Revolution and Afterward; Captain of the Margaretta and Diligent." New England Magazine, New Series XII (August 1895), 673-688.

1378. Smith, Myron J., Jr. "The Otter and the Defence: Victory or Draw?" Unpublished Papers, Files of the Maryland Department, Enoch Pratt Free Library, 1971.
Contends the British sloop was not "defeated" by the Maryland ship in March 1776. For an expanded version, see Appendix I, p. 177.

1379. -----. "The Virginia: Maryland's Ill-Fated Frigate of the Revolution." Unpublished Paper, Files of the Maryland Department, Enoch Pratt Free Library, 1971.
Lost on the Virginia capes in 1778 while attempting to escape for her first cruise.

1380. Smith, Page. John Adams, 1735-1826. 2 vols.; Garden City, N.Y.: Doubleday, 1962.

1380a. Smith, Paul H. "Sir Guy Carleton: Soldier-Statesman!" In George A. Billias, ed. George Washington's Opponents. New York: Morrow, 1964. p. 103-141.
The Canadian official who built the fleet which opposed Arnold's at Valcour Island.

1381. Smith, Philip C. F. and Russell W. Knight. "In Troubled Waters: The Elusive Schooner Hannah." American Neptune, XXX (April 1970), 86-116.

1382. Smith, Samuel. "General Samuel Smith's Account of the Defence of Fort Mifflin." Maryland Historical Magazine, V (September 1910), 205-229.

1383. Smith, Samuel S. Fight for the Delaware, 1777. Monmouth Beach, N.J.: Philip Freneau Press, 1970. 52p.

Smyth, Clifford

1384. Smyth, Clifford. John Paul Jones, the Man Who Carried the American Flag to Europe. Builders of America Series, v. 11. New York: Funk & Wagnalls, 1931. 176p.

1385. Snow, Elliot. "The Row Galley Bulldog." United States Naval Institute Proceedings, LXII (July 1936), 991-994.
Built by Emmanuel Eyre for use by the Colonies during the Revolution.

1386. Society of Old Brooklynites. A Christmas Reminder. Being the Names of About Eight Thousand Persons, a Small Portion of the Number Confined on board the British Prison Ships During the War of the Revolution. Brooklyn: Eagle Print., 1888. 61p.

1387. "Song of the Privateer Sloop Montgomery--1776." Rhode Island Mariner, I (April 1927), 6.
A Contemporary verse.

1388. "The South Carolina." In Burton E. Stevenson, ed. Poems of American History. Boston: Houghton, Mifflin, 1936. p. 228-229.
A poem of 1782.

1389. [South Carolina. Commissioners of the Navy Board.] Journal of the Commissioners of the Navy of South Carolina, October 9, 1776-March 1, 1779, July 22, 1779-March 23, 1780. Edited by A. S. Sally, Jr. 2 vols.; Columbia: Printed for the Historical Commission of South Carolina by the State Company, 1912-1913.
That portion of the journal between March 1 and July 22, 1779 has been lost.

1390. Spain. Navy. Noticia de los Sucesos de la Armada Combinada de Espagne y Francia Apostada a Esperar a la do Inglaterra, y de los Various Encuentros Pasta la Funcion--del dia 20 de Octubre de 1782. Madrid, 1782. 8p.
Claims of Franco-Spanish naval successes.

1391. Sparks, Jared. The Life and Treason of Benedict Arnold. Vol. III of The Library of American Biography. 25 vols.; Boston: Harper, 1835. 335p.

Devoted almost exclusively to his military career during the Revolution with useful coverage of the Valcour Island business.

1391a. -----., ed. Correspondence of the American Revolution; Being Letters of Eminent Men to George Washington. ... 4 vols.; Boston: Little, Brown, 1853.

1392. Spears, John R. "Benedict Arnold--Naval Patriot." Harpers New Monthly Magazine, CVI (January 1903), 276-281.

1392a. A Speech which was Spoken in the House of Assembly of St. Christopher Upon the 6th of November 1781 for Presenting an Address to His Majesty, Relative to the Proceedings of Admiral Rodney and General Vaughan at St. Eustatius. London: J. Debrett, 1782. 44p.

1393. Spencer, Frank. "Lord Sandwich, Russian Masts, and American Independence." Mariner's Mirror, XLIV (April 1958), 116-127.

1394. Spencer, John B. An Illustrated Historical Sketch of Jamestown, Williamsburg, and Yorktown. Petersburg, Va.: Franklin Press, 1907. 48p.

1395. Spilsbury, John. A Journal of the Siege of Gibraltar, 1779-1783. Edited by B. H. T. Frere. Gibraltar: Garrison Library, 1908. 143p.

1396. Spinny, David. Rodney. Annapolis: U.S. Naval Institute, 1969. 484p.

1397. Sprague, John F. "The Lexington of the Sea." Journal of American History, VI (1912), 403-415. Machais, Maine, 1775. Reprinted in Sprague's Journal of Maine History, I (October 1913), 157-164.

1398. -----. "The First Naval Battle." Journal of American History, VI (April-June 1912), 403-415. Actions of the Hannah.

1399. Stackpole, Edouard A. "John Paul Jones and His Nantucket Sea Fighters." Nantucket Historical

Association Proceedings, XLII (1936), 20-27.

1400. Stansbury, Joseph. "The Lords of the Main (1780)." In Moses C. Tyler The Literary History of the American Revolution. 2 vols.; New York: G. P. Putnam's Sons, 1897. II, 87-88.
A Tory song for use of British sailors engaging French and Spanish opponents in alliance with the colonies.

1401. Starbuck, Alexander. History of Nantucket County, Island, and Town. Boston: C. E. Goodspeed, 1924. 871p.
Raided by the British during the Revolution.

1402. Steadman, T. P. "The Regulation of Commerce and Navigation on the Great Lakes [1768-1846]." Unpublished M.A. thesis, University of Queens, 1938.

1402a. Steele, David. Steele's Original and Correct List of the Royal Navy, Improved: to which are Added their Stations, and a List of the Ships Lost Since the Commencement of the War, with their Commanders. Likewise, a list of the Enemies' Ships Taken or Destroyed. London: the Author, 1784. 34p.

1403. -----. The Elements and Practice of Rigging and Seamanship. 2 vols.; London: the Author, 1794. Rpr. 1958.
As practiced in the late 18th Century.

1404. -----. Steele's Naval Remembrancer; or, The Gentleman's Maritime Chronology of the Various Transactions of the Late War, from its Commencement to the Important Period of Signing the Preliminary Articles, on the 20th of January 1783. London: Printed for D. Steele, 1785. 104p.

1405. -----. Steele's Original and Correct List of the Royal Navy, Improved and Corrected to August 22, 1781. London: David Steele, 1781.
Published monthly at first and then quarterly to 1790; pagination varies.

1406. Stegmann, George H. and Howard I. Chapelle, comps. "A List of the Sailing Men-of-War and Packets of

the Continental Congress and the United States Navy, 1775-1852." Mariner, VII (October 1933), 111-126; VIII (January-October 1934), 11-26, 44-59, 77-92, 124-129.
    An alphabetical list with limited data on each vessel.

1407. Steiner, B. C. "Maryland Privateers in the Revolution." Maryland Historical Magazine, III (June 1908), 99-103.

1408. Stephen, Leslie and Sidney Lee, eds. The Dictionary of National Biography. 22 vols.; London: Oxford University Press, 1938.
    Reprint of the 1885-1901 edition; a basic source for biographies of important British naval officers involved in the American Revolution.

1409. Stephens, Frederick G. A History of Gibraltar and Its Sieges. 2nd ed. London: Provost, 1873. 280p.

1410. Stephenson, Orlando W. "The Supply of Gunpowder in 1776." American Historical Review, XXX (January 1925), 271-281.

1411. Stevens, Benjamin F. B. F. Stevens' Facsimiles of Manuscripts in European Archives Relating to America, 1773-1783. London: Photographed and Printed by Malby & Sons, 1889-1895. 24 portfolios. Rpr. 1970.
    Correspondence of French, British, and other ministries relating to neutrality, privateering, Continental cruisers, etc.

1412. -----. "Paul Jones: A Sketch." United Service, 3d Series IV (November 1903), 465-472.

1413. -----. Portrait of John Paul Jones, Presented to the Bostonian Society ... November 12, 1889. [Boston: The Society? 1889?] 8p.

1414. Stevens, John A. "The Duke de Lauzun in France and America." American Historical Magazine, II (September 1907), 343-375.

1415. -----. "The French in Rhode Island; With an

Stevens, William O.

Appendix." Magazine of American History, III (July 1879), 385-436.
Includes a list of the French fleet at Rhode Island under Admiral de Ternay and M. Destouches.

1416. -----. "The Return of the French, 1782-1783; With an Appendix." Magazine of American History, VII (July 1881), 1-35.
Features correspondence between Washington and De Grasse.

1417. Stevens, William O. and Allan Westcott. History of Seapower. New York: Doubleday, 1938. 426p.
Useful survey of the Battles of the Chesapeake and Saintes Passage plus Suffren's activities.

1418. Stevenson, Cornelius. "Description of John Paul Jones' Sword." United States Naval Institute Proceedings, XXXIII (June 1907), 711.

1419. [Stewart, Anthony.] "The Burning of the 'Peggy Stewart.'" Maryland Historical Magazine, V (September 1910), 235-245.
A memorial from owner Anthony Stewart, March 10, 1777, to the Lords Commissioners of His Majesty's Treasury and accompanying affidavits. Stewart's ship was burned off Annapolis in 1774.

1420. Stewart, Charles W., author. See United States, Congress, House, no. 1485.

1421. -----., ed. See United States, Navy Department, Naval History Division, no. 1496.

1422. Stewart, Robert A. The History of Virginia's Navy of the Revolution. Richmond: Mitchell and Hotchkiss, 1934. 279p.
"Roster of the Virginia Navy of the Revolution," p. 137-271.

1423. Stewart-Brown, Ronald. Liverpool Ships in the Eighteenth Century, Including the King's Ships Built There, with Notes on the Principal Shipwrights. London: Hodder & Stoughton, 1932. 148p.

1424. Stiles, Henry R. Letters from the Prison and Prison

Ships of the Revolution, with Notes. Wallabout Prison Ships Series, no. 1. New York: Priv. Print., 1865. 49p.

1425. Stiles, William C. I. "Paul Jones and Arnold." United States Naval Institute Proceedings, LXI (March 1935), 337-344.
A comparison.

1426. Stinchcombe, William C. The American Revolution and the French Alliance. Syracuse, N.Y.: Syracuse University Press, 1969. 246p.
Including the French fleets in American waters.

1427. Stoesen, Alexander R. "The British Occupation of Charleston, 1780-1782." South Carolina Historical Magazine, LXIII (April 1962), 71-82.

1428. Stone, Edwin M. History of Beverly [Mass.], Civil and Ecclesiastical, From its Settlement in 1630 to 1842. Boston: J. Munroe, 1843. 324p.

1429. -----. Our French Allies. Rochambeau and His Army, Lafayette and His Devotion, D'Estaing, De Ternay, Barras, De Grasse, and Their Fleets, in the Great War of the American Revolution, from 1778 to 1782, Including Military Operations in Rhode Island, the Surrender of Yorktown, Sketches of French and American Officers, and Incidents of Social Life in Newport, Providence, and Elsewhere. Providence: Providence Press Company, 1884. 632p.

1430. Stone, T. "Raid of British Barges." Maryland Historical Magazine, IV (December 1909), 381-382.
A letter from Stone dated April 8, 1781.

1431. Stone, William L., trans. See Pausch, Georg, no. 1210.

1432. Stone, William M., ed. See Thayer, Samuel, no. 1457.

1432a. Stoney, Mrs. S. Reed. "Fort Moultrie." American Monthly Magazine, XXV (December 1904), 911-915.

1433. Stout, Neil R. "The Royal Navy in American

Strittmatter, Isador P.

Waters, 1760-1775." Unpublished Ph.D. Dissertation, University of Wisconsin, 1961.
The role of the British fleet in the major pre-Revolutionary crises and problems afloat and ashore.

1434. -----. "U.S.S. Raleigh: Man-of-War." Marine Corps Gazette, XLVIII (May 1964), 31-2.

1435. Strittmatter, Isador P., ed. The Importance of the Campaign on the Delaware During the Revolutionary War--1777. Revised with Additions for the Pilgrimage of the Medical Club of Philadelphia, June 2, 1932. [Phila.?] 1932. 61p.
British naval efforts leading to the capture of Forts Mercer and Mifflin.

1436. Stryker, William S. The Forts on the Delaware in the Revolutionary War. Trenton, N.J.: Press of J. L. Murphy, 1901. 51p.

1437. Stuart, William M. "Paul Jones, Scottish Mason, American Patriot." Builder, XI (October 1925), 293-297.

1438. Substance of the Charge of Mismanagement in His Majesty's Naval Affairs, in the Year 1781, Compared with Authentic Papers Laid Before the House [of Commons], on Mr. [Charles] Fox's Motion, in the Month of February, 1782. To Which is Added a Complete List of the Division. London: J. Stockdale, 1782. 55p.
Primarily questions the Battle of the Chesapeake.

1439. Suffren Saint Tropez, Pierre Andre de. La Campagne des Indies: Letters Inedites du Bailli de Suffren. Edited by Regine Pernoud. Nantes, 1941. 86p.
The French admiral's letters on his battles with Hughes.

1440. -----. Journal de Bord du Bailli de Suffren Dans l'Inde, 1781-1784, Publie par Henri Moris. Avec Pref. par la Vice-Amiral Jurien de la Graviere. Paris: Challamel, 1888. 349p.

1441. Sullivan, James Y. F., jt. editor. See James, Bartholomew, no. 772.

1442. Sumner, William G. The Financier and Finance of the American Revolution. 2 vols.; New York: Dodd, Mead, 1891. Rpr. 1970.
The role of Robert Morris.

1443. "Supplies for the Galley Washington." Bulletin of the Fort Ticonderoga Museum, IV (1936), 21-22.
A list of victuals taken aboard on 2 October 1776.

1444. Sydenham, M. J. "Firing His Majesty's Dock-Yard: Jack the Painter and the American Mission to France, 1776-1777." History Today, XVI (May 1966), 324-331.

1445. Sylvester, Torrey A. "Down East Naval Defeat." Down East, XII (September, 1965), 32-33, 46-55.

1445a. Symonds, Craig L. "The American Naval Expedition to Penobscot, 1779." Naval War College Review, XXIV (April 1972), 64-72.

1446. Syrett, David. "The Disruption of H.M.S. Flora's Convoy, 1776." Mariner's Mirror, LVI (November 1970), 423-448.

1447. -----. "Living Conditions on the Navy Board's Transports During the American War, 1775-1783." Mariner's Mirror, LVIII (February 1969), 87-94.

1448. -----. Shipping and the American War, 1775-83: A Study in British Transport Organization. New York: Oxford University Press, 1970. 274p.
A unique study long needed.

1449. Talbot, George F. "The Capture of the Margaretta: The First Naval Battle of the Revolution." Collections and Proceedings of the Maine Historical Society, 2nd Series, II (1891), 1-17.
Machais, Maine, 1775.

1450. Talbot, Melvin F. "A Sketch of Fleet Maintenance in Nelson's Day." United States Naval Institute Proceedings, XLV (July 1939), 958-960.

Much of this data also applies to the British fleet of the Revolution.

1451. Tammany Society, or Columbian Order. Wallabout Committee. Account of the Interment of the Remains of American Patriots, who Perished on board the British Prison Ships during the American Revolution. With Notes and an Appendix by Henry R. Stiles. Wallabout Prison Ship Series, no. 2. New York: Priv. print., 1865. 246p.

1452. Tatum, Edward H., Jr., ed. See Serle, Ambrose, no. 1344.

1453. Taylor, A. H. "The French Fleet in the Channel, 1778 and 1779." Mariner's Mirror, XXIV (July 1938), 275-288.

1454. Taylor, George. Martyrs of the Revolution in the British Prison-Ships in the Wallabout Bay. New York: W. H. Arthur, 1855. 60p.

1455. [Taylor, Janette.] "New Light Upon the Career of John Paul Jones. A Letter from Janette Taylor to James Fenimore Cooper, 1843." United States Naval Institute Proceedings, XXXIII (June 1907), 683-706.

1456. Thacker, Joel D. and D. Michael O'Quinlivan. "A Double Anniversary." Marine Corps Gazette, XXXVIII (November 1954), 36-39.
    Concerns the November 10, 1775 resolution creating the Marine Corps.

1457. [Thayer, Simeon.] The Invasion of Canada in 1775. Including the Journal of Captain Simeon Thayer, Describing the Perils and Sufferings of the Army under Colonel Benedict Arnold, in its March through the Wilderness to Quebec. With Notes and an Appendix by Edwin M. Stone. Providence: Knowles, Anthony, 1867. 104p. Rpr. 1969.
    Includes the water-borne capture of St. Johns.

1458. Thiery, Maurice. Bougainville: Soldier and Sailor. London: Grayson & Grayson, 1932. 291p.
    The Count commanded the Auguste during the Battle of the Chesapeake.

1459. Thom, De Courcy W. "Captain Lambert Wickes, C. N. --A Maryland Forerunner of Commodore John Paul Jones, C. N." Maryland History Magazine, XXVII (Spring 1932), 1-17.

1460. Thomas, Sarah A. "John Barry: A Patriot of the Revolution." Cape May County Magazine of History and Genealogy, III (June 1948), 33-48.

1461. Thomson, Valentine. Knight of the Seas: the Adventurous Life of John Paul Jones. New York: Liveright, 1939. 608p.

1462. Thursfield, James R. "Paul Jones." In his Nelson and Other Studies. London: J. Murray, 1909. p. 170-257.

1463. Thurston, C. R. "Newport in the Revolution." New England Magazine, New Series XI (September 1894), 2-19.

1464. Tilly, Jean. "A Propos de la Bataille des Saintes, 1782." Bulletin de la Societé de Géographie de Rochefort, XXXIX (1926), 253-258.

1465. Todd, Charles B. "Whaleboat Privateersmen of the American Revolution." Magazine of American History, VIII (March 1882), 168-180.

1466. [Tomlinson, Robert and Nicholas.] The Tomlinson Papers, Selected from the Correspondence and Pamphlets of Captain Robert Tomlinson, Royal Navy, and Vice Admiral Nicholas Tomlinson. Edited by John G. Bulloche. Publications of the Navy Records Society, v. 74. London: Printed for the Navy Records Society, 1935. 400p.
   Admiral Tomlinson was presented aboard his ship, H. M. S. Bristol, at the fifth battle between Hughes and Suffren in 1783.

1467. Tooker, Dorothy. "The Strange Search for John Paul Jones." United States Naval Institute Proceedings, LXXXI (July 1955), 808-811.
   In quest of his French resting place.

1468. Tooker, Lewis F. John Paul Jones. True Stories of Great Americans. New York: Macmillan,

Tournquist, Carl G.

1925. 210p.

1469. Tournquist, Carl G. The Naval Campaigns of Count de Grasse during the American Revolution, 1781-1783. Translated from the Swedish with Introduction, Notes, and Appendices, Containing a list of Swedish Officers who took part in the Struggle, by Amandus Johnson. Philadelphia: Swedish Colonial Society, 1942. 208p.

1470. Tourtellot, Arthur B. "Rebels, Turn Out Your Dead!" American Heritage, XXI (August 1970), 16-17, 90-93.
Life--and death--on the prison ship Jersey.

1471. Toynbee, Mrs. Paget, ed. See Walpole, Horace, no. 1526.

1472. [Trevenen, James.] A Memoir of James Trevenen. Edited by Christopher Lloyd and R. C. Anderson. Publications of the Navy Records Society, v. 101. London: Printed for the Navy Records Society, 1959. 247p.
An officer with Nelson in the attempted recapture of St. Turks Island, in the West Indies, in July 1783.

1472a. Tribou, Agnes C. "Commodore Abraham Whipple." American Monthly Magazine, XXXV (August 1909), 369-375.

1473. Tricocke, George N. "La Prise du Nassau par les Loyalists de la Caroline du South en 1783." Revue Etudies Histoire, XC (1924), 345-358.

1474. Troude, O. Batailles Navales de la France. 4 vols.; Paris: Challamel Aine, 1867-1868.
Including those of the American Revolution.

1475. Trublet. Histoire de la Campagne d'Inde par Escadre Française Sous les Orderes Bailli de Suffren, Annees 1781, 1782, 1783. Paris: Rennes, 1803. 218p.
An early account of Suffren's efforts to help capture India from the British.

1476. Trumbell, J. H., ed. See Connecticut, no. 377.

1477. Tuckerman, Henry T. Life of Silas Talbot, a Commodore in the Navy of the United States. New York: J. C. Riker, 1850. 137p.
Reprinted in 1926 as Extra No. 120 of the Magazine of History.

1478. Turner, C. W. "Founder of the American Navy." Sewanee Review, IX (July 1901), 296-301.
John Paul Jones.

1479. Turner, Eunice H. "American Prisoners of War in Great Britain, 1777-1783." Mariner's Mirror, XLV (July 1959), 200-206.

1479a. Two Letters Addressed to Sir Thomas Charles Bunbury, Member of Parliament for the County of Suffolk, in February 1781, Previous to the Late Subscriptions Raised by the Noblemen and Gentlemen of that County, for Building a Ship of the Line for the Public Service. With Notes and Additions, by a Freeholder of Suffolk. Doncaster: the Author, 1782. 959p.

1480. Ubbelohde, Carl. The Vice Admiralty Courts and the Revolution. Chapel Hill: Published for the Institute of Early American History and Culture, Williamsburg, Va., by the University of North Carolina Press, 1960. 242p.

1481. Uhlendorf, Bernard A., ed. The Siege of Charleston: With an Account of the Province of South Carolina: Diaries and Letters of Hessian Officers from the Von Junghenn Papers in the William L. Clements Library. University of Michigan Publications in History and Political Science, v. 12. Ann Arbor: University of Michigan Press, 1938. 468p. Rpr. 1967.
Continental and Royal naval opposition featured.

1482. United States. Army. War College. Historical Section. The Virginia Campaign and the Blockade and Siege of Yorktown, 1781, Including a Brief Narrative of the French Participation in the Revolution Prior to the Southern Campaign, by H. L. Landers. Washington: U.S. Government Printing Office, 1931. 219p.

United States (cont.)

1483. -----. Congress. House. Report and Statement of the Commissioner of Pensions, Relative to the Armed National Ships Employed During the Revolutionary War and the Names of their Commanders. House Doc. 394, 23rd Cong., 1st Sess., 1834. 6p.

1484. -----. House. Committee on Naval Affairs. Heirs of John Paul Jones. House Doc. 206, 29th Cong., 1st Sess., 1846. 29p.

1485. -----. Joint Committee on Printing. John Paul Jones Commemoration at Annapolis, April 24, 1906. Comp. Under the Direction of the Joint Committee on Printing by Charles W. Stewart, Superintendent Library and Naval War Records. House Doc. 804, 59th Cong., 1st Sess., 1907. 210p.

1486. -----. Congress. Senate. Rochambeau; Army of de Rochambeau on Land and the Naval Exploits of de Ternay, des Touches, de Barras, and de Grasse in American Waters, 1780-1781. Edited by De B. Randolph Keim. 71sts Cong., 2nd Sess., Senate Doc. 211, 1931.

1487. -----. -----. -----. The Story of the Campaign and Siege of Yorktown, by Hamilton J. Eckenrode. Senate Doc. 318, 71st Cong., 3rd Sess., 1931. 54p.

1488. -----. Continental Congress. Extracts from the Journals of Congress, Relative to the Capture and Condemnation of Prizes, and the Fitting Out of Privateers; Together with the Rules and Regulations of the Navy, and Instructions to the Commanders of Private Ships of War. Philadelphia: John Dunlap, 1776. 45p.

1489. -----. -----. Journals of the Continental Congress, 1774-1789. Edited by Worthing C. Ford and Galliard Hunt. 34 vols.; Washington: Government Printing Office, 1904-1912.
    Much naval data.

1490. -----. -----. "Marine Committee. Orders of the Continental Marine Committee to Captain John

Barry." American Catholic Historical Researches New Series VI (October 1910), 322-333.
Covers period of 1778-1780.

1491. -----. Library of Congress. Naval Records of the American Revolution, 1775-1778. Washington, D. C.: Government Printing Office, 1906. 549p. Rpr. 1970.
Taken mostly from the Papers of the Continental Congress. Part II presents a chronological listing of letter of marque bonds.

1492. -----. Marine Corps. A Concise History of the United States Marine Corps, 1775-1969, by William D. Parker. Washington: U. S. Government Printing Office, 1971. 143p.

1493. -----. Navy Department, Naval Academy. Catalogue of Historic Objects at the United States Naval Academy, with an Introduction by Rear Admiral Henry B. Wilson. Baltimore: Industrial Printing, 1925. 250p.
Many items from the Revolution included.

1494. -----. -----. Naval History Division. American Ships of the Line. Washington: U. S. Government Printing Office, 1969. 44p.
Includes a discussion of the first U. S. battleship, the America, authorized in 1776, construction supervised by John Paul Jones, and when launched in 1782, given as a gift to the French government.

1495. -----. -----. -----. Dictionary of American Naval Fighting Ships. Washington: U. S. Government Printing Office, 1959--.
Vessels of the Revolution included; five volumes completed by the Fall of 1971.

1496. -----. -----. -----. John Paul Jones Autopsy Reports; Excerpts from the John Paul Jones Commemoration of Interest to the Medical Department, by Charles W. Stewart. Washington: U. S. Government Printing Office, 1965. 17p.

1497. -----. -----. -----. Naval Documents of the American Revolution. Edited by William B. Clark,

Usher, Roland G., Jr.

        et al. Washington: U.S. Government Printing Office, 1964--.
        Five volumes were completed by Fall 1971; upon the death of Mr. Clark, the editorship passed to Dr. William J. Morgan.

1498. -----. -----. -----. Riverine Warfare: The U.S. Navy's Operations on Inland Waters. Rev. ed. Washington: U.S. Government Printing Office, 1969. 60p.
        Section I, "Benedict Arnold on Lake Champlain."

1498a. -----. -----. -----. Uniforms of the U.S. Navy, 1776-1898. Washington: U.S. Government Printing Office, 1968.
        Twelve colored lithographs.

1499. -----. Yorktown Sesquicentennial Commission. The Yorktown Sesquicentennial. Proceedings of the United States Yorktown Sesquicentennial Commission in Connection with the Celebration of the Siege of Yorktown, 1781. Prepared by Schuyler O. Bland. Washington: U.S. Government Printing Office, 1932. 382p.

1500. Usher, Roland G., Jr. "The Civil Administration of the British Navy during the American Revolution." Unpublished Ph.D. Dissertation, University of Michigan, 1943.

1501. -----. "Royal Navy Impressment during the American Revolution." Mississippi Valley Historical Review, XXXVII (March 1951), 673-688.

1502. Valentine, Alan. Lord George Germain. Oxford, Eng.: Clarendon Press, 1962. 534p.

1503. Van Alstyne, Richard W. Empire and Independence: The International History of the American Revolution. New York: Wiley, 1955. 255p.

1504. Van Dusen, A. E. "The Trade of Revolutionary Connecticut." Unpublished Ph.D. Dissertation, University of Pennsylvania, 1948.

1505. Van Dyke, John. "The Jersey Prison-ship." Historical Magazine, X (December 1866), 7-11.

1505a. Van Tyne, Claude H. "French Aid before the Alliance of 1778." American Historical Review, 31 (October 1925), 20-40.

1506. Van Walden, Frederick H., jt. author. See Wachmeister, Hans F., no. 1517.

1507. Varg, Paul A., trans. See Wachmeister, Hans F., no. 1517.

1508. Venault, Raymond. "Une Tentative Contre Gibraltar: le Siège de 1782." Revue de France, III (Mai 1938), 271-274.

1509. [Vernon, William.] "Papers of William Vernon and the Navy Board, 1776-1794." Rhode Island Historical Publications," New Series VIII, (1900), 197-277.

1510. Verrill, Addison E. "Relations between Bermuda and the American Colonies During the Revolutionary War." Connecticut Academy of Arts and Sciences Transactions, XIII (1907), 47-64.

1511. Ver Steeg, Clarence L. Robert Morris: Revolutionary Financier. Philadelphia: University of Pennsylvania Press, 1954. 276p.

1512. "Vice Admiral Hugh Seymour, 1759-1801." In A. Audrey Lockey. The Seymour Family. Boston: Houghton, Mifflin, 1914. p. 318-320.

1512a. Vichot, Jacques. L'Oeuvre des Ozanne: Essai d'Inventaire Illustré. Paris: Edition Neptunia, 1971. 247p.
   A collection of articles (nos. 87-102, 1967-1971) from the illustrated naval journal presenting a useful record of French naval activities during the 18th Century, including the American Revolution.

1513. Viles, P. "The Shipping Interest of Bordeaux, 1774-1793." Unpublished Ph.D. Dissertation, Harvard University, 1965.

1514. Virginia. Navy Board. "Excerpts from the Letter Book of the Navy Board." Researcher, I

(October 1926, January-July 1927), 17-21, 77-81, 137-141, 204-207; II (October 1927, July 1928), 15-18, 127-129.
15 July 1776-17 August 1777.

1515. Vivier, Max. "De Grasse: Forgotten Hero." Legion d'Honneur, VI (1936), 233-243.

1516. Vreeland, Helen K., ed. See Austin, Mary S., no. 79.

1517. [Wachtmeister, Hans F. and Frederick H. Van Walden.] Two Swedes Under the Union Jack: A Manuscript Journal from the American War of Independence. Translated by Nils W. Olssom and Paul A. Varg, Edited by William Odelberg. Rock Island, Illinois: Augustana Book Concern, 1956. 120p.
The account of two Swedish-born Royal Navy officers of their training in New York Harbor and service in the Hudson River from 4 August 1775 to 21 December 1776.

1518. Wagner, Frederick R. Submarine Fighter of the American Revolution: The Story of David Bushnell. New York: Dodd, Mead, 1963. 145p.

1519. Waite, Henry E., comp. Extracts Relating to the Origin of the American Navy. Boston: New England Historic and Genealogical Society, 1890. 34p.
Concerned mostly with Washington's schooner flotilla.

1520. Waite, R. A., Jr. "Sir Home Riggs Popham: A Biography." Unpublished Ph.D. Dissertation, Harvard University, 1945.

1521. Waldo, Samuel P. Biographical Sketches of Distinguished American Naval Heroes in the War of the Revolution, Between the American Republic and the Kingdom of Great Britain: Comprising Sketches of Com. Nicholas Biddle, Com. John Paul Jones, Com. Edward Preble, and Col. Alexander Murray. With Incidental Allusions to Other Distinguished Characters. Hartford: S. Andrus, 1823. 392p. Rpr. 1970.

1522. Walker, Benjamin, ed. See Jones, John P., no. 804.

1523. Wall, John P. Commanders of New Brunswick's Navy in the War of the Revolution. [New Brunswick] Times Publishing, 1905. 6p.

1524. Wallace, David D. The History of South Carolina. 4 vols.; New York: American Historical Society, 1934.

1525. Wallace, W. M. "Benedict Arnold: Traitorous Hero." In George A. Billias, ed. George Washington's Generals. New York: Morrow, 1964. p. 163-192.

1526. [Walpole, Horace.] The Letters of Horace Walpole, Fourth Earl of Oxford. Edited by Mrs. Paget Toynbee. 16 vols.; Oxford: Oxford University Press, 1903-1905.
Includes his comments on the course of the American war as seen from his vantage point.

1527. Ward, Christopher. The War of the Revolution. Edited by John R. Alden. 2 vols.; New York: Macmillan, 1952.

1528. Ward, J. Paul Jones: A Naval Hero of the American Independence. Deeds of Daring Library. London: Dean & Sons, 1860. 158p.

1529. Wardle, A. C. "The King's Ships Named Liverpool, 1741-1941." Historical Society of Lancaster and Cheshire Transactions, XCIII (1942), 131-133.
A frigate by that name was very active on the American coast during the Revolution.

1530. Warner, J. H. "John Paul Jones: Fighting Sentimentalist." South Atlantic Quarterly, XLVII (January 1948), 35-44.

1531. Warner, Oliver. "The Action off Flamborough Head." American Heritage, XIV (August 1963), 42-49, 105.
Bonhomme Richard vs. Serapis. The chapter from the author's "Great Sea Battles."

1532. -----. Great Sea Battles. London: Weidenfeld and Nicolson, 1963. 303p.

1533. -----. Great Seamen. London: Bell, 1961. 226p. Including Lord Rodney.

1534. -----. "Paul Jones in Battle." History Today, XV (September 1965), 613-618.

1535. Warren, J. C. 'The Burning of Falmouth, Me., 1775." Pine Tree, VII (March 1907), 152-157.

1536. [Washington, George.] The Correspondence of General Washington and Comte de Grasse, 1781, August 17-November 4. With Supplementary Documents from the Washington Papers in the Manuscripts Division of the Library of Congress. Edited by the Institute Français de Washington. Washington: U.S. Government Printing Office, 1931. 107p. Rpr. 1970.

1537. -----. The Diaries of George Washington, 1748-1799. Edited by John C. Fitzpatrick. 4 vols.; New York: Houghton, Mifflin, 1925.

1538. -----. Washington, sa Correspondance avec D'Estaing. Paris: Publié par les Soins de la Fondation Nationale pour la Reproduction des Manuscrits Précieux et Pièces Rares d'Archives, 1937. 65p.

1539. -----. The Writings of George Washington, from the Original Manuscript Sources, 1745-1799. Prepared under the Direction of the United States George Washington Bicentennial Commission and Published by Authority of Congress. Edited by John C. Fitzpatrick. 39 vols.; Washington: U.S. Government Printing Office, 1931-1944.
No incoming letters recorded.

1540. Watson, D. H., ed. See Harrison, Joseph, no. 717.

1541. Watson, W. C. The Battle of Valcour Island on Lake Champlain in 1776. Plattsburg, N.Y., 1876. Unpaged.

1542. Weed, Richmond. The Battle of the Capes, 1781--

Victory of Comte de Grasse: the Prelude to the Yorktown Surrender. Norfolk Museum Papers, no. 2. Norfolk, Va.: The Museum, 1959. 13p.

1543. -----. "Battle of the Virginia Capes, 1781." United States Naval Institute Proceedings, LXVI (April 1940), 524-532.

1544. Weeks, Stephen B. "Paul Jones." Southern Historical Association Publications, X (July 1906, 228-232.

1545. Weelen, Jean. "The Embarking of General Rochambeau's Army in 1780." Sons of the American Revolution Magazine, XXV (October 1930), 225-227.
Aboard ships in Brest for the passage to America.

1546. Welch, Richard E. "Rufus King of Newburyport: the Formative Years (1767-1788)." Essex Institute Historical Collections, XCVI (October 1960), 241-276.

1547. Weller, M. I. "The Life of Commodore Joshua Barney." Columbia Historical Society Proceedings, XIV (1911), 67-183.

1548. Wells, D. F. "The Trial of Admiral Keppel, 1779: A Study of Political Opposition to the North Ministry." Unpublished Ph.D. Dissertation, University of Kentucky, 1957.

1549. Wells, G. Harlan. "The British Campaign of 1777 in Maryland Prior to the Battle of the Brandywine." Maryland Historical Magazine, XXX (March 1938), 3-13.
Includes the passage of Lord Howe's fleet to Head of Elk.

1550. Wertenbaker, Thomas J. Norfolk: Historic Southern Port. Duke University Studies. Durham, N.C.: Duke University Press, 1931. 378p.

1551. West, Charles E. "Prison ships in the American Revolution." Journal of American History, V (January-March, 1911), 121-128.

1552. West, Richard S., Jr. "Barrington on the Leeward Station." United States Naval Institute Proceedings, LXVIII (September 1942), 1288-1294.

1553. Westcott, Allan, jt. author. See Stevens, William O., no. 1417.

1554. Wharton, Francis, ed. The Revolutionary Diplomatic Correspondence of the United States. 6 vols.; Washington: Government Printing Office, 1886.

1555. [Wharton, James.] "Chandlery Supplied to the Continental Fleet." In U.S. Navy Department, Naval History Division. Naval Documents of the American Revolution. Edited by William B. Clark, et al. Washington: U.S. Government Printing Office, 1964--. III, 1377-1391.
Day book of a Philadelphia ship chandler during the winter of 1775-1776.

1555a. Wheeler, George A. Castine Past and Present. Boston: Rockwell and Churchill, 1896.
Some discussion of the Penobscot Expedition of 1779.

1556. Wheeler, S. A. "The Last Voyage of John Paul Jones." American Mercury, LXXXI (July 1955), 39-42.
To his Annapolis tomb.

1557. Whipple, William. "Letter" and "Stray Leaves from an Autograph Collection: Correspondence of Josiah Bartlett, of N.H., during the American Revolution." Historical Magazine, VI (March 1862), 73-78.
Whipple and Bartlett, both members of the Continental Congress from New Hampshire, corresponded during 1778 on the "pernicious consequences" of privateering.

1558. White, Thomas. Naval Researches; or, a Candid Inquiry into the Conduct of Admirals Byron, Graves, Hood, and Rodney, in the Actions off Grenada, Chesapeake, St. Christopher's, and of the Ninth and Twelfth of April 1782. Being a Refutation of the Plans and Statements of Mr. Clark, Rear Admiral Ekins, and Others. Founded on Authentic Documents, or Actual Observation.

London: Whittaker, Treacher, and Arnott, 1830. 136p.
By a Royal Navy captain.

1559. Whitehead, William A., ed. See New Jersey, no. 1127.

1560. Whitridge, Arnold. Rochambeau. New York: Macmillan, 1965. 340p.

1561. Whitton, Frederich E. "The Great Siege of Gibraltar, 1779-1783." Blackwood's Magazine, CCXLII (July 1937), 35-55.

1562. -----. "Washington's One Victory." Blackwood's Magazine, CCXXXI (March 1932), 348-359.
Yorktown.

1562a. Wiatt, Aaron. "Marine Notes of Salem: Privateers in the Revolution. From the Account Books of Aaron Wiatt in the Possession of the Essex Institute." Essex Institute Historical Collections, LXVIII (1932), 147-152.

1563. Wickwire, M. B. "Lord Sandwich and the King's Ships: British Naval Administration, 1771-1782." Unpublished Ph.D. Dissertation, Yale University, 1962.

1563a. [Widger, William.] "The Diary of William Widger of Marblehead, Kept at Mill Prison, England, 1781." Essex Institute Historical Collections, LXXIII (1937), 311-347; LXXIV (1938), 22-48, 142-158.
The diarist was taken aboard a Yankee privateer.

1564. Wiener, Frederick B. "Notes on the Rhode Island Admiralty, 1727-1790." Harvard Law Review, XLVI (November 1932), 44-90.

1564a. Wiener, Joel H., ed. Great Britain: Foreign Policy and the Span of Empire, A Documentary History, 1689-1971. 4 vols.; New York: McGraw-Hill, 1972.
Volume III contains a chapter, "The Loss of the American Colonies."

1565. Wilkinson, H. C. Bermuda in the Old Empire: a History of the Island from the Dissolution of the Somers Island Company until the end of the American Revolution, 1684-1784. London: Oxford University Press, 1950. 457p.

1566. Willcox, William B. "Admiral Rodney Warns of Invasion, 1776-1777." American Neptune, IV (July 1944), 193-198.
Memoranda sent by the naval officer to Lord Shelburne commenting on the dangers and possibilities of a French landing in the British Isles.

1567. -----. "Arbuthnot, Gambier, and Graves: 'Old Women.'" In George A. Billias, ed. George Washington's Opponents: British Generals and Admirals in the American Revolution. New York: Morrow, 1969. p. 260-290.

1568. -----. "The Battle of Porto Praya, 1781." American Neptune, V (January 1945), 64-78.
Suffren vs. Johnstone.

1569. -----. "British [Naval] Strategy in America, 1778." Journal of Modern History, XIX (June 1947), 97-121.

1570. -----. "The British Road to Yorktown: A Study in Divided Command." American Historical Review, LII (October 1946), 1-36.
An important essay on the infighting between British Admirals and Generals.

1571. -----. Portrait of a General: Sir Henry Clinton in the War of Independence. New York: Knopf, 1964. 534p.
Great detail on his relations with the Royal Navy; their co-operation and mutual dissatisfaction.

1572. -----. "Rhode Island in British Strategy, 1780-1781." Journal of Modern History, (December 1945), 306-307, 309-313, 316-317.
The inability of General Clinton and Admiral Arbuthnot to co-operate to the extent of destroying the French in the Newport area.

1572a. -----. "Sir Henry Clinton: Paralysis of Command."

In George A. Billias, ed. George Washington's Opponents. New York: Morrow, 1964. p. 73-102.
Further comments on the general's inability to cooperate with the Royal Navy.

1573. Williams, M. J. "The Naval Administration of the Fourth Earl of Sandwich, 1771-1782." Unpublished D Phill Dissertation, Oxford University, 1962.

1574. Williamson, James A. The English Channel: A History. Cleveland: World, 1959. 381p.

1575. Williamson, Joseph. "Correspondence Pertaining to Penobscot." Collections of the Maine Historical Society, 3rd Series II (1906), 223-240.

1576. -----. "The British Occupation of Penobscot During the Revolution." Collections and Proceedings of the Maine Historical Society, 2nd Series I (1890), 389-400.

1577. Wilmington, North Carolina. Proceedings of the Safety Council for the Town of Wilmington, North Carolina, from 1774 to 1776--Printed from the Original Record. Raleigh: T. Loring, 1844. 76p.

1578. Wilson, Henry W. "Howe." In Twelve British Admirals. London: Navy League, 1904. p. 91-95.

1579. Wilson, Thomas. The Biography of the Principal American Military and Naval Heroes: Comprehending Details of Their Achievements During the Revolutionary and Late Wars. Interspersed with Authentic Anecdotes not Found in Any Other Work. 2nd ed., rev. 2 vols.; New York: J. Low, 1821.
John Paul Jones and Joshua Barney included.

1579a. Winchell, Mrs. A. G. "History of the British Prison Ships." American Monthly Magazine, XXXV (July 1909), 7-17.

1580. Wolkins, George G. "The Seizure of John Hancock's Sloop Liberty." Massachusetts Historical Society Proceedings, LV (1923), 239-284.

1581. Wood, Walter. Famous British Warships and Their

Woods, John A.

Commanders. London: Hurst & Blackett, 1897. 312p.
"The Formidable and Lord Rodney."

1582. Woods, John A. "The City of London and Impressment, 1776-1777." Proceedings of the Leeds Philosophical and Literary Society, VIII (1956), 111-127.
Widespread opposition to the practice.

1583. Worchester, Donald. "Miranda's Diary of the Siege of Pensacola, 1781." Florida Historical Quarterly, XXIX (January 1951), 163-196.

1584. Wright, M. W. E., trans. See Rochambeau, Jean B. D. de Vimeur, Comte de, no. 1291.

1585. Wrong, George M. Washington and His Comrades in Arms: A Chronicle of the War of Independence. Vol. XII of The Chronicles of America Series, edited by Allen Johnson. New Haven: Yale University Press, 1921. 296p.

1586. Wuslin, Eugene. "The Political Consequences of the Burning of the Gaspee." Rhode Island History, III (January-April 1944), 1-11, 55-64.

1587. Wyatt, Thomas. Memoirs of the Generals, Commodores, and Other Commanders Who Distinguished Themselves in the American Army and Navy During the Wars of the Revolution and 1812, and Who were Presented with Medals by Congress for Their Gallant Services. Philadelphia: Carey and Hart, 1848. 315p.
John Paul Jones and Joshua Barney included.

1588. Wyndham, Horace. "The Siege of 'The Rock.'" National Review, CXV (December 1940), 699-705.
Gibraltar, 1779-1783.

1589. "The Yankee Man-of-War." In Burton E. Stevenson, ed. Poems of American History. Boston: Houghton, Mifflin, 1936. p. 223.
A poem of 1778 on John Paul Jones and the Ranger.

1590. Yeager, Philip B. "Last in the Hearts of His

Countrymen." United States Naval Institute Proceedings, XCIV (October 1968), 80-88.
　　The naval achievements of B. Arnold.

1591. Yela Utrilla, Juan F. España Ante la Independcia de los Estados Unidos. 2 vols.; Lérida: Graficos, 1925.

1592. Yonge, Charles D. The History of the British Navy, From the Earliest Period to the Present Time. 2nd ed. 3 vols.; London: R. Bentley, 1786.

1593. Zimmerman, J. F. "The Impressment of American Seamen." Unpublished Ph.D. Dissertation, Columbia University, 1925.
　　During the Revolutionary period.

1594. Zlatick, Marko and Peter F. Copeland. "The Virginia State Navy, 1776-1780." Military Collector and Historian, XX (Summer 1968), 49-52.

APPENDIX A

The Otter and the Defence:
A 1776 Naval Episode in Maryland Waters

The role of the state navies in the Revolution has received little attention in the past half century and is today largely unknown by most Americans. At one time or another, nearly every colony possessed a locally controlled naval force, among them Maryland. Of the many vessels which composed her fleet, the ship Defence was by far the largest and most important. Around the outcome of her premier cruise there yet remains considerable leeway for debate and confusion.

For nearly two centuries, we have been told that a brave band of volunteers put out aboard this state vessel and easily drove away the British sloop-of-war Otter which threatened Baltimore in 1776. During the years since, the British have been consistently derided for an apparent retreat while Yankee tars, led by Captain James Nicholson, have been toasted for their great success. The spirit of the forthcoming Bicentennial demands no less than a fair reexamination of this episode. This essay, by demonstrating the temper and preparations of Marylanders, as well as the physical difficulties confronting their enemy, will attempt that more balanced assessment. [1]

The English decision to open the issue came as the direct result of faulty intelligence. Early in 1776 Captain Andrew Snape Hamond, senior King's officer on the Chesapeake and Delaware blockade, learned of significant enemy cruiser activity. Two American "privateers," engaged in escorting traders out to sea were reported off Baltimore. [2] In hopes of bringing these "pirates" to action, he penned orders on February 26 from his flagship H. M. 44-gun frigate Roebuck, anchored in the Elizabeth River near the ashes of Norfolk, for Captain Matthew Squire to take the 16-gun Otter and sail in search of them. [3]

Hamond's directions were very specific. Should the Otter arrive at Baltimore without detecting her quarry, her men were to cut out of the harbor any vessels having "the appearance of being proper for Arming" to prevent their conversion into Continental or private warships. No chances were to be taken in these operations and under no circumstances was the ship or "His Majesty's Arms" to suffer such "an insult" as defeat or destruction. Along with the usual task of "inspecting" and seizing Rebel coasters, Squire was to obtain fresh provisions and complete his cruise within two weeks. On February 28 the Otter, accompanied by her swivel-equipped tender Samuel and the Edward, 6-gun schooner escort of H. M. frigate Liverpool, set sail into a driving rainstorm. Only the Roebuck and Liverpool plus a few tenders were left to guard the Virginia capes, an inadequate force for a close watch.[4]

The tiny British squadron was above the Potomac by March 5. About noon that day, a colonial sail was sighted in the mouth of the Patuxent. The Edward, sent to investigate, soon apprehended a fine New England schooner outward bound for Casco Bay with a shipment of flour. As the Otter and Samuel lay to some six miles off shore awaiting her return, they were spied about suppertime by a pair of Maryland picket boats. Never before in this conflict had a regular English cruiser ascended the Bay so far and the patriot vessels quickly put about and sped toward Annapolis to warn the Council of Safety.[5]

It was dark when the scouts tied up at the Annapolis wharf. Within minutes, however, the fear of attack was moving through the town. Drums were sounded and city militia companies rushed to arms. Shopkeepers and men of means hurriedly made arrangements to evacuate their goods and households further inland. Each succeeding whisper magnified the threat and through the night a violent storm, complete with thunder, lightning, rain, and high winds, sounded ominously.[6]

Rumors, doubtless stoked by memory of the Norfolk disaster, were rampant when the Council convened. Some members believed the fleet, mistaken now as the Roebuck and two sloops, would anchor in the South or Severn and open a bombardment later that night. Others were not so fast to assume Annapolis to be the British target. Everyone from Chairman Daniel of St. Thomas Jenifer on down was puzzled over the enemy intent and destination, but all agreed

Appendix A

that preparations should be made on the chance of imminent attack. Mobilization orders were sent to outlying militia units and precautionary warnings hurried off by "express" to Baltimore and other towns.[7]

When the Baltimore Committee assembled on Wednesday morning, the great tempest was still blowing. The urgent appeal of the Annapolis group to "be on your Guard and make all the Preparations in your Power for your Defence," was read and discussed. Unanimously the local body, chaired by Samuel Purviance, Jr., passed a series of resolutions including a militia alert, an embargo on shipping, a call to Congress for powder and ball, and the removal of county records. As in the capital, many women, children, and valuables soon were headed out of town.[8]

Rather than risk the Bay during the dirty wet weather, Captain Squire lay by much of the sixth with his topgallant masts struck and lower yards down. Patriot observers at Thomas's Point, studying the whitecaps caused by the stiff northwest breeze, were unable to spot the enemy even "with the best Glasses." All morning and into the afternoon, heavy sheets of rain hid them from sight. Later toward dusk the wind shifted around and they were able to proceed, following the western shoreline.

Thursday was a busy day for the raiders. The Samuel chased two sail under Popular Island while the Otter's gig was sent after a sloop running to the Eastern Shore. The sloop and a schooner were captured. The English sailed past Annapolis in midafternoon coming to only long enough to burn an oat-laden shallop near the head of Kent Island. When the warship steered toward the Patapsco at sundown, four or five small prizes trailed in her wake.[9]

As the Otter cruised above Kent Island, further expresses from the Council of Safety were dispatched to Baltimore. "The Man of War with her Tenders," read one, "Have passed by this Harbour and are standing up the Bay, we presume for your Town." Another advised, "if there be any vessels loaded in your River, we would have you fall on the best Expedients you can to secure them." There was some commerce in port, but the gravest concern was felt for a recently departed coaster.[10]

Sometime before the enemy alert reached Baltimore, a large unnamed ship belonging to a Mr. Jonathan Hudson had cleared for New England. The vessel, transporting a wheat and flour cargo under Congressional contract, soon grounded in the shallows near North Point. Three small vessels were sent to lighten her on Thursday afternoon, but they never arrived. Coming down near Sparrows Point Friday morning, the Marylanders saw the Edward and Samuel, flying the Union Jack, headed inshore to add the colonial to their prizelist. Leary of capture, the skippers of the three put about and returned to town expressing the fear that the trader, estimated in value at 14,000 pounds, would soon be lost.[11]

    The little gunboats had no difficulty in securing the grain ship; however, the shallows were such that she could not be cleared even when the prizes taken earlier were ordered to the Point where their crews might bear a hand. While the English salts struggled to float her, the Otter, slowly ascending from her position abreast Gibson Island, was hailed by a man in a small boat. Invited aboard, the stranger identified himself as William Eddis, former Surveyor of Annapolis Port and messenger from His Excellency Robert Eden. The governor, last Royal appointee to that post, had not been warned of her coming and desired to know the nature of Squire's business. The captain, recognized for his humanity by such patriots as St. Thomas Jenifer, spoke freely of his duty and penned a note assuring Eden of his city's safety: 'I must beg Leave to assure you nothing ... will happen from Me: I am on a cruise here in Order to procure fresh Provisions for the Kings Ships." Satisfied, Eddis took his leave about 4 p.m. as the ship prepared to move to the assistance of her tenders.[12]

    The letterbearer, while passing down, watched the sloop sail boldly off and was amazed to see her suddenly shudder, running her bow onto a shoal. Arriving at Annapolis about 9 a.m., he delivered his papers and intelligence to Eden, who dutifully passed them along to the Council. Only now did the leaders find that they were plagued by the Otter, not the frigates Roebuck or Liverpool. St. Thomas Jenifer, grasping the significance of Eddis' "certain Intelligence," immediately summoned a rider to speed to Baltimore with word that the warship's poor luck would spare the town "Till seven or eight o'clock in the morning."[13]

    These British of long ago share with countless successors the disbelief that any stream could be as difficult to navigate as the Patapsco. A native later reported that there

Appendix A   181

was seldom as much as 14 or 15 feet of water in the main
channel and much less elsewhere--data the captain of the
Otter could surely have used to advantage had he known it.
Hundreds of rocks, some huge, broke the surface to be
washed by sharp waves whenever the wind shifted. Lacking
experience in this tributary, Squire's Virginia pilot had
conned the vessel directly onto the Bodkin Point Shoal. The
sloop was "high and dry," caught at lowtide in less than 10
feet of water. She would not be movable until the river
rose hours later.

The tide toward 10 p.m. was sufficiently high to begin working the Otter's stern into deeper water. Orders
were passed for her topsails and foresail to be loosed and
braced. The forward guns were manhandled aft and all
hands summoned to lend their weight by assembling on the
quarterdeck. After considerable sweat and waiting, the
swelling river finally permitted her to slip off. The evening
was so far advanced by the completion of the ordeal that,
just as the Council had predicted, Squire postponed all offensive action until the morrow. The anchor was dropped
and the prizes sent in earlier were signalled to remain inshore with the tenders.[14]

Even before learning of the Britisher's vulnerability,
Baltimorians, according to one journal, "seemed animated
with the most undaunted and unanimous spirit; and prepared
for a determined opposition at the utmost hazzard." While
that description is perhaps a bit too colorful, local defensive
arrangements were ordered and made in exceedingly short
order.

To begin with, a battery was thrown up at Fells
Point and many of the older traders were ordered down to
Whetstone Point preparatory to scuttling as a channel barrier. If time permitted, the "engineers," on orders from
Captain James Nicholson, would pass a chain across their
hulks to the opposite side of the river. The alarms sounded
on Wednesday and Thursday were bearing fruit as hundreds
of militiamen, most poorly armed if at all, flocked into
town. At Whetstone, where Fort McHenry would stand,
regular Maryland contingents of the Continental Army under
Major, later General, Mordecai Gist arrived to dig in.
Despite these precautions, salvation seemed to lie in the
speedy finish of a colonial cruiser then receiving her outfits
at one of the Fells Point boatyards.[15]

Responding to the excitement Lord Dunmore and the Royal Navy were causing in the lower Bay, especially the raids on patriot shipping, "rebellious" Marylanders saw the need for some type of naval protection. Continental warships were too few and those available, such as Wasp and Hornet, were frequently needed outside the Chesapeake. In the fall of 1775, the Baltimore Committee, aided and authorized by the Maryland Council, began the conversion of a square-rigged, three-masted merchantman. Agents for the project were the wealthy Committee member William Lux and Daniel Bowley.

As the work neared an end, many began thinking of practical ways to employ the new man-of-war, aptly named the Defence. Some officials felt she could effectively escort convoys of merchantmen past the Norfolk-based enemy out into the Atlantic. Others agreed with this and added the hope that a warship under Maryland bunting might clear enemy raiders from the Bay and as "Occasion may require," pursue those infesting the Potomac. The ultimate objective would be for her captain to cruise under instructions "to contribute every Thing in his Power to the common Defence on all Occasions" by actively aiding the growing Virginia Navy by moving to the offensive.[16]

The "Dimensions of the Ship Defence" as compiled by First Lieutenant John Thomas Boucher, later Commodore of the Virginia Navy, give the craft an overall length of 85 feet and a beam (width) of about 10 feet. Her draft when fully loaded was close to 13 feet and her total complement put at 180-200 officers and men. Eighteen 6-pounds would line the gundeck with two 4-pounds on the quarter and swivels on the rails.[17] James Nicholson, a native of Chestertown and former Royal Navy officer, was chosen skipper and throughout the winter actively oversaw the ship's metamorphosis. Much of the outfitting was completed when the Otter emerged off the Patuxent; it only remained to mount her guns and assemble a crew.[18]

Manning a state or Continental warship during the Revolution was often quite difficult as most sailors preferred the more profitable berths available aboard privateers. The Otter's sortee proved a God-send to the Baltimore recruiting officers. Hundreds of volunteers, including militiamen led by Captain, later General, Samuel Smith, men from idle merchantmen, and a few bounty-takers, rushed to ship aboard the Defence. So many turned out that additional

Appendix A

small craft were chartered or commandeered so that these surplus fellows might accompany Nicholson's ship in the hoped-for attack on the King's men.

The bulk of the cannon contracted for months earlier fortuitously came into town from the foundry on Thursday evening. With the aid of the many volunteers, these were manhandled aboard the Defence by mid-day on the eighth. By sundown the gunners and recruits had stacked the various equipments around the deck, but as one witness reported, the whole was "in very bad order." Orders were passed along with a towline and soon the ship was anchored "a little Way down the River" with her guns bearing in the direction of any possible enemy advance.

In the small hours of Saturday morning, Samuel Purviance, Jr., was awakened with intelligence of the Otter's identity and grounding. Clad in his nightshirt, he immediately penned directions for Nicholson to sail, hoping he could reach and retake Hudson's ship before the enemy cruiser was refloated. When the Defence, aided and surrounded by no less than three local schooners, put down later toward sunrise, the captain was reported extremely confident that his 220 men could recapture the supply vessel--and perhaps the English sloop as well.[19]

There exists some question as to whether Nicholson was actually ordered to attempt the capture of the Otter. A search among the extant contemporary documents and letters[20] reveals the belief among patriots of diverse authority that he would make the effort. One is led to believe, from the lack of available evidence, that if the Committee officially directed it, the order was either verbal or subsequently lost. What does emerge from such reading is the vivid impression of a mission primarily dispatched to effect the speedy dispersement of the enemy tenders and recovery of the flour ship. Any decision to attack what was believed a stranded warship was a matter left to the judgment of the captain.

It was clear to Nicholson that many of his fellow Baltimorians believed their safety rested on the guns of his vessel--even to the extent of using them as a floating battery, for which purpose she was positioned downstream the previous night. That the Defence was not to be risked is clearly shown in the following dispatch from Purviance, sent by rider after the ship weighed:

I am directed by the Committee of Baltimore to inform you, that, should the Tenders escape you before you get down to Mr. Hudson's Ship and join the Otter, it is their opinion, it would [be] improper for you to attack them all together, and that if you think there is a Probability of their coming to attack you, it would be most adviseable for you to return to Whetstone Point or Fells Point.

The captain was free to engage only if his opponent was grounded nearby in helpless condition or forced battle. Always his vessel was to be kept "ready to protect the Town."[21]

March 9 was one of those hazy winter days when a heavy fog and constant drizzel replaced the sun on the upper Bay; in short, a perfect day for a surprise raid. As the Defence and her escorts, "Manned with a parcel of Buckskin-Heroes," slowly made their way downriver, the rain slackened off increasing visibility. Suddenly a lookout aboard one of the leading schooners sighted a cluster of small craft laying near North Point, about two miles away. "As soon as we saw them," recalled a volunteer, "all hands gave three loud cheers that made the very welkin [sky] ring."[22]

The Yankee holler was answered by an alarm gun fired by one of the English tenders. Out in the Bay, Captain Squire saw the shapes of the unidentified craft hovering "above the Narrows." Shaken by the previous night's accident and distrustful of his pilot, the seadog was fearful of rushing again into those dangerous shallows. Nevertheless, he gave orders to maneuver slowly deeper into the rivermouth only to be rewarded for his effort by again briefly striking shoal. Unable to locate the main channel, the recall signal was hoisted and longboats sent to aid the Edward and Samuel in securing those prizes yet afloat.

The small British raiders were no match for the numerous, noisy, and rapidly approaching Americans. When the recall signal was seen flying from the mother ship, the tenders and seaworthy prizes made sail. Abandoning Hudson's still-grounded ship to the enemy and reinforced by the rowboats, most reached the safety of Squire's guns about 11 a.m.[23]

The returning Edward brought alongside the Otter Bridger Goodrich, a son of the notorious Virginia Loyalist

Appendix A

and privateer John Goodrich, who as an acting pilot had conned the schooner inshore of the point. This worthy informed Squire--wrongly as it turned out--that the Americans had fixed a number of large guns along the channel leading to Baltimore and placed chains across the Patapsco. Additionally, the marker trees, those in the forest lining the bank cut to indicate the river's depth, had all been felled by the patriots.[24] Faced with these new obstacles and already past due in reporting to Captain Hamond at Norfolk, the British skipper decided to forgo the pleasure of engaging the "privateer" and abort the foray. "At 2 p.m.," reads the Otter's log, "weighed & came to sail and ran down the Bay, the 2 Tenders & 5 Prizes in Company."[25]

Most accounts agree that Captain Nicholson, with guns run out, pursued the enemy small craft a short distance beyond North Point. Holding his men in check and mindful of Purviance's last note, he did not sally forth to battle. Instead, he put about and came to abreast the Hudson wreck, ready to meet the Otter if she ran in to reclaim her lost capture. Later when the sloop had weighed, most of the Americans, not appreciating the difficulties man and nature had placed before their adversary, were amazed and delighted when she bore away to the south "without thinking of her prize." Nicholson remained on the station while an express was sent off to the Committee. A number of light vessels were again dispatched to offload the grain ship and by 9 a.m. Sunday morning, all were once more tied up safely at Fells Point.[26]

When the Otter put down the Bay that Saturday, the prospect of her immediate visit to Baltimore evaporated. The excited patriot press, starving for victories, immediately proclaimed her departure a great American triumph. Maryland authorities added to the confusion by making Captain Nicholson an instant hero, a move which would eventually see him confirmed as senior officer of the Continental Navy. For 200 years now, chroniclers have based their histories upon these reports and repeated the contention that the English were so "intimidated by the determined action and formidable appearance" of the Defence that they immediately took flight. While this may have been true with respect to the tenders, a recapitulation of the facts must show this belief no longer valid in the case of the Otter.[27]

Although it is evident from his journal that Matthew Squire did not know the true strength of the colonials before him, he was plainly not "intimidated" into leaving the Patapsco. The record is positive: H.M.S. Otter hauled away more than three hours after the Marylanders appeared. Yet if she were not "chased away," what explains this delay in departure and the lack of an engagement? We have already noted that Captain Nicholson was under orders not to risk his ship except under certain specific eventualities. While Captain Squire was under much the same type of instruction, in his case the chief reason for inaction was the Patapsco itself.

The long period aground Friday evening was anything but enjoyable for the British and when pilot Goodrich returned from North Point on Saturday to report the marker trees replaced by cannon and chain, the captain's decision was practically made for him. It is probable that in the time between the return of the tenders and his departure, he groped for any idea which would have allowed him to seek action. After all, the capture of the mysterious privateer plus the recovery of the flour ship would have brought considerable prize money. When one considers his attempted rescue of the Edward and Samuel, no other explanation can fairly be advanced. 28

After much thought and discussion with his officers and the unknowledgeable pilots, a single thought probably came to haunt Squire. With or without the Yankee presence and already behind schedule, he could not ascend the river to Baltimore; a sane man minus a skilled pilot, no matter what the prize, simply could not again risk a vessel as deeply-drafted as the Otter in such tricky waters. If she were lost or "insulted," it could be ruinous; it was a truism in the Royal Navy of 1776 (just as in the present U.S. Navy) that the loss of a sorely needed ship could have meant his naval career. Possibly recalling the Shakespearean line on discretion and valor, Squire elected not to try the latter. 29

This account must end with "victory" assigned to neither force. Baltimore Town was safe for the moment, but as many expressed it, the marauder was free to return or strike anywhere else along the Bay. There was even fear that, as James Smith of the York Committee put it in a letter to Purviance, "a greater force may be sent to harrass you in revenge for Capt. Squire's bad success." Fortunately for Maryland, Captain Hamond had another mission in mind for the Otter and no vessels to spare in

Appendix A 187

vengeance; unfortunately for history, the Defence and her late opponent would never lie yardarm to yardarm where in the flash of broadside and boarding pike the chief superiority would be known. Perhaps in the end, it is sufficient for all to admit that courage and boldness of full measure were present in both. [30]

Notes

1. Representative portraits include: J. Thomas Scharf, History of Maryland (3 vols; Baltimore: 1879), II, 210-22, and Chronicles of Baltimore (Baltimore: 1874), p. 142; Clayton C. Hall, Baltimore: Its History and Its People (3 vols; New York: 1912), I, 29; Ester M. Dole, Maryland During the Revolution (Baltimore: 1941), p. 185; Hamilton Owens, Baltimore on the Chesapeake (New York: 1941), pp. 97-100. Our two "survey" histories of the naval war also mention the Defence: Charles O. Paullin, The Navy of the American Revolution (Cleveland: 1906), p. 449; and Gardner Allen, The Naval History of the American Revolution (2 vols; Boston: 1913), I, 138-139.

2. These were the Continental ships Wasp and Hornet which did not return but continued to sea to join Esek Hopkins' squadron enroute to the West Indies. Allen, op. cit., 193-94.

3. "Journal of H.M. Sloop Otter, Captain Matthew Squire, February 26, 1776, Admiralty Records 51/663, Public Record Office, London, cited hereafter as Otter Journal; Andrew S. Hamond to Matthew Squire, February 26, 1776, Hamond Papers, University of Virginia Library, Charlottesville, cited hereafter as Hamond Papers. Norfolk was burned by the British and Tories during the first days of the year. Much of the Otter's poor reputation among colonials stemmed from her involvement in this deed. For the comment 'It is glorious to see the blaze of the town and shipping,'" see the letter from one of the ship's party in The Morning Chronicle and London Advertiser, March 5, 1776; for an account of the burning, see The [London] Public Advertiser, March 13, 1776 and the journal of one of the Otter's midshipmen quoted in Henry B.

Dawson, Battles of the United States, By Sea and Land (2 vols; Boston: 1858), I, 126-127.

4. Hamond to Squire, loc cit.; Otter Journal, February 28, 1776; "Examination of Captain Thomas Wirt," Revolutionary Papers, Box 15, Maryland State Archives, Hall of Records, Annapolis, cited hereafter as Wirt Examination. Tenders were small, often captured, vessels employed to gather supplies and intelligence. When armed in the manner of Edward and Samuel, they could arrest prizes in waters too shoaly for their parent ships. For the force left at Norfolk upon Squire's departure, see the letter dated February 28 in Lloyds Evening Post and British Chronicle of April 15, 1776; for the strategic tomfoolery behind that problem, consult Piers Mackesy, The War for America, 1775-1783 (Cambridge, Mass.: 1964), pp. 97-100.

5. Otter Journal, March 5, 1776; "Narrative of the Alarm over the Sloop Otter," Revolutionary Papers, Box 10, Maryland State Archives, Hall of Records, Annapolis, cited hereafter as "Narrative"; Calvert County Committee to the Maryland Council, March 6, 1776, Correspondence of the Council of Safety, Maryland State Archives, Hall of Records, Annapolis, cited hereafter as C.S. Correspondence; John A. Thomas to the Maryland Council, March 8, 1776, C.S. Correspondence; and Maryland Council to Virginia Committee of Safety, March 9, 1776, Council of Safety Letterbook, no. 1, Maryland State Archives, Hall of Records, Annapolis, cited hereafter as C.S. Letterbook.

6. Morning Chronicle and London Advertiser, May 24, 1776.

7. "Narrative"; Maryland Council to Baltimore Committee of Observation, March 5, 1776, Baltimore Committee Papers, Library of Congress, cited hereafter as B.C. Papers; Maryland Council to Virginia Committee, loc cit. Colonel John Weem's battalion was sent to guard the South River Ferry and repel any landing attempted there. Journal of the Maryland Council, March 7, 1776, Council of Safety Journal, 29 August 1775 to 20 March 1777, Maryland State Archives, Hall of Records, Annapolis.

Appendix A   189

8. Minutes of the Baltimore Committee, March 6, 1776, B. C. Papers; Colonel Joseph Reed to George Washington, March 15, 1776, Washington Papers, Library of Congress; Dunlap's Maryland Gazette, March 19, 1776. A ton of powder was forwarded overland from Philadelphia on March 9 in hopes that it "may possibly with the utmost Diligence get to Baltimore Town [in] Time enough to be of service." The Otter was gone before any of it arrived. Thomas Johnson, Jr. and Robert Alexander to Henry Hollingworth, March 9, 1776, Red Book, IV, Maryland State Archives, Hall of Records, Annapolis, cited hereafter as Red Book followed by a comma and the volume number in Roman numerals.

9. "Narrative"; Otter Journal, March 6-7, 1776; Morning Chronicle and London Advertiser, May 24, 1776; Dunlap's Maryland Gazette, March 14, 1776.

10. Council of Safety to Baltimore Committee, March 7, 1776, C. S. Letterbook.

11. Otter Journal, March 8, 1776; Baltimore Committee to Maryland Council, March 8, 1776, Red Book, XIII; Morning Chronicle and London Advertiser, May 24, 1776. A little after the lighters tied up, an express rode off to Philadelphia spreading the fear that the ship, yet believed the Roebuck, would attack Baltimore sometime Friday. Pennsylvania Packet, March 11, 1776.

12. Squire to Eden, March 8, 1776, Purviance Papers, Maryland Historical Society, Baltimore, cited hereafter as Purviance Papers. Of Squire, St. Thomas Jenifer wrote: "[he] behaved politely ... and was he to come here in peaceable times I should be glad to shew him the Civility due to a gentleman." St. Thomas Jenifer to Charles Carroll, Barrister, March 8, 1776, C. S. Correspondence.

13. Maryland Council to Virginia Committee, loc cit.; St. Thomas Jenifer to Carroll, loc cit. Eden gingerly held his position by deferring to the Council; his finish would come later in the summer. Bernard C. Steiner, The Life and Administration of Sir Robert Eden (Baltimore: 1898), pp. 125-138.

14. Otter Journal, March 8, 1776; Morning Chronicle and London Advertizer, May 24, 1776.

15. Dunlap's Maryland Gazette, March 12, 1776; Samuel Purviance, Jr. to Daniel of St. Thomas Jenifer, March 8, 1776, Red Book, XXIV, and to Benjamin Griffith, March 9, 1776, Executive Papers, Box 2, Maryland State Archives, Hall of Records, Annapolis; Baltimore Committee to Maryland Council, March 8, 1776, loc cit.; Charles Carroll, Barrister, to Thomas Dorsey, March 8, 1776, C.S. Correspondence; Minutes of the Baltimore Committee, March 8, 1776, Red Book, XXIV.

16. Maryland Council to Virginia Committee, February 8, 1776, C.S. Letterbook; Baltimore Committee to Maryland Council, March 16, 1776, C.S. Correspondence; Richard H. Lee to Samuel Purviance, Jr., March 17, 1776, Purviance Papers; Hall, loc. cit. South Carolina, Massachusetts, and Connecticut also sent forth state warships christened Defence. Allen, op. cit., passim.

17. "Dimensions of the Ship Defence," Revolutionary Papers, Ship Defence, Maryland Historical Society, Baltimore, cited hereafter as Defence Papers. For comparison, Samuel Eliot Morison tells us that a British sloop-of-war, or "corvette," also carried three masts and ranged between 80 and 120 feet in length. With a crew averaged at 200 men and a normal armament of between 16 and 20 6-pounders, one can readily believe a correlation between Otter and Defence and Bon Homme Richard and Serapis. John Paul Jones: A Sailor's Biography (Boston: 1959), p. 99.

18. Charles O. Paullin, "James Nicholson," in The Dictionary of American Biography (20 vols; New York: 1930), XIII, 502-503; "Receipts for Labor and Expenses on Board the Maryland Armed Ship Defence," November 1775-March 1776, Defence Papers. Little thought was given to the total cost of alteration which, with the Lux bill for cordage and the Purviance total for new sail canvass, came to a huge 11,272 pounds, 18 shillings, 8 pence--at the current exchange rate, nearly $25,000! "An Estimate of the Cost of the Ship Defence," Defence Papers.

Appendix A 191

19. Baltimore Committee to Maryland Council, March 8, 1776, loc cit.; Purviance to Charles Carroll, Barrister, March 9, 1776, Red Book, XIII; Charles Carroll, Barrister, to Daniel of St. Thomas Jenifer, March 9, 1776, C. S. Correspondence; Maryland Council to Maryland Delegates in the Continental Congress, March 20, 1776, Red Book, IV; Smith letter; "Ship's Company Defence" in Muster Rolls and Other Records of Maryland Troops in the American Revolution, 1775-1783, Vol. XVIII of The Maryland Archives (Baltimore: 1900), pp. 654-661. Green as they were, these patriotic tars were in their innocence perhaps more eager for action than the hardened but sickly "pressed" crew aboard the Otter. During this cruise, Squire lost in death six ill members of his crew. Otter Journal, 2 February-21 March 1776; Andrew S. Hamond to Vice Admiral Molyneux Shuldham, March 3, 1776, Hamond Papers.

20. In preparing this paper, the author has chosen to explore whenever possible the original documents as housed in their respective archives. For copies of British Admiralty records and English newspapers, I am indebted to Dr. William J. Morgan, editor of The Naval Documents of the American Revolution, within whose work many have appeared.

21. Purviance for the Baltimore Committee to James Nicholson in Minutes of the Baltimore Committee, March 9, 1776, B. C. Papers, and to Charles Carroll, Barrister, March 9, 1776, Red Book, XIII. Barrister Carroll wrote in the spirit of the moment, "the Defence will I think be a match for the Otter." When Charles Carroll of Carrolton away at the Philadelphia Congress heard the rumors of impending battle, he dismissed them believing Baltimorians "will think better of it: as I fancy the Otter is superior to Nicholson's ship." Charles Carroll, Barrister, to Daniel of St. Thomas Jenifer, March 9, 1776, C. S. Correspondence; and Charles Carroll of Carrolton to Charles Carroll, Barrister, March 12, 1776, Carroll Papers, Maryland Historical Society, Baltimore.

22. Smith letter.

23. Smith letter; Otter Journal, March 9, 1776; Maryland Council to Maryland Delegates, loc cit.; Dunlap's Maryland Gazette, March 19, 1776; Minutes of the Baltimore Committee, March 9, 1776, loc cit.; The Morning Chronicle and London Advertizer, May 24, 1776. When Major Gist learned of Squire's new difficulties, reinforcements were dispatched to hopefully "add one more ship to our stock." These expectations were dashed when the arriving militiamen found the Otter cautiously rounding under light sail, no longer stuck on the rocks. Charles Carroll, Barrister, to St. Thomas Jenifer, March 9, 1776, loc cit.

24. Otter Journal, March 9, 1776. As late as mid-March, the Fells and Whetstone Point batteries were incomplete, the channel-blocking vessels unsunk, and the great chain unstretched. Baltimore Committee to Maryland Council, March 16, 1776, C.S. Correspondence; Minutes of the Baltimore Committee, March 15, 1776, B.C. Papers; Dunlap's Maryland Gazette, March 19, 1776.

25. Otter Journal, March 9, 1776. The Otter hove to off Annapolis that night and the following day in an unsuccessful attempt to purchase supplies. When refused, her prisoners were landed and she continued down the Chesapeake capturing coasters and seeking foodstuffs. After an absence of 21 days, she dropped anchor in the Elizabeth River on March 20 with six "grocery"-laden prizes. Otter Journal, March 9-20, 1776; Squire to Eden and Eden to Squire, March 9, 1776, Naval Papers, Maryland Historical Society, Baltimore; "Narrative"; Maryland Council to Robert Eden, March 10, 1776, C.S. Letterbook; Lord Howe's Prize List, March 31, 1777, Admiralty Records 1/487, Public Records Office, London.

26. Smith letter; Maryland Journal, March 13, 1776; Minutes of the Baltimore Committee, March 12, 1776, B.C. Papers; Purdie's Virginia Gazette, March 22, 1776; Baltimore Committee to Maryland Council, March 9-10, 1776, Red Book, XIII; "Journal of Captain Andrew S. Hamond, March 20, 1776, Admiralty Records 1/487, Public Records Office, London.

Appendix A   193

27. Scharf, History of Maryland, II, 211; Allen, op. cit., I, 139; Paullin, "James Nicholson," op. cit.; Maryland Council to Maryland Delegates, March 20, 1776, loc cit.; Maryland Council to James Nicholson, March 15, 1776, C. S. Letterbook; Morning Chronicle and London Advertizer, May 24, 1776; Dunlap's Maryland Gazette, March 12, 1776.

28. Even the partisan Maryland Gazette in its March 14 issue conceded that the Otter lay to apparently "wanting capt. Nicholson to come down." When he did not, she "at length bore away."

29. "Journal of Andrew S. Hamond," March 9, 1776, loc cit. A daylight small boat raid might have been attempted, but the British sailors available for the raid would doubtless have been outnumbered--to say nothing of outgunned!

30. Smith to Purviance, March 10, 1776, Purviance Papers; Kent County Committee to Maryland Council, March 13, 1776, C. S. Correspondence; Morning Chronicle and London Advertizer, May 24, 1776; "Narrative." The Otter was left at Norfolk to aid Lord Dunmore while the Roebuck and Liverpool cruised off the Delaware. Two years later she would again threaten the upper Bay as part of a larger Royal Navy task force. The Defence operated in the Bay throughout the summer and when Nicholson assumed command of the frigate Virginia, she was given to Captain George Cooke of St. Mary's County who began a two month cruise in the lower Atlantic that September. Several prizes were taken and the vessel returned safely to Baltimore before New Years completing her last important cruise. Scharf, History of Maryland, II, 272; Allen, op. cit., I, passim.; Maryland Council to George Cooke, September 13, 1776, C. S. Correspondence; Vol. XII of The Maryland Archives (Baltimore: 1893), passim.

APPENDIX B

Vessels in the Public Service
of the United States, 1775-1785

In the decade 1775-1785, nearly a hundred vessels were outfitted for the public service of the United States. The following list of Continental craft, including the schooners of Washington's New England flotilla and the assorted boats employed by Benedict Arnold on Lake Champlain, is an effort to provide in convenient form available and brief data on each. The sources for this information (proper citations given in the bibliography) are Chapelle's History of the American Sailing Navy and the Naval History Division's Dictionary of American Naval Fighting Ships.

Abbreviations:
- A.   Armament
- L.   Length
- B.   Beam
- Dph.   Depth (in hold)
- T.   Tonnage
- Cpl.   Complement of men

Numbers--e.g., "(2nd)"--refer to a vessel's position on the Navy's historical registers of ships bearing the given name. Unless otherwise noted, all were the first to carry their names.

WASHINGTON'S SCHOONERS. During the 1775 siege of Boston, the colonial army sent some small schooners to sea armed to capture desperately needed supplies and munitions. Three remained in service as late as 1777.

Franklin. Schooner. A. 6 guns. Dimensions and builder unknown. Ex-Marblehead fishing vessel. Fitted out by Washington's order. Returned to owner in 1776.

Hancock. Schooner. A. 6 4-pndrs. Dimensions: L. 60';

194

Appendix B

B. 20'; T. 72. Cpl. 70. Ex-merchantman Speedwell. Chartered by Washington's order from Thomas Grant of Marblehead in October 1775. Returned to owner in early 1777.

Hannah. Schooner. A. 4 4-pndrs. Dimensions and builder unknown. Originally owned by John Glover of Marblehead. Decommissioned in late 1775.

Harrison. Schooner. A. 6 guns. Dimensions and builder unknown. Ex-New England fishing vessel. Fitted out by Washington's order. Decommissioned in early 1776.

Lee. Schooner. A. 4 4-pndrs. Dimensions unknown. T. 74. Builder unknown. Ex-merchantman Two Brothers. Chartered in October 1775 as a replacement for the Hannah. Returned to owners in October 1777.

Lynch. Schooner. A. 4 guns. Dimensions and builder unknown. Fitted out by Washington's order in late 1775. Captured off Belle Isle by H.M. ship-of-the-line Feudroyant, 19 May 1777.

Warren. Schooner. Armament, dimensions, and builder unknown. Ex-Marblehead fishing vessel. Fitted out by Washington's order in late 1775. Captured by H.M.S. Milford in 1776.

ARNOLD'S FLOTILLA. In addition to Washington's fleet, another army squadron was put together on Lake Champlain under General Arnold to slow the British advance from Canada in 1775-1776. While most of it was destroyed in the October 1776 Battle of Valcour Island, several elements escaped--only to be destroyed by the Americans in the face of the 1777 invasions of Burgoyne's army.

Congress (2nd). Galley. A. 2 18-pndrs., 2 12-pndrs., 4 6-pndrs. Dimensions: L. 72'4"; B. 19'7"; T. 123. Cpl. 80. Built near Skenesboro or present-day Whitehall, New York. Burned near Crown Point, October 15, 1776.

Connecticut. Gundalow. Armament and dimensions approximately the same as Philadelphia (below). Cpl. 45. Built at Skenesboro. Burned October 13, 1776.

Enterprize. Sloop. A. 12 4-pndrs. Dimensions and builder

unknown. Cpl. 50. Taken from the British at St. Johns, on the Canadian Richelieu River, in 1775. Blown up at Skenesboro in 1777 to prevent capture.

Gates. Galley. A. 8 guns. Dimensions: L. 60'6"; B. 19'; Dph. 6'2"; T. 128. Cpl. 80. Built near Skenesboro in 1776, but not completed in time for Valcour Island. Blown up in 1777 to prevent capture.

Jersey. Gundalow. Armament and dimensions approximately the same as Philadelphia (below). Cpl. 45. Built near Skenesboro. Captured by the British on October 13, 1776, and taken into the Royal Navy.

Lee (2nd). Cutter galley. A. 1 12-pndr., 1 9-pndr., 4 4-pndrs. Dimensions: L. 43'9"; B. 16'3 1/2"; Dph. 4'8"; T. 48. Cpl. 86. Built at Skenesboro in 1776 from frames captured by the colonials at St. Johns. Sunk August 13, 1776. Raised by the British in 1777 and taken into the Royal Navy.

Liberty. Schooner. A. 4 4-pndrs., 4 2-pndrs. Dimensions unknown. Built at Skenesboro for land owner Philip Skene. Captured by Arnold in 1775. Destroyed in 1777.

New Haven. Gundalow. Armament and dimensions approximately the same as Philadelphia (below). Cpl. 45. Built on Lake Champlain in 1776 by an unknown contractor. Burned October 13, 1776.

New York. Gundalow. Armament and dimensions approximately the same as Philadelphia (below). Cpl. 45. As with all the gundalows, built by an unknown contractor near or at Skenesboro sometime in 1776. Believed captured; fate uncertain.

Philadelphia. Gundalow. A. 1 12-pndrs., 2 9-pndrs. Dimensions: L. 53'4"; B. 15'6"; Dph. 3'10". Cpl. 45. Built at Skenesboro by an unknown contractor. Sunk in battle October 15, 1776. Raised in 1932. Presently on display at the History and Technology Building of the Smithsonian Institution.

Providence (3rd). Gundalow. Armament and dimensions approximately the same as Philadelphia (above). Built at Skenesboro by an unknown contractor. Sunk October 12, 1776.

Appendix B 197

Revenge. Schooner. A. 4 4-pndrs., 4 2-pndrs., swivels. Dimensions unknown. Cpl. 50. Built at Ticonderoga, New York, in 1776 by an unknown contractor. Captured by the British in 1777 and subsequently burned.

Royal Savage. Schooner. A. 4 6-pndrs., 8 4-pndrs., swivels. Dimensions unknown. T. 70. Cpl. 50. Builder unknown. British vessel captured at St. Johns in November 1775. Burned October 11, 1776.

Spitfire. Gundalow. Armament and dimensions approximately the same as Philadelphia (above). Built at Skenesboro by an unknown contractor. Burned October 13, 1776.

Success. Gundalow. Name apparently altered as no record exists.

Trumbell (2nd). Galley. A. 1 18-pndr., 1 12-pndr., 2 9-pndrs., 4 4-pndrs. Dimensions approximately the same as Washington (3rd), below. Built at Skenesboro in 1776 by an unknown contractor. Captured by the British and destroyed in 1777.

Washington (3rd). Galley. A. 2 18-pndrs., 2 12-pndrs., 2 9-pndrs., 4 4-pndrs., 1 2-pndrs., 8 swivels. Dimensions: L. 72'4"; B. 19'7"; Dph. 6'2"; T. 123. Built at Skenesboro in 1776 by an unknown contractor. Captured by the British, 13 October 1776. Rerigged as a brig and taken into the Royal Navy.

SHIPS AND PACKETS OF THE CONTINENTAL NAVY.

Active. Brigantine. Armament and dimensions unknown. T. 60. Cpl. 15. Builder unknown. Continental packet captured 23 March 1782 by H.M.S. Prosperine.

Alfred. Ship. A. 24 9-pndrs., later 20 9-pndrs. Dimensions unknown. T. 440. Cpl. 220. Ex-merchantman Black Prince purchased into service at Philadelphia in 1775. Captured by H.M. ships Ariadne and Ceres, 9 March 1778.

Alliance. Frigate. A. 28 18-pndrs., 12 9-pndrs. Dimensions: L. 151'; B. 36'; Dph. 12'6". Built by James and William Hackett at Salisbury, Mass., in 1777. Sold at Philadelphia, 3 June 1785, the last ship of the

Continental navy.

America. Ship-of-the-Line. A. 30 18-pndrs., 14 9-pndrs., 32 12-pndrs. Dimensions: L. 182'6"; B. 50'6"; Dph. 23'; T. 1,982 (?). Built by Hacket et al. at Portsmouth, N.H. Supervised by John Paul Jones. First line-of-battle ship constructed in North America and the only one built here during the Revolution. Given as a gift to France, 3 September 1782. Broken up by the French sometime in 1786.

Andrew Doria. Brig. A. 14 4-pndrs. Dimensions unknown. Cpl. 130. Builder unknown. Ex-merchantman purchased in 1775. Captured by H.M.S. Racehorse in December 1776.

Argo. Sloop. A. 12 6-pndrs. Dimensions and builder unknown. In the Continental service in 1779. Fate unknown. See also Pigot (below).

Ariel. Ship. A. 20 guns. Dimensions unknown. T. 435. Cpl. 45. Builder unknown. Loaned by the French government in 1779 and returned to it after the war.

Baltimore. Brigantine. Armament, dimensions, and builder unknown. Continental packet lost off Cape Henry, 29 January 1780.

Bon Homme Richard. Ship. A. 6 18-pndrs., 28 12-pndrs., 8 9-pndrs. Dimensions and builder unknown. Ex-French East Indiaman Duc de Duras purchased in France. Sunk after capture of H.M.S. Serapis, 23 September 1779.

Boston. Frigate. A. 24 guns. Dimensions: L. 114'3"; B. 32'; Dph. 10'3"; T. 514. Built in Newburyport, Mass., in 1776 by Jonathan Greenleaf and Stephen and Ralph Cross. Captured at Charleston, S.C., in 1780. Taken into the Royal Navy under the name H.M.S. Charleston and rerated as a 20-gunner. Sold out in March 1783 and broken up.

Bourbon. Frigate. A. 36 guns. Dimensions and builder unknown. Laid down at Chatham, Conn., in 1780 under the supervision of John Cotton. Thomas Read slated as her first captain. Launched July 1783; sold two months later.

Appendix B   199

Cabot. Brig. A. 14 guns. Dimensions: L. 74'9 1/2";
B. 24'8"; Dph. 11'4"; T. 189. Former merchantman
purchased in Philadelphia in 1775. Taken by H. M. S.
Milford in March 1777--the first vessel of the Continental Navy to be captured by the British. Added to
the Royal Navy as a 12-gun brig. Sold out in June
1783.

Champion. Xebec. A. 2 24-pndrs., 2 18-pndrs., 4 9-
pndrs. A Pennsylvania State Navy vessel loaned to the
Continental service about mid-1777. Destroyed that
fall off Philadelphia.

Columbus. Ship. A. 24 guns. Dimensions and builder unknown. Ex-merchantman Sally purchased into the Continental service in November 1775. Driven ashore on
Point Judith, R. I., abandoned by her crew, and burned
by the British on 1 April 1778.

Confederacy. Frigate. A. 32 guns. Dimensions: L.
154'9"; B. 37'; Dph. 12'3"; T. 970. Built by Jedidiah
Willets at Norwich, Conn., in 1778. Taken by H. M.
ships Orpheus and Roebuck in 1781. Added to the Royal
Navy as 36-gun H. M. S. Confederate.

Congress. Frigate. A. 28 guns. Approximate dimensions:
L. 126'; B. 34'10"; Dph. 10'6". Built by Lancaster
Burling at Poughkeepsie, N. Y., in 1776. Burned in
the Hudson River in October 1777 to prevent capture.

Deane. Frigate. A. 24 12-pndrs., 8 4-pndrs., 2 6-pndrs.
Dimensions: L. (on the keel) 96'; B. 32'; T. 550.
Built in Nantes, France, in 1777 for the Americans.
Renamed Hague in 1782. Sold in 1783.

Delaware. Frigate. A. 24 guns. Dimensions: L. 117'
9 1/2"; B. 32' 10 1/2"; Dph. 9'8 1/2"; T. 563. Built
by Warwick Coates at Philadelphia in 1776. Captured
by the British in the Delaware on 27 September 1777
and taken into the Royal Navy. Sold out in March 1783.

Despatch. Armament, dimensions, and builder unknown.
Continental packet in service in 1778. Fate unknown.

Diligent (or Diligence). Brig. A. 14 guns. Dimensions:
L. 88' 5 3/4"; B. 24' 8"; Dph. 10' 10"; T. 236. Cpl.
100. Captured by the sloop Providence on 7 May 1779

and taken into the Continental service. Burned on the Penobscot to prevent capture, 14 August 1779.

Dolphin. Cutter. Armament, dimensions, and builder unknown. Purchased in France in 1776; "seized" by the French in 1777 for possible use as a receiving ship.

Duc de Lauzun. Armed ship. Armament, dimensions, and builder unknown. Purchased in France in 1782. Took a complement of French troops home from America in 1783 and was sold upon arrival.

Effingham. Frigate. A. 28 guns. Dimensions uncertain, approximately the same as frigate Delaware (above). Built by Grice and Company in Philadelphia in 1776 with John Barry slated as first captain. Burned in the Delaware on 7 May 1778 to prevent capture.

Enterprize (2nd). Schooner. A. 8 guns. Dimensions unknown. T. 25. Cpl. 60. Builder unknown. Ex-privateer converted into a Continental packet to serve on the Chesapeake Bay in 1776. Fate unknown.

Fame. Schooner. Armament, dimensions, and builder unknown. Continental packet of 1776. Fate unknown.

Fly. Schooner. A. 6 9-pndrs. Dimensions and builder unknown. Purchased in Baltimore in 1775 for use as a dispatch vessel. Destroyed in the Delaware in 1778.

General Arnold. Schooner. Armament, dimensions, and builder unknown. Purchased in 1776 for use as a dispatch vessel. In service as late as the end of 1778 under John Ayers of Massachusetts. Fate unknown.

General Gates. Ship sloop. A. 18 guns. Dimensions unknown. Ex-British brigantine Industrious Bee built at Bristol, England, in 1764. Captured 29 August 1777 by schooner Lee. Taken into the Continental service. Sold in 1779.

General Mifflin. Sloop. Armament, dimensions, and builder unknown. Fitted out at New York City in 1776 by Washington's order to cruise about Long Island Sound. Fate uncertain.

General Washington. Ship. A. 24 9-pndrs. Dimensions:

Appendix B

L. 130' 9"; B. 32' 8". Builder unknown. Ex-Rhode Island privateer General Washington captured by the British and renamed General Monk. Taken by Pennsylvania state ship Hyder Ali, 8 April 1782, and purchased into the Continental service that August under her original name. Sold out during the summer of 1784.

Georgia Packet. Schooner. Armament, dimensions, and builder unknown. Employed as a packet between Philadelphia and Georgia in 1776-1777. Fate unknown.

Hampden. Brigantine. A. 14 guns. Dimensions and builder unknown. Former West Indian trader purchased into the Continental service during the summer of 1776. Sold at Providence, R.I., in late 1777.

Hancock (2nd). Frigate. A. 32 guns. Dimensions: L. 136' 7"; B. 35' 6"; Dph. 11'; T. 750. Built by Jonathan Greenleaf and Stephen and Ralph Cross at Newburyport, Mass., in 1776. Captured by H.M. ships Rainbow, Flora, and Victor on 7 July 1777. Taken into the Royal Navy under the name H.M.S. Iris. Captured by the French in 1781 and blown up at Toulon in 1793.

Hague. See Deane (above).

Hornet. Sloop. A. 10 9-pndrs. Dimensions and builder unknown. Ex-merchantman Falcon purchased at Baltimore in 1775. Employed in the Delaware in 1776 and as escort to merchantmen sailing to Charleston in 1777. Apparently taken somewhere off Charleston in the summer of 1777.

Hornsnake. Schooner. Armament, dimensions, and builder unknown. Continental packet of 1775-1776. Fate unknown.

Independence. Sloop. A. 10 guns. Dimensions and builder unknown. Purchased into the Continental service in mid-1776. Wrecked on a bar while attempting to enter Okracoke Inlet, N.C., 24 April 1778.

Independence (2nd). Brig. A. 12 guns. Purchased into the Continental service in 1777. Sold out in 1779.

Lady Washington. Galley. Armament, dimensions, and builder unknown. Possible New York state gunboat.

Fitted out at New York City by Washington's order in 1776. Active through June 1777. Fate unknown.

Lexington. Brigantine. A. 14 4-pndrs., 2 6-pndrs., 12 swivels. Dimensions: L. 86'; B. 24' 6". Cpl. 110. Ex-merchantman Wild Duck purchased in 1775. Captured off the French coast by H.M.S. Alert, 20 September 1777.

Mercury. Ketch. Armament unknown. Dimensions: L. 72' 6"; B. 20' 6"; Dph. 8' 9 1/2"; T. 135. Built by Wharton and Humphreys in Philadelphia. Taken off Newfoundland by H.M. ships Vestal and Fairy, 10 September 1780.

Mercury (2nd). Schooner. Armament and dimensions unknown. Built by John Peck at Plymouth, Mass., in 1781. A packet in the Continental service. Fate unknown.

Montgomery. Frigate. A. 24 guns. Dimensions uncertain. Built by Burling at Poughkeepsie, N.Y., in 1776. Burned in the Hudson to prevent capture.

Morris. Ship. A. 24 guns. Dimensions and builder unknown. Prize merchantman Rebecca purchased into the Continental service at New Orlenas in 1778. Wrecked by a Gulf hurricane, 18 August 1779.

Morris (2nd). Schooner. Armament, dimensions, and builder unknown. Presented to the Continental navy by Louisiana in 1779 to replace the first Morris. Fate unknown.

Mosquito. Sloop. A. 4 guns. Dimensions and builder unknown. Purchased into the Continental service in 1775. Destroyed in the Delaware in October 1777.

Pallas. Ship. A. 30 guns. Dimensions and builder unknown. French merchant frigate loaned to the Continental navy in 1779. Most noted for her capture of H.M.S. Countess of Scarborough in September 1779. Returned to owners at the close of the war.

Phoenix. Rig, armament, dimensions, and builder unknown. Continental packet of 1778. Fate unknown.

Appendix B

Pigot. Brig galley. A. 8 guns. Dimensions and builder unknown. British transport cut down. Taken by Silas Talbot's sloop Hawke, 28 October 1778. Renamed Argo in 1779 and employed as a guard vessel on Narragansett Bay. Fate unknown. See also Argo (above).

Providence. Sloop. A. 12 guns. Dimensions unknown. Cpl. 90. Builder unknown. Ex-merchantman Katy purchased into the Continental service at Providence, R. I., in 1775. Blown up in the Penobscot to prevent capture, 14 August 1779.

Providence (2nd). Frigate. A. 28 guns. Dimensions: L. 126' 6 1/2"; B. 33' 8"; Dph. 10' 5"; T. 632. Built by Sylvester Bowers at Providence, R. I., in 1776. Captured by the British at Charleston, S. C., in May 1780. Taken into the Royal Navy and sold out in March 1783.

Queen of France. Frigate. A. 28 guns. Dimensions and builder unknown. Purchased from the French in 1777. Sunk at Charleston, S. C., in May 1780.

Race Horse. Sloop or schooner. A. 10 9-pndrs. Dimensions and builder unknown. Captured from the British in 1776 and burned in the Delaware the following year.

Raleigh. Frigate. A. 32 guns. Dimensions: L. 131' 5"; B. 34' 5"; Dph. 11'; T. 697. Built by James K. Hackett at Portsmouth, N. H., in 1776. Captured by H. M. ships Experiment and Unicorn off Penobscot Bay, 27 September 1778. Taken into the Royal Navy and sold out in July 1783.

Randolph. Frigate. A. 32 guns. Dimensions: L. 132' 9"; B. 34' 6"; Dph. 10' 6". Blown up in battle with H. M. S. Yarmouth in the West Indies, 17 March 1778.

Ranger. Ship sloop. A. 18 6-pndrs. Dimensions: L. 116'; B. 34'; Dph. 13' 6"; T. 308. Cpl. 140. Built by James K. Hackett at Portsmouth, N. H., in 1777. Captured at Charleston, S. C., in May 1780. Taken into the Royal Navy under the name H. M. S. Halifax.

Reprisal. Brig. A. 16 guns. Dimensions and builder unknown. Purchased into the Continental service in 1775. Floundered off the Banks of Newfoundland in 1778.

Repulse. Xebec. A. 8 guns. Dimensions and builder unknown. Pennsylvania State Navy vessel loaned to the Continental service about mid-1777. Destroyed that fall off Philadelphia.

Resistance. Brigantine. A. 10 4-pndrs. Dimensions and builder unknown. Purchased into the Continental service at New London, Conn., in 1777. Captured by the British in 1778.

Revenge (2nd). Cutter. A. 14 6-pndrs., 22 swivels. Dimensions unknown. Cpl. 106. Builder unknown. Purchased at Dunkirk, France, in 1777. Sold out at Philadelphia in 1780.

Sachem. Sloop. A. 10 9-pndrs. Dimensions and builder unknown. Ex-British tender Edward captured by the Lexington in 1776--the first prize of a regularly commissioned ship of the Continental navy. Destroyed in the Delaware in 1777.

Saratoga. Ship sloop. A. 18 guns. Dimensions unknown. Built by Wharton and Humphreys in Philadelphia in 1777. Lost at sea sometime in 1780.

South Carolina. Frigate. A. 28 36-pndrs., 12 12-pndrs. Dimensions: L. 154'; B. 40'; Dph. 16' 6"; T. 1,186 (?). Built at Amsterdam, Holland, 1776-1777 as L'Indien. Purchased from France in 1777 and returned. Loaned by the French to the South Carolina State Navy. Taken off the Delaware by H.M. ships Astrea, Quebec, and Diomede, 19 December 1782.

Spy. Schooner. Armament, dimensions, and builder unknown. Continental packet of 1776. Fate unknown.

Surprize. Sloop. Armament, dimensions, and builder unknown. Purchased into the Continental service in 1777. Fate unknown.

Surprize (2nd). Cutter. A. 10 guns. Dimensions unknown. Cpl. 50. Builder unknown. Purchased at Dover, England, fitted out at Dunkirk, France, and seized by the French government in 1777.

Trumbell. Frigate. A. 28 guns. Dimensions uncertain. Built by John Cotten at Chatham, Conn., in 1776.

Appendix B

Captured off the Delaware capes by H.M. ships Iris (ex-Hancock) and General Monk (ex-General Washington), 8 August 1781.

Vengeance. Brig. A. 12 guns. Dimensions and builder unknown. Purchased in France in 1779. Sold there at an uncertain later date.

Virginia. Frigate. A. 28 guns. Dimensions: L. 126' 3 1/2"; B. 34' 4"; Dph. 10' 5 1/2"; T. 681. Built by George Wells at Baltimore in 1776. Captured at the mouth of the Chesapeake by H.M. ships Emerald and Conqueror in April 1778. Taken into the Royal Navy under her original name and sold out sometime after 1783.

Warren (2nd). Frigate. A. 32 guns. Dimensions: L. 132' 1"; B. 34' 5 1/2"; Dph. 11". Built by Sylvester Bowers in Providence, R.I., in 1776. Burned in Penobscot Bay, 14 August 1779.

Washington. Brigantine. Armament, dimensions, and builder unknown. Fitted out at Plymouth, Mass., in mid-1775. Taken off Cape Ann by H.M.S. Fowey in December of that year.

Washington (2nd). Frigate. A. 32 guns. Dimensions approximately the same as Randolph. Built by Manuel, John, and Benjamin Eyre at Philadelphia in 1776-1778. Burned in the Delaware in 1778 before completion.

Washington (4th). Galley. Armament, dimensions, and builder unknown. Fitted out on the Hudson River in 1776. Fate unknown.

Wasp. Schooner. A. 8 guns. Dimensions and builder unknown. Ex-merchantman Scorpion purchased into the Continental service at Baltimore in 1775. Destroyed in the Delaware two years later.

West Florida. Sloop. Armament, dimensions, and builder unknown. British vessel taken by schooner Morris in 1779 and subsequently purchased into the Continental service. Sold at Philadelphia in 1780.

SUBJECT INDEX

All vessels, places, officers, and men referred to in this index are keyed to the entry numbers of references in the bibliography. In most instances, place names have been abbreviated or shortened, e.g., Eng. for England, N.H. for New Hampshire. The appendices are not included in the index. Standard abbreviations used throughout include the following:

For public and private vessels:

CN   Continental Navy Ship
HCMS   His Christian Majesty's [French] Ship
HMS   His Majesty's [British] Ship
PR   Privateer
SS   State (or colony) Ship

For public personnel:

AAO--American Army Officer
AMO--American Marine Officer
ANO--American Naval Officer
AP--American Politician

BAO--British Army Officer
BMO--British Marine Officer
BNO--British Naval Officer
BP--British Politician

FAO--French Army Officer
FMO--French Marine Officer
FNO--French Naval Officer
FP--French Politician

SAO--Spanish Army Officer
SMO--Spanish Marine Officer
SNO--Spanish Naval Officer
SP--Spanish Politician

Certain general categories familiar to many have been inserted, e.g., Strategy and tactics, or Shipbuilding and outfitting. No references are made to national navies or marine corps by name; the services of the various states are included as entries pertain to them.

Active, SS, 604
Adamant, HMS, 167
Adams, John, AP, 308, 726, 1380
Administration, American naval see Continental Congress
Administration, British naval see Sandwich, John M.
Admiralty, British see Sandwich, John M.
Adventure, 220
Aigle, HMS, 1314a
Alfred, CN, 334, 400, 959, 960
Alliance, CN, 96, 225, 582, 736, 862, 907, 1115
America, CN, 1120, 1242, 1357, 1494
America, PR, 406
Andrew Doria, CN, 1064
Antilles see West Indies
Arbuthnot, Marriot, BNO, 351, 352, 653, 661, 745, 1029, 1567
Ariadne, HMS, 159
Ariel, CN, 96
Armed Neutrality see Diplomacy
Arnold, Benedict, AAO, 15a, 53, 76, 127, 211, 223, 372, 517, 764, 781, 872, 902, 958, 977a, 1022, 1278, 1341, 1365, 1380a, 1391, 1392, 1425, 1457, 1498, 1525, 1590
Auguste, HCMS, 1458
Aurora, PR, 586

Baltimore, Md., 499, 693, 1158, 1250, 1329
Barbadoes see West Indies
Barfleur, HMS, 152
Barham, Charles Lord, BNO, 92, 1229
Barney, Joshua, ANO, 19, 99, 548, 577, 579, 590, 1165, 1175, 1547, 1579, 1587
Barras, Jacques-Melchior Saint-Laurent, Comte de, FNO, 618, 1429, 1486
Barrington, Samuel, BNO, 184, 1552
Barry, John, ANO, 129, 208, 267, 339, 438, 531, 582, 590, 671, 672, 673, 674, 681, 782, 1018, 1239, 1249, 1317, 1460, 1490
Bartlett, Josiah, 1204
Baton Rouge, La., 420
Beaumarchais, Pierre A. de, FP see Diplomacy
Bedford, HMS, 1107
Berbice see West Indies
Berkeley, George C., BNO, 182
Bermuda see West Indies
Berwick, HMS, 148
Betsey, 71
Beverly, Mass., 117, 140, 144, 322, 750, 1075, 1428
Biddle, Nicholas, ANO, 134, 336, 578, 580, 590, 1077, 1103, 1521
Black Prince see Alfred, CN

Blane, Gilbert see Medicine, naval
Bonhomme Richard, CN, 128, 229, 581, 739, 767, 797, 862, 1132, 1187, 1531
Boston, CN, 51
Boston, Mass., 156, 240, 291, 322, 717, 759, 850, 1112a, 1126
Bougainville, Louis A. de, FNO, 823, 1458
Bouillon, Philip d'Auvergne, Duke of, BNO, 157
Brandywine, Battle of, 1198
Bristol, Eng., 1299, 1327
Bristol, HMS, 1466
Britannia, HMS, 821
Broughton, Nicholas, ANO, 545
Buell, Augustus C., 698
Bulldog, CN, 1385
Bunker Hill see Boston, Mass.
Burgoyne, John, BAO, 454, 457a, 1210
Bushnell, David, 2, 532, 595, 676, 713, 857, 983a, 1324, 1518
Byron, John, BNO, 230, 1558

Calder, Robert, BNO, 176
Caldwell, Benjamin, BNO, 146
Campbell, John, 900
Canada, 457a, 827, 861, 977a, 1363, 1457
Cannon see Ordnance
Carew, Benjamin H., BNO, 283
Carleton, Guy, BAO, 457a, 902, 1380a
Cathcart, James, ANO, 282
Cato, PR, 1253
Charleston, S. C., 15a, 80, 221, 270, 351, 352, 557, 745, 849, 958, 1086, 1090, 1091, 1342, 1349, 1364, 1427, 1432a, 1481
Charts see Maps
Chesapeake, Battle of the see Yorktown, battle of
Chesapeake Bay, 594, 617, 1058, 1160, 1245
Chester, Peter, BP, 1, 1308
Chevaux-de-Frize, 507
Clerk, John, 464, 841, 1112, 1113, 1558
Clinton, Henry, BAO, 618, 745, 785, 1571, 1572, 1572a
Coffin, Isaac, BNO, 54, 167
Collier, George, BNO, 163
Collingwood, Cuthbert, BNO, 1096
Colpoys, John, BNO, 169
Concord, Mass., 1258
Confederacy, CN, 310, 1284
Congress, CN, 1116, 1272
Connecticut, 365, 740, 988, 989, 1504
Connecticut, 1117
Connecticut State Navy, 365, 1199
Continental Congress (including Marine Committee), 721, 723, 726, 762, 1056, 1112a, 1195, 1204, 1205, 1206, 1207, 1368, 1557
Convoys, 43, 301, 976, 1088, 1316
Conyingham, Gustavus, ANO, 95, 793
Cooke, John, BNO, 148
Cornett, William, BNO, 206
Cornwall, HMS, 169
Cornwallis, Charles Lord, BAO, 353, 618
Cornwallis, William, BNO,

209

185, 392
Cotton, Charles, BNO, 1110
Countess of Scarborough,
    HMS, 6
Crowell, Samuel, 405
Curtis, Roger, BNO, 178
Customs Service, British,
    107, 324, 359, 456, 759,
    957

Dacres, Richard, BNO,
    150, 1109
Dale, Richard, ANO, 383,
    590, 908, 1339
Dalrymple, Alexander, BNO,
    1108
Danbury, Conn., 794
Dance, Nathan, BNO, 172
Dean, George, BNO, 753
Deane, Silias, AP, 331
Defence, SS (Conn.), 1044
Defence, SS (Md.), 439,
    1004, 1160, 1161, 1378
Defence, SS (S.C.), 1089
Delaware, 1330
Delaware River and Bay
    (including naval actions
    in), 124, 141, 143, 148,
    248, 252, 507, 551, 813,
    1055, 1222, 1314a, 1382,
    1383, 1435, 1436
Demerara see West Indies
Derby, Elias H., 966
Derby, John, 1258
Desbarres, J. F. W., 915a
Destouches, Charles R. D.
    G., FNO, 1415, 1486
Digby, Robert, BNO, 183
Diligent, SS, 607, 1377
Diplomacy, 37, 78, 82, 88,
    126, 263, 325, 379, 462,
    463, 473, 490, 545a,
    564, 623, 675, 690, 833,
    858, 927, 930, 938, 941,
    1037, 1040, 1187, 1220,
    1236, 1248, 1265, 1266,
    1275, 1281, 1282, 1303,
    1306, 1373, 1426, 1453,
    1505a, 1554, 1591
Dispatch, HMS, 296
Dominica or Dominique see
    West Indies
Douglas, Andrew S., BNO,
    1028
Douglas, Howard, BAO,
    1112, 1113
Downman, Hugh, BNO, 1021
Duke, HMS, 197
Dunmore, John M., 281,
    372, 484

Eagle, HMS, 189
Ellison, Joseph, BNO, 149
Elphinstone, George K. see
    Keith, George K. E.
    Lord
Enterprise, CN, 738, 956
Essequibo see West Indies
Estaing, Charles H., Comte
    d', 65, 132, 156, 506,
    508, 627, 631, 732, 746,
    792, 842, 886, 945, 994,
    1036, 1359, 1429, 1538
Exmouth, Edward P. Lord,
    161, 538, 1156, 1178

Fair American, PR, 407
Fairfield, Conn., 1044
Falcon, HMS, 220, 916
Falmouth, Me. see Portland, Me.
Fanning, Nathaniel, ANO,
    257
Farmer, Robert, 1370
Flamborough Head, battle
    off see Jones, John P.
Fleury, Francois L. de,
    FAO, 1055
Flora, HMS, 1446
Flying Fish, 977
Formidable, HMS, 1581

Forten Gaol see Prisons, prisoners-of-war, and prisonships
Fort George see Pensacola, Fla.
Fort Mercer see Delaware River and Bay
Fort Mifflin see Delaware River and Bay
Fort Moultrie see Charleston, S. C.
Fowey, HMS, 391
Fox, Charles, BP, 1438
Fox, Montagu, BP, 1265
Franklin, Benjamin, AP, 335, 797, 873
Franklin, CN, 144, 467
French aid and alliance see Diplomacy
Freneau, Philip, 79, 887

Gage, Thomas, BAO, 27, 454
Galvez, Bernardo de, SAO, 304, 305, 306, 330, 518, 1137, 1155
Gambier, James, BNO, 1567
Gardner, A. Gardner Lord, 197
Gaspee, HMS, 108, 267a, 386, 733, 946, 1053, 1586
General Greene, SS, 251
General Monk, HMS, 579, 624
General Sullivan, PR, 123
George III, 635, 1099
Georgia, 294, 360, 468, 1091, 1124
Germain, George S. Lord, 262, 353, 679, 1502
Gibraltar, Siege of, 62, 376, 848, 962, 1303, 1311, 1395, 1409, 1508, 1561, 1588

Gillon, Alexander, ANO, 375
Glasgow, HMS, 1185
Glover, John, AAO, 141, 142, 143, 1323
Good Man Richard, CN see Bonhomme Richard, CN
Gower, Erasmus, BNO, 162
Grand Union, 1019
Grant, Alexander, ANO, 1251
Grasse, Francois J. P., Comte de, FNO, 7, 67, 100, 239, 244, 290, 298, 299, 378, 380, 418, 429, 440, 441, 458, 459, 539, 627, 640, 732, 812, 823, 855, 903, 1320, 1335, 1416, 1429, 1486, 1536, 1542
Graves, Thomas, BNO, 646a, 1107
Graves, Thomas Lord, BNO, 201, 353, 567, 575, 645, 1107, 1558, 1567
Greenwood, John, ANO, 666
Greenwood, William, 977
Grosvenor, 832, 895
Guadaloupe see West Indies
Gunnery see Ordnance

Hackensack Valley see New Jersey
Halifax see Nova Scotia
Hallock, William, ANO, 693a
Hamond, Andrew S., BNO, 1059
Hancock, CN (1st), 144
Hancock, John, AP, 115, 456, 717, 1580
Hannah, CN, 368, 545, 592, 889, 1381, 1398
Harding, Seth, ANO, 748
Hargood, William, BNO, 46

211

Harris, John, ANO, 953
Haskin, Jonathan, 33
Head of Elk, Md., 1549
Heermann, Lewis, ANO, 1228
Hempstead, N.Y., 361
Hercules, HMS, 244
Hero, SS, 384
Hewes, Joseph, AP, 800
Hinman, Elisha, ANO, 334
Holker, PR, 343
Hood, Samuel, BNO, 152, 742a
Hood, Samuel Lord, BNO, 114, 200, 253, 699, 742a, 1063, 1360, 1558
Hope, HMS, 467
Hope, PR, 465
Hopkins, Esek, ANO, 41, 398, 527, 670, 706, 1241
Hopkinson, Francis, 721
Horsburgh, James, BNO, 1104
Hotham, William Lord, BNO, 203
Howe, Richard Lord, BNO, 9, 18, 60, 106, 154, 158, 178, 189, 262, 285, 417, 454, 550, 552, 596, 631, 678, 678a, 679, 680, 752, 771, 983, 1063, 1144, 1344, 1549, 1578
Howe, William, BAO, 9, 60, 454, 552, 678a, 1058
Hoyt, S., 1212
Hudson River, 504, 507, 509, 744, 846, 847, 1035, 1315, 1517
Hughes, Edward, BNO, 85, 86, 460, 1111, 1274, 1304, 1466
Hunolstein, Aglae de, 638
Hunter, CN, 1153a
Hunter, John, BNO, 148
Hyder Ali, SS, 624

Hygiene, naval see Medicine, naval

Impressment, 277, 326, 373, 426, 498a, 498b, 1328, 1501, 1582, 1593
Independence, PR, 519
Independence, SS, 605
Independent, PR, 755
Inman, Henry, BNO, 1025
Instructions, permanent see Strategy and tactics
Invasion of England, projected 1779 see Diplomacy
Iris, HMS, 586

Jack the Painter see John the Painter
Jamaica see West Indies
James River Naval Office, 777
Jason, PR, 426
Jefferson, Thomas, AP, 211
Jersey, HMS see Prisons, prisoners-of-war, and prisonships
Jervis, John see St. Vincent, John J.
Jervis, William H., BNO, 1023
John, 1208
John the Painter, 341, 593
Johnstone, George, BNO, 1314, 1568
Jones, John P., ANO, 4, 6, 25, 34, 35, 71, 83, 94, 96, 114a, 120, 128, 241, 242, 257, 261, 268, 323, 383, 394, 399, 410, 411, 427, 444, 475, 479, 482, 485, 495, 512, 515, 531, 535, 540, 569, 581, 589, 590, 621, 628, 638, 659, 696, 698, 704, 709,

719, 736, 767, 786, 790,
810, 829, 835, 836, 875,
905, 906, 910, 911, 912,
919, 933, 934, 935, 937,
973, 979, 983b, 984, 987,
996, 1003, 1070, 1073,
1074, 1076, 1077, 1093,
1103, 1120, 1142, 1189,
1190, 1191, 1192, 1193,
1194, 1201, 1208, 1213,
1224, 1227, 1233, 1268,
1280, 1309, 1313, 1321,
1333, 1337, 1338, 1340,
1352, 1353, 1354, 1384,
1399, 1412, 1413, 1418,
1425, 1437, 1455, 1459,
1461, 1462, 1467, 1468,
1478, 1484, 1485, 1494,
1496, 1521, 1528, 1530,
1531, 1534, 1544, 1556,
1579, 1587, 1589
Jones, Willie, 394, 1076
Junius Brutus, PR, 1247
Jupiter, HMS, 1185

Keith, Lord George K. E.,
   BNO, 39, 196, 815a
Kempenfelt, Richard, BNO,
   1105
Keppell, August, BNO, 186,
   259, 285, 321a, 648,
   736a, 822, 902a, 1007a,
   1063, 1145, 1548
King, Richard, BNO, 174
King, Rufus, 1546
Kingsmill, Robert, BNO,
   177
Kingston, N. Y., 556
Knight, John, BNO, 156

Lady Margareta, 541
Lady Washington, CN, 856
Lafayette, Marquis de,
   FAO, 618, 638, 834,
   1429

La Graviere, Jurien de,
   1113
La Hebe, HCMS, 164
L'Aigle, PR, 159
Lake Champlain see Valcour Island, battle of
Lamotte-Piquet, Admiral,
   FNO, 301
Landais, Pierre, ANO, 1201
Langdon, John, AP, 1016
Lanquedot, HCMS, 501
Lark, HMS, 205
La Surveillante, HCMS, 940
Latona, HMS, 198
Lauzun, Armand L., Duc
   de, FAO, 870, 1414
Lauzun Legion see Lauzun,
   Armand L.
Lee, CN, 144, 972
Lee, Ezra, 676
Leeward Islands see West
   Indies
Le Sagittaire, HCMS, 119
Liberty, 115, 717, 1334,
   1580
Liberty, HMS, 1356
Lincoln, Benjamin, AAO,
   746, 1359
Lincoln, SS, 603
Lind, James see Medicine,
   naval
Linzee, John, BNO, 916
Lists of ships see Ship
   registers
Liverpool, Eng., 256, 763,
   1423
Liverpool, HMS, 1529
Locker, William, BNO, 153
London, HMS, 567
Long Island see New York
   City
Lord Dartmouth, 1083
Louis, Thomas, BNO, 179
Louis XVI, 719, 854
Lovell, Solomon, AAO, 280
Lowestoffe, HMS, 153
Lynch, CN, 393

213

Macbride, John, BNO, 190
McClenachan, Blair, 343
Machais, Me., 421, 516, 931, 963, 1098, 1377, 1397
Machais Liberty, SS, 611, 620
McLean, Francis, BAO, 280
McNeill, Hector, ANO, 40, 1069
Maine, 22, 38, 1050, 1153a, 1255
Maintenance, naval see Shipbuilding and outfitting
Manley, John, ANO, 466, 665, 1211
Maps, 322, 449, 682, 915a, 988, 989, 1224, 1225, 1226, 1270
Margaretta, 421, 1174, 1377, 1449
Marine Committee see Continental Congress
Marquis Lafayette, PR, 397
Mars, SS, 608
Maryland, 461, 1253, 1331, 1407
Massachusetts State Navy, 1196, 1202
Mead, John, BNO, 391
Medicine, naval, 647, 757, 795, 814, 914, 924, 1177, 1294
Meserve, William C., 1041
Middleton, Charles, BNO see Barham, Charles Lord
Mill Prison see Prisons, prisoners-of-war, and prisonships
Milne, David, BNO, 1106
Mississippi River, 304, 305, 307a, 720a
Montgomery, CN, 1272
Montgomery, PR, 1387
Moris, Henri, 1113

Morris, Robert, AP, 435, 718, 1143, 1144, 1442, 1511
Mowat, Henry, BNO, 636
Mugford, John, ANO, 315, 467
Mulgrave, Constantine Lord, BNO, 191
Murray, Alexander, ANO, 590, 907, 1521

Nafey, Peter, 1114
Nagent, Charles E., BNO, 151
Nancy, HMS, 388, 972
Narragansett Bay, 108, 1298
Nassau see West Indies
Nautilus, HMS, 368
Nautilus, PR, 1253
Naval policy see Strategy and tactics
Navigation Acts, 457
Navy Board, British see Sandwich, John M.
Nelson, Horatio, BNO, 199, 240, 538, 1472
Newburyport, Mass., 278, 357, 851, 852
New Hampshire, 1336, 1357, 1557
New Jersey, 900
New London, Conn., 221, 309, 1300
Newman, John N., BNO, 188
Newport, R.I., 100, 109, 455, 576, 1140, 1429, 1463
New York City, 5, 142, 158, 227, 315, 364, 530, 1006, 1345, 1517
Nicholas, Samuel, AMO, 510, 904
Norfolk, Va., 1550
North, Frederick Lord,

214

BP, 263, 1548
North Carolina, 293, 402, 403, 445, 468, 541
North Carolina State Navy, 729
Northesk, William Lord, BNO, 202
Norwich, Conn., 310
Nova Scotia, 38, 245, 1130, 1254, 1261

O'Brien, Jeremiah, ANO, 620, 1077, 1098, 1355
Oliver Cromwell, PR, 221, 811, 1047
Olmstead, Gideon, 1043
Onslow, Richard, BNO, 175
Orde, John, BNO, 171
Ordnance, 247, 483, 655, 1087
Otter, HMS, 1378
Otway, William A., BNO, 205

Pallas, HMS, 174
Pallister, Hugh, BNO, 194, 259, 736a, 820, 1145
Parker, Hyde, BNO, 166, 847
Parker, Peter, BNO, 173, 199, 352
Parker, William, BNO, 538
Parsons, Abraham, 1237
Pasley, Thomas, BNO, 180, 1183
Patton, Andrew, 541
Payne, John W., BNO, 158
Pearson, Richard, BNO, 581, 1033
Peggy Stewart, 238a, 274, 443, 1419
Pellow, Edward see Exmouth, Edward P. Lord
Pennsylvania, 731
Pennsylvania State Navy, 133, 1217
Penobscot, Me., 171, 280, 639, 730, 770, 913, 948, 1008, 1336, 1347, 1445a, 1555a, 1575, 1576
Penrose, Charles V., BNO, 1219
Pensacola, Fla., 408, 518, 597, 598, 1094, 1155, 1310, 1370, 1583
Philadelphia, 687, 951
Philadelphia, Pa., 551, 784, 1058, 1332, 1555
Phillip, Arthur, BNO, 120, 145
Pilgrim, PR, 1075
Pole, Charles M., BNO, 1020
Pollock, Oliver, AP, 773, 1364a
Pomona, HMS, 204
Pope, Nathaniel, ANO, 497
Popham, Home R., BNO, 201, 1520
Portland, Me., 273, 636, 1535
Porto Praya, Battle of, 1568
Portsmouth, Eng., 593, 1345
Portsmouth, N.H., 15, 629, 1242
Portsmouth, Va., 362a, 1158
Poughkeepsie, N.Y., 988
Preble, Edward, ANO, 1521
Princeton, Battle of, 956
Prince William, HMS, 162
Pringle, Captain, 1153
Prisons, Prisoners-of-War, and Prisonships, 31, 32, 33, 49, 52, 55, 56, 57, 64, 68, 69, 70, 91, 131, 217, 218, 236, 266, 291, 299a, 315, 401, 469, 537, 547, 578, 659, 724, 736, 783, 953, 1150,

1151, 1180, 1246, 1293,
1366, 1386, 1424, 1451,
1454, 1470, 1479, 1505,
1551, 1563a, 1579a
Privateering, Privateers,
 and Privateersmen, 31,
42, 45, 68, 75, 130,
131, 256, 278, 329a,
365, 367, 424, 431, 465,
477, 478, 563, 564a,
689, 693, 750, 753, 754,
755, 758, 791, 838, 900,
917, 971, 988, 989, 999,
1000, 1006, 1041, 1075,
1082, 1084, 1085, 1114,
1130, 1166, 1167, 1226,
1247, 1253, 1255, 1266,
1271, 1277, 1281, 1348,
1376, 1407, 1411, 1465,
1488, 1557, 1563a
Prosper, SS, 1090
Protector, SS, 609
Provence, France, 1173
Providence, CN, 77
Providence, PR, 689
Providence, R.I., 386,
 1244, 1429

Quebec, HMS, 624, 940
Quero, 1258

Radstock, William Lord,
 BNO, 204
Rainbow, HMS, 164, 362
Raleigh, CN, 51, 334, 561,
 1357, 1434
Ramillies, HMS, 1088
Randolph, CN, 430, 936,
 944
Ranger, CN, 658, 799, 817,
 1119, 1357, 1589
Rathbun, John, ANO, 1259
Rattlesnake, HMS, 209
Rattlesnake, PR, 50
Republic, SS, 612

Resistance, CN, 337
Revenge, 1216
Rhode Island, 65, 396, 528,
 918, 945, 946, 988, 989,
 1007, 1039, 1279, 1348,
 1359, 1415, 1429, 1564,
 1572
Richmond, Va., 15a
Rigging see Shipbuilding
 and outfitting
Riou, Edward, BNO, 147,
 538
Rising Empire, SS, 606
Roberts, George, 1280
Robust, HMS, 206
Rochambeau, Jean, Comte
 de, FAO, 1244, 1429,
 1486, 1545, 1560
Roddam, Robert, BNO, 160
Rodney, Lord George, BNO,
 18, 56, 98, 105, 161,
 192, 193, 197, 202, 244,
 285, 301, 349, 415, 416,
 464, 489, 539, 669, 700,
 707, 720, 841, 874, 923,
 989, 1063, 1064, 1092,
 1177, 1263, 1269, 1392a,
 1396, 1558, 1566, 1581
Roebuck, HMS, 1059
Romney, HMS, 115
Rose, HMS, 1298
Ross, John L., BNO, 163
Rowley, Joshua, BNO, 1032
Royal George, HMS, 17,
 451, 790a, 1105, 1367
Royal Savage, 1365

St. Albans, HMS, 175
Saint Christophe see West
 Indies
Saintes, Battle of the, 7, 74,
 105, 120, 193, 197, 202,
 215, 216, 244, 246a,
 303, 349, 350, 400a,
 414, 428, 464, 471, 539,
 555, 564, 626, 823,

216

1107, 1181, 1263, 1417, 1464, 1469, 1558
Saint Eustatius see West Indies
St. Johns, Canada, 958, 977a, 1457
St. Kitts see West Indies
St. Lucia see West Indies
Saint-Simon, Marquis de, 378
St. Vincent, John J., Earl of, BNO, 195, 776, 785
Salem, Mass., 322, 405, 406, 641, 890, 1166, 1167, 1226, 1562a
Sally, 1091
Sandwich, John M., 4th Earl of, 113, 258, 423, 602, 998, 1081, 1097, 1230, 1393, 1500, 1563, 1573
Sartine, HCMS, 231
Saumarez, James, BNO, 168, 538, 1305
Savannah, Ga., 72, 360, 453, 502, 746, 792, 886, 893
Saxton, Charles, BNO, 1031
Selkirk, D. H. Lord, 34, 808
Serapis, HMS, 6, 96, 581, 767, 797, 862, 1531
Seymour, Hugh, BNO, 198, 1512
Shipbuilding and Outfitting, 23, 58, 89, 249, 250, 252, 297, 316, 317, 320a, 321, 637, 763, 888, 890, 991, 1014, 1393, 1403, 1450
Ship Registers, 112, 219, 317, 321, 358, 498, 588, 830, 892, 1240, 1242, 1372, 1406, 1423, 1483, 1494, 1495
Shortland, John, BNO, 1026
Shrewsbury, HMS, 170
Shuldham, Molyneux, BNO, 1030
Skene, Philip, 1215
Skenesborough, N.Y., 517, 1215
Smedley, Samuel, 1044
Smith, William S., BNO, 181
Smuggling see Customs service, British
South Carolina, 468, 1091, 1524
South Carolina, SS, 1045, 1388
South Carolina State Navy, 855, 933, 1076
Spanish aid see Diplomacy
Sproat, David, 91
Strategy and Tactics, 138, 139, 237, 288, 302, 314, 333, 370, 389, 390, 400a, 422, 440, 464, 492, 573, 649, 650, 652, 656, 668, 841, 845, 968, 1017, 1112, 1113, 1286, 1569, 1572
Sturdy Beggar, PR, 387
Suffren de Saint Tropez, Pierre, FNO, 85, 86, 87, 238, 302, 311, 361a, 413, 425, 442, 460, 627, 714, 725, 875, 883, 884, 1065, 1111, 1172, 1274, 1304, 1314, 1343, 1417, 1466, 1475, 1568
Sullivan's Island see Charleston, S.C.
Sybil, HMS, 1185
Syren, HMS, 1051

Tactics see Strategy and tactics
Talbot, Silas, AAO, 1477
Tartar, PR, 1299
Tartar, SS, 610

Ternay, Chevalier de, FNO, 505, 732, 1415, 1429, 1486
Thesiger, Frederick, BNO, 193
Thompson, Edward, BNO, 187
Thompson, Thomas, ANO, 334
Three Friends, 293
Timber and masts see Shipbuilding and outfitting
Tomlinson, Nicholas, BNO, 1022
Tracy family, 278
Trenton, Battle of, 956
Trevenen, James, BNO, 1219
Trincomalee, Ceylon, 361a
Trollope, Henry, BNO, 164
Trotter, Thomas see Medicine, naval
Troubridge, Thomas, BNO, 1034
Trumbell, CN, 907
Truscott, William, BNO, 207
Truxton, Thomas, ANO, 524
Tucker, Daniel, ANO, 412
Tucker, Samuel, ANO, 279, 932, 1350
Turnor, John, BNO, 1027
Turtle see Bushnell, David
Tyrannicide, SS, 296

Ushant, Battle of, 170, 488, 819, 902a, 992, 1154a

Valcour Island, Battle of, 110, 111, 210, 223, 457a, 516, 517, 546, 622, 657, 685, 697, 703, 781, 861, 902, 951, 982, 1095, 1109, 1153, 1156, 1170, 1178, 1210, 1216, 1363, 1365, 1372, 1380a, 1498, 1541
Vaughan, John, BAO, 970, 1392a
Vengeance, PR, 753
Victoire, HCMS, 834
Vigilant, HMS, 177
Virginia, 356, 362, 363, 372, 480, 484, 837, 872, 964, 1022, 1125, 1158, 1278
Virginia, CN, 249, 1160, 1379
Virginia Capes, Battle of the see Yorktown, battle of
Virginia State Navy, 15a, 255a, 284, 872, 953, 1171, 1196, 1422, 1594

Wallace, James, BNO, 847, 1298
Warren, CN (1st), 144
Warren, CN (2nd), 77, 452
Warren, John B., BNO, 159
Washington, 1443
Washington, George, AAO, 117, 141, 142, 143, 144, 252, 340, 393, 490a, 545, 570, 571, 618, 727, 844, 941, 1238, 1391a, 1416, 1562, 1585
Washington, PR, 1371
Wasp, CN, 693a
Wasp, PR, 511
West Florida, British see Pensacola, Fla.
West Indies, 6, 71, 74, 122, 148, 153, 175, 199, 234, 301, 378, 380, 416, 419, 429, 471, 472, 664, 688, 706, 737, 772, 778, 826, 831, 915, 928, 957, 959, 970, 986, 994, 999, 1012, 1019, 1038, 1064,

1123, 1147, 1162, 1226, 1259, 1262, 1296, 1297, 1472, 1473, 1510, 1552, 1558, 1565
Whaleboat warfare see Privateering, privateers, and privateersmen
Wharton, James, 319
Whipple, Abraham, ANO, 985
Whitley, John, BNO, 209
Wickes, Lambert, ANO, 224, 342, 710, 1459
Willing, James, AAO, 720a
Willing Raid, 1, 307a, 720a
Wilmington, Del., 521
Wilson, Henry B., 1156
Winthrop, SS, 613
Wood, James A., BNO, 1024

Yarmouth, HMS, 430, 578
York River, 525
Yorktown, Battle of (including the Battle of the Chesapeake), 67, 119, 152, 206, 214, 233, 246, 348, 353, 354, 378, 400a, 409, 418, 455, 471, 480, 543, 544, 567, 591, 646, 692, 761, 772, 780, 855, 868, 869, 1048, 1049, 1068, 1071, 1131, 1188, 1288, 1292, 1320, 1335, 1346, 1374, 1394, 1417, 1429, 1438, 1458, 1469, 1482, 1487, 1499, 1542, 1543, 1558
Young, George, BNO, 155
Young, John, ANO, 338

Zaffarine Islands, 1358